PRIMARY LOVE AND PSYCHO-ANALYTIC TECHNIQUE

PRIMARY LOVE AND PSYCHO-ANALYTIC TECHNIQUE

Michael Balint

M.D., Ph.D., M.Sc., L.R.C.P., L.R.C.S.

MARESFIELD LIBRARY
LONDON

First published in 1952
Reprinted 1985
with permission of The Hogarth Press
by H. Karnac (Books) Ltd.,
58 Gloucester Rd., London S.W.7
England

ISBN 0 946439 11 7

Printed and bound in Great Britain
by A. Wheaton & Co. Ltd., Exeter

Preface

AFTER having highly ambivalently criticised *The Interpretation of Dreams* and *The Psychopathology of Everyday Life*, I was at the age of 21 decisively and definitely conquered for psycho-analysis by the *Three Contributions* and *Totem and Taboo*. In some form or other these two directions of research—the development of the individual sexual function and the development of human relationships—have remained in the focus of my interest ever since. Coming from medicine, and strongly biased by my predilection for the exact sciences, my approach to these two problems was mainly, though not exclusively, through clinical observation; this meant studying the processes as they develop and change under the impact of the analytical situation in the patient, that is, studying the psycho-analyst's technique and the patient's responses to it.

This volume collects my papers written during the years 1930–1952 on these three intimately interlinked topics—human sexuality, object-relations and psycho-analytic technique. Apart from minor stylistic corrections the papers are printed here without any alteration, giving a fair picture of my own development. The reason why I decided to publish this collection now is that I feel that my ideas have reached a certain completeness with my two last papers, 'On Love and Hate' and 'New Beginning and the Paranoid and the Depressive Syndromes'. Ever since Freud's *Beyond the Pleasure Principle*, Ferenczi's *Thalassa* and his later technical papers, the rôle and place of destructiveness and hate in the development of the human mind have been a puzzling problem to psycho-analytic thinking. Apart from its theoretical significance, any answer to this problem fundamentally influences our ideas about the therapeutic processes in the patient, and thus our interpretations, in fact our whole behaviour in the analytic situation. I think that, at last, I have been able to clarify certain aspects of these interrelations.

Returning to 1917, *Totem and Taboo* was lent to me by a young girl who was then studying pure mathematics (as I also was as a sideline) because there were no facilities for studying anthropology at the Budapest University. We were already great friends. We married soon after I had finished my medical studies, and a few months later started our analytic training with Dr. H. Sachs in Berlin on the same day. After some time both of us changed over to Ferenczi, and we finished our training under him. Starting with our shared enthusiasm for *Totem and Taboo* till her death in 1939, Alice and I read, studied, lived and worked together. All our ideas—no matter in whose mind they had first arisen—were enjoyed and then tested, probed and criticised in our endless discussions. Quite often it was just chance that decided which of us should publish a particular idea. Apart from psychoanalysis, Alice's main interests were anthropology and education, mine biology and medicine, and usually this factor decided who should write about the idea. We published only one paper jointly, although almost all of them could have been printed under our joint names. In fact, our development was so intertwined that this book would be incomplete, in the true sense of the word, without her contribution; that was one of my reasons for including in this volume the last paper she published 'Love for the Mother and Mother-love'.

I wish to express my thanks to Miss Barbara Cooke, Miss Ursula Todd-Naylor and to Mr. Francis Stuart for helping me to translate some papers published only in Hungarian or German. Mr. Ivo Jarosy proved invaluable as an inexorable critic of my English, and as a reliable censor of the references to literature.

M. B.

LONDON,
April 1952

Contents

PART ONE

INSTINCTS AND OBJECT-RELATIONS

1 Psychosexual Parallels to the Fundamental Law of Biogenetics (1930)   11

2 Two Notes on the Erotic Component of the Ego-Instincts (1933)   42

3 Critical Notes on the Theory of the Pregenital Organisations of the Libido (1935)   49

4 Eros and Aphrodite (1936)   73

5 Early Developmental States of the Ego. Primary Object-love (1937)   90

6 [Alice Balint] Love for the Mother and Mother Love (1939)   109

7 On Genital Love (1947)   128

8 On Love and Hate (1951)   141

PART TWO

PROBLEMS OF TECHNIQUE

9 Character Analysis and New Beginning (1932)   159

10 On Transference of Emotions (1933)   174

11 The Final Goal of Psycho-analytic Treatment (1934)   188

12 Strength of the Ego and Ego-pedagogy (1938)   200

13 [with Alice Balint] On Transference and Counter-transference (1939)   213

14 Changing Therapeutical Aims and Techniques in Psycho-analysis (1949)   221

15 On the Termination of Analysis (1949)   236

16 New Beginning and the Paranoid and the Depressive Syndromes (1952)   244

Index   266

Part One

INSTINCTS AND OBJECT-RELATIONS

I

PSYCHOSEXUAL PARALLELS TO THE FUNDAMENTAL LAW OF BIOGENETICS [1]
(1930)

1. *The Career of Eros*

In discussions about biology, and especially about the great variety of forms of life, it is often said (Freud also made the remark) [2] that biology is indeed a realm of unlimited possibilities. Is not the psychological meaning of such an exclamation one of astonishment that our boldest fantasies have not been able to conjure up anything not actually found in the living world? For a long time I made use of the recognition of this fact merely as a theme for conversation, and in the company of analysts often passed the time by quoting some type of animal that corresponded to every perverse activity, however absurd, to every myth or every infantile theory of sex.

I was finally startled by the exactitude of the parallel. If true, it must mean that the human mind knows all about phylogenesis, indeed that it knows nothing else but phylogenesis and cannot really produce anything that has never existed before. Perhaps this can be put the other way round: The human id contains potentially the entire phylogenesis, and the actual experience only releases the one or the other form of reaction.

A corresponding law exists in biology, although it is not of very long standing. It was first formulated by Haeckel and is often called the fundamental law of biogenetics. In order to make the similarity plain I will state it in a form somewhat different from the usual: 'The fertilised human egg knows all about phylogenesis; it recapitulates it in its own development.' Naturally this statement of Haeckel refers only to the body.

[1] Paper read at the Second Conference of the German Psycho-analytic Society, Dresden, 1930.
[2] In: *Beyond the Pleasure Principle*, Int. PsA. Lib., London, 1950.

I now want to show that not only the body but also the mind recapitulates the development of the species. If this can be proved, the statement quoted at the beginning of this paper is no longer an enigma. Knowledge of phylogenesis can then be reduced to knowledge of one's own genesis, which is something that need not astonish us. This idea, if not so explicitly stated, guided Ferenczi in the interpretation of the eternal fish symbol.[1]

I can naturally give no general proof because we know too little about mental development, especially that of the higher systems of the mind. I will confine myself to psychosexuality. In the first place, this is perhaps the most primitive mental stratum and thus closest to biology. Secondly, it is a sphere that has been fairly thoroughly explored, both from the phenomenological and the genetic point of view. Furthermore, we psycho-analysts have what might be called some conqueror's rights in this sphere, for it was here that our master, Freud, was the first and certainly a most successful explorer.

Since he opened the way with his *Three Contributions to the Theory of Sex* [2] we have learnt that the concept of sexuality embraces a great deal more than is usually understood from impressions gained from normal, adult sexuality. We know that sexuality goes through a long and complex process of evolution before arriving at the final, mature form which Freud called genitality. It is now possible to show the main landmarks along this path, the so-called stages in organisation, which are named after those regions of the body that play the principal part in the particular organisation. These, in their order of appearance, are: the oral, the anal and the genital zones, and thus the individual phases are called oral, anal and genital. But it has not yet been asked why human sexuality, without exception, organises itself at first around the mouth, then around the anus, before reaching the adult genital form.

The only man to have put this question and brought its solution considerably nearer was Abraham. In his essay

[1] Ferenczi: *Versuch einer Genitaltheorie*, Chap. VI. Int. PsA. Verlag (1924). (English translation: *Thalassa*, New York, 1938.)

[2] Freud: *Three Contributions to the Theory of Sex*. New York: Nerv. & Ment. Dis. Pub. Co., 1910.　First German Edition, 1905.

'Origins and Growth of Object-love' [1] he pointed to a very remarkable correspondence between the sequence followed in embryogenesis and that of the development of psychosexuality. In embryogenesis the first organs to be formed are the primitive mouth and the primitive intestine. In many chordates, especially in the simplest, the primitive mouth moves away from the final oral region of the body to the opposite pole and becomes there the anus. At the same time the muscles appear, first of all the jaw-muscle system, and only far later the sexual glands. All this has long been known, but we have to thank Abraham for having pointed out that the principal sexual regions appear in exactly the same sequence. He propounded another 'special law' according to which the psychosexual development 'lags a long way behind this somatic development, like a late version or repetition of the same processes.' [2] I consider that this 'special law' of Abraham, which I want here to emphasise as the principle of retardation, is one of the most important laws in the whole mental and bodily evolution of man. But I must postpone any detailed treatment of this subject to another occasion.

We know, then, that the development of the body and that of psychosexuality take the same path; we also know that while in the case of the body the development takes place in a matter of weeks, the mind requires years for it; what we do not yet know is why just this path—oral, anal, genital—is the one traversed both by body and mind. I would like now to show that in animals sexual behaviour has been observed that is immediately recognisable as equivalent to the stages in the organisation of sexuality already known to us, and that the three phases of the psychosexual development of man discovered by Freud correspond to a similar triple gradation in phylogenetic sexual evolution. Thus it becomes understandable why there are neither more nor less than three stages in human sexual organisation, a fact at which, curiously enough, no one hitherto seems to have wondered.

Since the discovery of cells, biologists divide the sexual func-

[1] Printed in: *A Short Study of the Development of the Libido* (1924). (English translation in *Selected Papers*, Hogarth Press, London, 1942.)
[2] op. cit., p. 499.

tions into two large groups: *fertilisation* and *mating*. By 'fertilisation' is understood the union of two, generally sexually differentiated, cells, called gametes (this may be reduced to the union of two mere nuclei). Closely related to this process is a remarkable phenomenon, the nuclear reduction, which will be discussed later. To the group of functions called 'mating' belong all the processes necessary to union of the gametes, but which are not carried out by the gametes themselves.

Now, in the case of many unicellulars, among them the most simple, sexuality consists exclusively of fertilisation. The ways and means by which this is brought about in the different species is astonishingly multiform. What is important to our thesis is that all biologists have interpreted this process as a mutual devouring; and that, in all unicellular forms of life which take in solid food, the union takes place, without exception, in the place where nourishment is otherwise taken in; that is to say, where a cell mouth has already been formed, through this cell mouth. The original form of sexuality is, then, closely related to the intake of solid food. There are, from the first, two possible explanations: either the sexual development and that from liquid to solid food took place independently of each other, and only later did the cell-mouth region become the sexual one, or else the pleasure experienced by these organisms at sexual union matures in them the desire for the intake of solid particles. The disturbing presence in their own plasma of substances of a type foreign to their own released a sequence of defensive processes which, in successful cases, led to the assimilation of the particles and so converted the originally merely pleasurable act into a practical one.

Biological factual material does not point to one rather than the other of these two hypotheses. All that we can gather from it suggests, however, a very close relation between nourishment and sexuality.[1]

---

[1] As we have seen, union of the unicellular forms of life takes place through the cell mouth. The oral zone in higher animals plays a similarly important rôle, though naturally only in the sexual play that leads up to mating. And this is not only true of mammals, but also of birds, amphibians (tritons, for instance), arthropodes, etc. By far the greatest number of sense organs that take any considerable part in mating are, then, arranged around the mouth or in its neighbourhood, even when

We are very often faced with a similar antinomy in biology: Does sexuality attach itself to already existing somatic functions, or, vice versa, does sexuality determine the development of new somatic functions? It is interesting that this very question crops up at the very beginnings of human psychosexuality. With infants we are not in a position to decide how far sucking is to be ascribed to the sexual and how far to the feeding instinct.

In the protists we see still another type of sexual phenomena. The above-mentioned living beings propagate themselves by dividing for a time, until for some reason sexual union takes place. The so-called vegetative individuals in whom no sexual function is observable are exactly similar to the sexual ones; *the individual is the gamete itself* (isogamous example: Pyramidomonas, Dunaliella; anisogamous: Chlamydomonas braunii).[1] We can, however, observe in the case of the more highly developed protists that individuals produced through ordinary

the sexual orifices have already long moved away from it. Language, or the Hungarian language at least, has the same expression, 'csorog a nyála' (his mouth waters) for the desire for food or for a woman.

It has long been known that change of food, and particularly starvation, can suddenly start sexual cycles in unicellulars. Now fertilisation does not at first mean an increase but rather a reduction of the number of individuals by half. Very often there follows after fertilisation a period of rest, and even encystment, but the assimilation of food is always discontinued during fertilisation and for some time afterwards. Here one is reminded of the psychological concept of repletion and, anthropomorphically speaking, one might say that these protists are seeking a substitute in fertilisation for the nourishment denied them in reality. So that if they do not get enough to eat they devour each other. The resorption of the nuclear material during reduction can be interpreted on similar lines. We might even say that all unicellular sexual acts are released by nourishment difficulties and that their actual aim is to overcome these. (Hertwig's nucleus-plasma relation, etc.)

In those species where sex is not determined genetically, the undifferentiated young can be reared to either sex by a suitable choice of nourishment (e.g. in the case of the worm Bonellia viridis).

And finally an impressive example is offered us in the fundamentally different methods of nourishment and of sexual functions between the animal and vegetable world. (See pp. 26-27.)

[1] I have taken all my examples of primitive forms from the group of Volvocales, partly because they have been fairly thoroughly investigated and partly to keep in accord with the time-honoured custom in all text-books.

division never fertilise each other. Multiplication by division continues until one such 'vegetative' individual divides in a particular manner departing from the normal. The cells thus produced are as a rule easily distinguishable from the 'vegetative' ones; morphologically they may either be similar (isogamous: Stephanosphaera, Haematococcus, Gonium pectorale) or already show sexual differentiation (anisogamous: Eudorina elegans, Volvox). These are the gametes which perform the sexual union. The 'vegetative' cells, on the other hand, represent a completely new phenomenon, that is to say a new generation. To distinguish them from the gametes they are known as gametocytes. While they never fertilise each other, they have their own sexual functions, only of a different kind— the formation and evacuation of gametes. This function can easily be interpreted as an equivalent of anal satisfaction, i.e. the formation and evacuation of excrement.

The more simple multicellular protists (Eudorina, Pandorina, etc.) are actually several unicellulars grouped and existing together, all similar to each other and having the same functions. From the point of view of sexuality this means that they represent a colony of gametes or, respectively, gametocytes. It is different when we come to the next higher stage in this group (Volvox). Here it is only certain specific cells which can produce gametes while the remainder cannot do so. Here a third generation is superimposed on the gametes and gametocytes, which Meisenheimer calls the 'gametocyte-carrier'. At first it is cut off from all sexual activity and, in contrast to the 'germ cell', is known as 'soma'. While it is doubtful if the soma is asexual or bisexual, it is certain that no sexual function can be observed in it. It produces the gametocytes, then lets the completed gametes escape in some manner, mostly through a fissure, and is then finished with them.[1] For the time being, no sexual differentiation is to be found in it, and so it remains in the lowest category of multicellular animals such as sponges and coelenterates, and also many worms.

It looks as if the newly evolved soma had secured an advantage over Eros. In fact, it has remained independent of him for

---

[1] Although it soon dies after the evacuation of the last gametocyte.

quite a long time, and developed itself into complex, highly efficient forms whose sexual activity is almost completely confined to the primitive evacuation of gametes. But untiring Eros refused to leave the soma for long with this advantage. Step by step he subdued it and pressed it into his service. The history of this eventful process, which runs a different course in animals and plants, could be called the career of Eros.[1]

I can here do no more than follow this interesting path in merest outline and only point to its main landmarks. The two original forms of sexual function are at first, as we have seen, absolutely independent of each other; the gametes unite with each other while the gametocytes evacuate, and the two generations exert no influence on each other. Already in the lowest group, however, often before the formation of the third generation, exceptions arise which show tentative attempts at the great evolution which is to follow. This takes place in two ways. At first the sexual differentiation of the gametes is hereditarily established; that is to say it is made independent of environment. Then the gametocytes are gradually compelled to sexual differentiation. In the case of Chlorogonium euchlorum, to keep to the Volvocales, morphologically the gametes resemble each other, while physiologically they are already sexually differentiated, and it is the same with the gametocytes. Determination of sex takes place at the first division after fertilisation; of the four cells produced two are of one sex and two of the other. Similar conditions prevail in the colony-forming Gonium and Pandorina. In the case of Eudorina elegans, on the other hand, the gametes are also morphologically different, while the gametocytes are still similar, although physiologically strictly differentiated in sex. It is the same with the Pleodorina. The next step forward is taken by the Volvox. Here the gametocytes are also heteromorphous and easily recognisable as male antheridia or female oogonia. The already evolved soma is, on the contrary, still undifferentiated sexually.

The other evolutionary path is that in which the other generations, besides the gametes, are slowly drawn into the

[1] The following paragraphs should be omitted by readers not particularly interested in biology. The main argument is resumed on p. 24.

function of uniting; and so mating begins. Thus in the higher species of all groups the female gamete loses mobility and finally becomes a motionless egg. (Example: Chlamydomonas coccifera.) The egg is then no longer evacuated but remains in the oogonium until fertilisation (Eudorina elegans, etc.). In many types the oogon then helps with the fertilising. A famous case is that of the Coleochaeta. In the case of this Chlorophycea the oogon must open itself to the fertilising spermatozoa, and becomes after fertilisation the so-called 'fruit'. With many fungi, such as Albugo Bliti, Pyronema, Mucor and so on, no more gametes whatsoever are formed; it is the four-celled gametocytes that perform the sexual union.[1]

Actually, the same thing happens with the Ciliates, the most highly evolved animal protists. Here the inter-pairing individuals are gametocytes, while the gamete generation is atrophied, and is only represented by the two different kinds of nuclei, the stationary and the mobile nuclei (Paramecia). In another respect these forms are still primitive; the gametocyte, i.e. the individual, is not yet sexually differentiated. In the case of the other sessile family in the same group, the Vorticellides, this step has already been taken. With them the female gametocyte remains in her place while the male swims about until he meets and fertilises her. This process, that can already be called mating, has become the rule in the plant world. We know that the pollen is a perfectly homologous

---

[1] Fungi offer a rich field for the study of these transitional phenomena. The very complex situation that prevails in this group unfortunately prevents me from going into further detail. I want only to mention that the complexity of sexual functions in fungi is intimately connected with the circumstance that momentous changes of habit took place within this group. These are the transition from existence in the sea to existence on land, and from an independent to a parasitic form of life. The types existing freely in water are from the sexual point of view very similar to the original forms; and vice versa. It is the same, as we shall see shortly, with the worms and still later with the amphibians that are also transitional types. What the fungi stand for in the eroticising of the gametocyte functions, the worms and amphibians do for the gametocyte-carrier. Thus the assumption of Ferenczi, according to which the complex mating functions only became necessary after the drying up of the earth, is strengthened (op. cit., *passim*, p. 68, for example), although he only postulated this for the vertebrates.

counterpart of the gametocyte generation;[1] it produces the fertilising male gametes on the stigma of the female blossom and—the similarity to the anal function is to be observed here—makes them reach the egg cells through a duct. With few exceptions the sexual functions in plants are not evolved beyond this, which means that their soma is not further eroticised.

It is different with animals.[2] Here the gametocytes never become independent, but are slowly drawn together to form an organ, the gonad, that is called, respectively, ovary or spermary. This organ, that from its inception plays an important part in the organisational plan of the animal body, is gradually being removed farther and farther from the surface, towards the interior. Parallel with this process goes the participation of the soma in the sexual function of the gametocytes. In the more primitive types, in which the gametocytes are still somewhere on the surface of the body, a rent in them can release the gametes (Sponges, Hydra, Hydromedusa, etc.). In the higher coelenterates the gonads empty themselves into the interior of the body (the gastro-vascular space) and then reach the external world through the mouth. As we see, the soma is not affected by any sexual functions in either of these groups (sponges and coelenterates). Asexual propagation is correspondingly common (gemmulae in sponges, buds in polyps). In the next higher evolved group, that of worms, the picture suddenly becomes very varied. This is undoubtedly partly due to their polyphyletic origin; not for nothing has this group been called 'the lumber-room of zoology'. I think, however, that there is another factor which has added to the complexity here. This factor is the alteration in habits. In this group the transition from forms swimming freely in the water to those living on land, or living parasitically, took place on several occasions, as in the case of the Platyhelminthes, Nemathelminthes, Annelids etc.; and everywhere one finds that the free water worms show simpler sexual functions than the next related parasitic or land

[1] With the one difference that it belongs to the haploid generation, while the infusoria are diploid and thus bisexual. I will refer to this difference later.

[2] The following examples are almost all taken from the important work of J. Meisenheimer, even where I do not expressly quote him. (*Geschlecht und Geschlechter*, **1**, G. Fischer Jena, 1921.)

forms. It is interesting to note that already in the worms almost all mating functions or organs can be observed, at least in their rudimentary form, which later play so important a part. But the old, primitive sexual functions also remain in other types, and non-sexual propagation and metagenesis occur. It looks as if it was in this group that the decisive battle between Eros and soma was fought out, while in the higher groups the victor had only to consolidate his domination over quite isolated rebellions. Soma has become the servant of Eros.

Eros compelled soma in the first phase of the struggle to take over the functions of the gametocytes. At the formation of the coelom the gonads were drawn into the interior of the body and so isolated from the external world. From now on the soma had to be responsible for the evacuation of the gametes. This probably took place at first through a fissure in the wall of the body, produced for this purpose, as in the case of the Volvox already mentioned, and further in many Turbellaria, Annelida and Balanoglossus, as well as in the Appendicularia (which already belong to the chordates). In many polychaete Annelida special parts are formed in the body, the so-called (epitocic) sexual parts which, tightly packed with gametes, release themselves from the mother body and so effect the discharge of the gametes. And, just as with the Volvox, many animals die in this process.

In other types evacuation ducts are then formed. The transition to this group is provided by species in which the fissure formed for the purpose quickly heals up. To this group are joined those which develop ducts only at the time of the ripening of the gametes, such as certain Nemertines and the Crinoides among the Echinoderms, etc. Next come the types whose ducts are permanent; these ducts are often connected already with the channels of evacuation of the nephridia, representing the first rudiments of the later uro-genital system (cf. Ferenczi, op. cit., p. 80 ff.). In these, therefore, the soma has completely taken over the evacuation function. Such species are extremely common and are still to be found in the highest groups, as in many Turbellaria, primitive Snails, most marine Mussels, Echinoderms, Tunicates and many Fishes.

In the next stage we see Eros compelling the gametocyte-carrier to expel the gametes simultaneously, as may be easily observed in sessile aquatic animals in an aquarium. If one starts with the evacuation, the others follow. It is almost always the males that begin first. The most perfect example of this is to be found in the behaviour of herrings. At this state there appear the first distinct traces of mutual sexual stimulation, perhaps already in some species of Medusa but definitely in Brachiopods, Chitons and Prosobranchiata.

Another evolutionary line is embarked on actually before the worms. In this only the male, and not the female, gametes are evacuated. The male gametes must then bring about the fertilisation inside the mother animal (the so-called 'internal fertilisation'). This happens with the red coral, many Tubicolae and Mussels (Unio, Anodonta) and with the famous Callistochiton viviparus, which lives up to its name. The father animal, however, has as yet nothing to do with the process; his gametes have to fulfil the task independently.

Now Eros again intervenes and compels the individual, the gametocyte-carrier—after it has already partly taken over the work of the gametocytes—to play the rôle of the gamete as well. The beginnings of this process are again to be found in the worms. In many nemertines several individuals join together for the general evacuation; in other species the number is soon reduced to two, and so it remains up to the highest animals. Examples are to be found in all the higher species, the best known being that of the amphibians. Here, however, special measures have to be taken to replace the water necessary in the case of dry-land species. (Cf. Ferenczi, op. cit., *passim*, p. 50.) Rudiments are found again among the worms where, for instance, the earthworms cover themselves in viscous slime during the period of the transfer of sperms, the spermatozoa being enclosed in spermatophores as a protection against drying up. Spermatophores are still given out by the males and actively taken up by the females among the salamanders and tritons, and more or less viscous secreta make up for the lack of water in the case of many toads and frogs. Everywhere at this stage, however, the males still empty their gametes into the external world, although already in the proximity of, or directly on to the body of, the females.

What happens next surely forms the most fantastic chapter of biology. All that Eros has done towards making a so-called 'internal fertilisation' possible is truly astonishing. One may say without exaggeration that every part of the body has been tried out for this purpose. The arthropods in particular, those miracles of mechanical precision, show many remarkable examples. Feelers, chelicerae, parts of the mouth, legs, etc., are utilised in order to bring the spermatozoa, mostly joined to spermatophores, to the female sexual orifice, and in some cases to push them into it. Evolution then goes on to produce a far-reaching division of labour, and for each phase of the sexual act only certain appointed parts of the body are used, and these are refashioned correspondingly. Thus the gonopodes were produced, those decidedly male organs which were orginally either appendages of the body or organs of motion, and now perform the task of transmitting the sperm. Organs for grasping, trapping and holding, pincers, pouches, hooks, vesicles, conductor grooves and channels, pumps, dilators and so on are formed, no matter out of what. They all have the task of provisionally taking up the freely deposited sperm and then transporting it into the body of the female. Even more remarkable are the gadgets found in cuttlefish. Here an arm or a pair of arms can take over the function of the gonopodes or can also be formed into conductor grooves. In the argonautids this arm detaches itself from the male body and, laden with the spermatozoa, succeeds in independently reaching the female mantle cavity. Biology was for long undecided about the nature of this discovery, and the detached arms were for some time thought to be parasites; hence their name, hectocotylus. We also find gonopodes produced from the anal fin of certain fishes, such as the viviparous cyprinodontides.

Another evolutionary process that is actually only a special form of the foregoing begins early, once again among the worms. The sperm is transferred directly out of one sexual orifice into the other without reaching the outside world. Organs are developed for this purpose which, however, differentiate from the external ducts of the genital glands, and on this account are called copulative organs proper. The simplest method of copulation is by mere pressing against each other of the sexual orifices, as may be observed in many vivi-parous fishes and a few salamanders. Many types develop auxiliary organs for the purpose, called mixipodes, that either fasten the two orifices more firmly together or, by penetrating into the female orifice, widen it. The roundworm possesses such a gadget (in this case known as a spicula), as well as many insects such as crickets and locusts, and also sharks. The functioning of this apparatus is often aided by glandular secretion. A proper penis first appears in the platyhelminthes, although in other worms, too, we find either tubular- or conical-shaped formations capable of swelling and protruding. This is so among many turbellarians, oligochaetes and hirudinea. Snails and many arthropods of almost all the groups in this class form similar organs which become erect either by muscles or already by the inflowing body fluid, conditions which are completely similar to those obtaining among the highest group of animals. The most complicated are perhaps the organs of the higher insects, but in principle these are also a repetition of the two original types of functioning: by muscular action or by increase in blood-pressure. The position as regards the vertebrates shows, in the main, no new features.

Before summarising the conclusions from these digressions I would like to describe one further achievement of Eros. It is only the gametes, as we have seen, that are at first sexually differentiated. This difference may, primarily, be only a physiological one; the gametes still exhibit perfect similarity of shape, except that some of them only copulate with some, and not with all, others. We cannot here speak of male and female, and biologists distinguish the two sexes by a $+$ and a $-$ respectively. Soon the two differ morphologically as well, and this differentiation is extended to the gametocyte generation. For some time, however, the soma remains unaffected. The most that Eros was able to achieve in the case of sponges and coelenterates is that some types are dioecious. We know extremely little, however, about how this was accomplished. In some species which are at this stage Eros even succeeded in conjuring up a kind of sexual dimorphism. Many ovaries are coloured conspicuously different from the corresponding spermaries, and thus in some dioecious types the individuals producing male gametes are distinguishable from those producing female gametes, as in red coral. Whether these can already be called male or female animals is still an open question, as all other parts of the body are absolutely similar. In rare cases it sometimes happens that the soma also, or, more exactly, a part of it, is differently coloured (Meisenheimer can only enumerate two such species of medusa, op. cit., p. 442). Such non-sexual forms are also to be found among the worms; we need only think of the very common metagenesis and of the even commoner non-sexual propagation that frequently occurs in this group, and which does not appear in any higher one (excepting the tunicates). Here too we have a victory won by Eros. All higher animals are sexually differentiated; at first the differentiation may be hermaphroditic, but in the highest forms, such as insects and amniotic vertebrates, it is only isolated individuals, probably evolutionary failures, that are not strictly monosexual. This is another confirmation of Ferenczi's genital theory, because these two groups actually contain only land animals, of which only a few species secondarily reverted to an aquatic existence. Now according to Ferenczi mating proper first became obligatory among land animals, and the strict sexual differentiation in whole classes of animals is undoubtedly closely related to the fact of this compulsory mating.

In the various groups of animals Eros has explored various trails, one might almost say 'conducted many experiments'. Of these some were abandoned as useless, but many others were utilised again in improved forms. The principal lines of this evolution almost all lead up to adult human genitality. Eros first compelled the gametocyte-carriers to take over the function of the gametocytes. For this he had to form ducts to secure a safe outlet for the completed gametes into the open, that is to say, into the water. Then we find him no longer leaving the moment of evacuation to chance but inducing the gametocyte-carriers to expel their gametes simultaneously. Then the soma had also to perform part of the work of the gametes and had to seek a place in the proximity of the partner in which to deposit the sex cells. Eros finally developed all kinds of tools and gadgets to bring about a close union of the partners and so to ensure that the coming together of the gametes was not subject to accident; and eventually he evolved copulative organs proper in the land animals. The sexualising of the soma runs parallel to this evolution. Non-sexual at first, it later had to develop sexual parts, until finally a sex (or both sexes) were imposed on it. The determination of sex takes place among the higher animals already at the commencement of the ontogenesis, and is fixed hereditarily. Thus the soma that in the beginning was independent of sexuality became the servant of Eros and was sexualised through and through. It made itself responsible for carrying out all the activities which biologists summarise under the concept of 'mating'. As a reward for its service it then received from its mighty lord, Eros, a truly princely gift: the love rapture, or orgasm, the highest pleasure on earth.

Looking back, we recognise the psychosexual evolution of man as a repetitive phenomenon. Not only the body but also the mind must recapitulate the principal points of phylogenesis before arriving at its final form. Phylogenetic evolution begins in the unicellular gametes—the first organ to be formed in embryogenesis is the mouth—and so the psychosexual evolution commences with the gametes' own particular way of obtaining satisfaction: *oral incorporation*. The same parallelism is found at the next stage. Here the development of the anal region and the muscular system, there the setting up of the anal-sadistic organisation, corresponding to the sexual function of the gametocytes: *anal evacuation*. And finally the formation of the sexual parts of the body, including the centralisation of sexuality in the genital primacy, runs parallel to the sexual function of the gametocyte-carrier, which is *genital mating*.

These facts give fresh biological support to Freud's theory of sexuality. Independently of Freud, biologists have for long comprised in the idea of sexuality phenomena which have nothing to do with what is generally understood by that concept. The biological and psycho-analytical concepts, however, are in complete agreement. From the biological viewpoint pregenital sexuality appears to us as the remnant of a long-vanished epoch; having lost its biological purpose, it is rather like an old paid-off mercenary who willingly offers his services to any bidder—a conception closely corresponding to that of psycho-analysis.

There is, however, one other fact to be considered. We have found three forms of sexuality in biology, of which only one, the genital mating, has actually 'existed before'. Compelled by Eros, the soma imitated the union of the gametes, although in an improved manner adapted to the changed circumstances. The two partners in sexual intercourse merge into each other, as do the two gametes, so that Ferenczi did not hesitate to call them megaloon and megalosperm respectively. The genital union is, therefore, actually a regression.

Thus there are only two original forms of sexual functioning: union and evacuation. Apart from the most primitive species, *union has become the characteristic form in the animal world*. This has resulted in a high degree of mobility, strong sexual dimorphism, well-developed sensory organs, sharply defined individuality, and participation by the whole animal in the sexual act; that is to say, the individuals imitate the gametes. In the *plant world* quite other conditions obtain. Almost everywhere there, *evacuation* is the form in which the gametocyte-carriers, that is the soma, perform the sexual act. The bringing together of the sex cells (actually sex individuals) is left more or less to chance, being effected by water currents, winds and, in the case of the highest plants, the agency of animals (principally arthropods). Dimorphism is correspondingly hardly ever found; plants are in general sessile, have no sensory organs, are not in fact individuals but colonies with vague individuality boundaries, and only a part of them is affected by sexuality. The reason for this difference may perhaps be found in the method of feeding. Animals generally take in solid organic food, and do so through the mouth. Plants, on the contrary, absorb dissolved or gaseous inorganic substances by means of diffusion. When we consider how intimately connected the intake of food through the mouth is with the sexual function of union, we can perhaps recognise in the circumstance that plants do not eat, one reason for their different sexual behaviour. The work of assimilation in plants is also undoubtedly much greater, and this may be another reason for their less developed sexuality. Thus among plants the genital stage is not reached; the actual sexual individual, the gametophyte, is very rudimentary, and is represented by the pollen or, respectively, the female cell (the embryo sac), which is scarcely more than a gametocyte.

The path we have followed led us principally through the sexual behaviour of the male. A similar evolutionary path can be traced through the development of female sexual functions or organs. This would, however, be considerably more complex and require much more time. The many forms of breeding and rearing by means of the mother's body would have to be taken into account in any such presentation. As is well known, this function transformed the maternal body to a much greater degree than the fertilising function the paternal body. One consequence of this can be anticipated: what the male can accomplish in a single act is split up in the case of the female. In addition to the sexual union, female sexuality includes breeding and rearing, i.e. gravidity, followed by parturition and lactation. In the sexual union the female is the receptive part and takes a foreign element, the penis and the sperm, into herself. The similarity between this and the oral-sucking activity is further stressed by the successive contractions of the vagina. The other component of the female sexual function has more resemblance to anal phenomena. It appears then that in females the two original sexual functions, union and evacuation, were not synthesised; in this sense the female has remained at a more primitive stage. The mating function in the male, on the other hand, represents a further development towards synthesis by means of regression. The union with a partner, a rather late achievement in phylogenesis, is biologically a regression, an imitating of the function of the gametes by the gametocyte-carrier. With the male, sexual union and the expulsion of sex cells, i.e. the gametocyte function proper, are indivisibly merged. Females undoubtedly possess characteristics, both physical and mental, which appear much more primitive than the corresponding ones in males. But conversely there are other features in the male which show the same kind of primitiveness. Perhaps some of these respective primitive characteristics can be better explained by referring them to the actual biological difference. This difference has much similarity to that between animal and plant. The rearing process, as is well known, is very strongly developed in plants. This may be the reason why poetical language so often compares women to plants and also why, as far as I know, in all European languages plants have a feminine gender, while animals are masculine or neuter.

2. *Individuality and Orgasm*

It is time to pause and reflect. Hitherto, in order to explain the evolution of sexual organs and functions, I have presented Eros as governed by the spirit of conquest. Thus I am doubly guilty of transgressing the command against anthropomorphising. Is it not simpler and more scientific, it might be asked, to seek the reason for these phylogenetic phenomena in external conditions, in changes of environment? This is what I have, in fact, partly done. The variegated picture offered us by the fungi in their fertilisation function, or by the worms in their mating function, I have tried to explain by pointing out that it was in these groups that the transition from marine to land, or to a parasitic way of life, was achieved. The absence of water unconditionally demanded special provisions which were unnecessary in the sea. In the biological part we discussed several of such provisions. In his biological investigations Ferenczi came to the conclusion [1] that it was the absence of water—or, psychologically speaking, the desire for the more friendly sea—on the part of the land animals that was responsible for the evolution of genitality. This desire or, as he called it, the *thalassal regressive impulse* was the motive power behind the development of true mating organs, of internal fertilisation, and, in the embryo, of protective organs containing the foetal fluid, i.e. the amnion. Now this triad is actually found only in land animals, or in those former land animals that returned to the sea, but not in all of them—only in the higher vertebrates such as mammals, birds and reptiles. Insects, these purely land animals, certainly possess true organs of mating and internal fertilisation, but no amnion fluid. The other land species (which

[1] op. cit., Chap. VI.

incidentally are very rare indeed compared with these two large groups), are in this respect similar to the insects. It is just because of this difference that the higher vertebrates are grouped under the general name of 'amniota'. We are thus compelled to abandon one characteristic of Ferenczi's triad as not universal, or else to limit his law to the vertebrates. This solution is supported by the fundamental difference between the ontogenesis of the chordates and that of the arthropods. The first are deuterostomia, while the second are protostomia; the migration of the primitive mouth to the anal region, mentioned in the first chapter, takes place only in the former group.

This, however, is only one reason for limiting the ecological explanation. We find proper organs of mating and internal fertilisation also in quite a few marine animals. Many fishes, for instance, mate by pressing together their cloacal openings, others (cyprinodontides) with the help of gonopods, and others again (sharks) by means of mixipods. Finally, the clinus species develop an organ like a penis, which lies behind the anus, but already contains the urethra and the sperm duct, and is certainly used for mating, the species being viviparous. And all these exist side by side with such purely evacuating species as the herrings! We find similar extremes of divergence among the worms, and indeed, to a lesser degree, among all groups containing marine animals. This divergence in the forms of sexuality decreases as life adapts itself to a dry-land existence and becomes more and more uniform. I am therefore not of the opinion that the environmental conditions were responsible for the development of internal fertilisation and of proper mating organs, but that, on the contrary, they caused the eradication of all other fertilising methods. Thus the conclusions arrived at by Ferenczi are not weakened but merely put in another light. Of the many available forms of mating it was the one which met the greatest number of demands that was selected and further developed. And this was the genital one, firstly because it was best suited to the new environment, and secondly because it gave the fullest measure of satisfaction to the thalassal regressive impulse. I must stress that this limitation of the effect of the dry-land environment just mentioned only holds good as regards the two phenomena of internal fertilisation and the possession of true organs of mating. Compared to these, the formation of amnion in the higher vertebrates appears to be an entirely new acquisition; at least no marine prototype is to be found. For this phenomenon the ideas put forward by Ferenczi remain completely valid.

The problem, however, is still far from solved. What was it that compelled animals while still in the sea to develop these mating organs? I think it might be useful to examine, as our provisional working hypothesis, the tendency to conquer which we ascribed to Eros. If we glance once more at the many forms which I reported in the previous chapter, we shall find ourselves constantly brought up against this general conquering tendency of sexuality. Ever more parts of the soma, which at first was asexual, were sexualised; and in such a way that it was in some manner compelled to undertake the work that in past generations had been carried out by the gametes and gametocytes. At first it performed these supplementary tasks with organs that had actually been formed for quite other purposes, such as elimination through the mouth in the coelenterates, through the metanephridia in many coelhelminthes, the use of limbs and body appendages for sperm transmission in the articulated animals, and so on. In man, too, the sexual channels are still excretory ducts belonging to the kidneys. Soon, however, the soma was forced to form special organs, and we see it finally completely permeated by sexuality. With what weapon did Eros achieve this victory? The answer is easy to find when we examine human behaviour. The magic weapon used by Eros can have been none other than the orgasm.

The rudiments of this pleasure are already demonstrable in the case of quite primitive marine animals, possibly even in worms, and certainly in all higher groups. The signs which can be observed are exactly similar to those of fully developed genitality: extreme excitement, a tetanus-like rigidity or clonic convulsions, violence, unusual positions taken up before and during the mating; while afterwards peace, complete relaxation, often followed by a cataleptic-like state. Pleasure experiences, that is to say, a high degree of excitation which is extremely quickly spent,[1] probably also play a part in the other

[1] Cf. Freud: *Beyond the Pleasure Principle*, Int. PsA. Lib. (London, 1950); Ferenczi: op. cit., Chap. V.

two sexual functions—the union of the gametes and the evacuation by the gametocytes—although a true intensity can be observed solely in the pairing of the gametocyte-carriers. A convincing psychological parallel is offered us by the clinical fact that at a pre-genital level no orgasm is observable, only a pleasurable excitation which does not, however, increase to a proper climax. Men patients under analysis often admit to having experienced their first actual orgasm at the first emission, and women tell of a possibly similar difference between clitoral and vaginal excitation. Another fact that probably has a bearing on this is that in all extra-genital perversions, however absurd, the final satisfaction is arrived at through genital masturbation. But whence, we may ask, comes the intensity?

The only analyst to have concerned himself with the source of this intensity is Ferenczi. I will quote his conclusions word for word.[1]

'Considered from a purely physiological standpoint coitus seemed to us to be the periodically occurring terminal episode in the equalising and adjustment of an unpleasure-producing state of libidinal tension which accumulates throughout the entire life of the individual as the accompaniment of every non-erotic activity on the part of the various organs, and which is transferred from these organs in an "amphimictic" manner to the genitals. It looks as if under the conditions of coitus a tension which has been keyed up to a maximum is released unexpectedly and extremely easily so that a large amount of cathectic energy becomes suddenly superfluous. Hence the enormously great sensation of pleasure. . . . 'To this sensation some "genitofugal" backflow of libido into the bodily organs might run parallel—the opposite of that "genitopetal" flow which conducted the excitation from the organs to the genital during the period of tension.'

This revealing *physiological* explanation partly solves the problem. Ferenczi goes on to show that the soma strives to unite all its unfulfilled, or (in the real world) unfulfillable desires, either really or symbolically, in the mating function, in order to get rid of them as far as possible. The first to be mentioned here are the ontogenetic desire for the mother and the phylogenetic one for the sea.

[1] op. cit. pp. 37 ff.

We can see how Eros still keeps his servant under his domination. He rewards him by fulfilling his real desires and lures him on by the promise of granting all his other desires. We do not yet know, however, why at this—the genital—stage of evolution these rewards and promises have to be so much greater than at the other two. Or, to put it more exactly, why the excitation in the sexual function of the gametocyte-carriers is so much more intense than in that of the gametocytes and the gametes.

We saw in the first chapter that the gametocyte-carriers actually imitate their own gametes during mating. *The union of the gametocyte-carriers in copulation is, however, only temporary and partial, while that of the gametes, on the other hand, is total and final.* Now the unicellulars are not actual individuals; they propagate by dividing, and the very meaning of the word individual connotes indivisibility. This is not a mere play on words. Freud suggested [1] that the structure of the body of the metazoa may be regarded as arising from the life instincts of the single cells taking one another as love-objects. The more intense and stable these bonds, the more worthy is the animal in question of the proud name of individual. This individuality is threatened from two directions: from without by death, and from within by falling in love. It is a commonplace that those in love have no appetite, grow pale, sleep badly, and, as we know from fairy tales, stories of chivalry and romantic films, are ready to suffer all sorts of privations. It is remarkable that biology can make similar observations in the animal kingdom; but not in that of the plants, which are not individuals. The conclusion is clear: falling in love in some way loosens the texture of individuality, the bonds between the cells. With that we certainly have taken a step beyond physiology. Beyond this we cannot as yet go; our knowledge so far can do no more than confirm the fact of the close connection between individuality, sexuality and death.

The vegetative unicellulars are, as the experiments of Woodruff,[2] Max Hartmann [3] and others have shown, potentially

---

[1] Freud: *Beyond the Pleasure Principle*, Int. PsA. Lib., London, 1950 pp. 67–8.

[2] Woodruff: *Proc. Nat. Ac. Sc.*, (1921) **7**.

[3] M. Hartmann: *Arch. f. Protisten Kunde* (1921), **43**, 223.

immortal. The first individuals to make their appearance in the above sense of the word, that is to say, forms of life no longer capable of dividing, are the male gametes. These die when they cannot fertilise, and we have here the first example of death from internal causes. The female gametes retain their capacity for dividing for a considerable time; according to Schreiber [1] the famous immortal Eudorina cultures of Hartmann are all female. We see here that sexual differentiation can, although it need not necessarily, lead to death.

With the gametocytes the opposite is the case. In many species it happens that in the gamete formation the entire body of the gametocyte is not used up; the remainder, the so-called 'body remnant' ('Restkörper'), is inevitably doomed to death. The same thing repeats itself in the first gametocyte-carrier, the Volvox. After the evacuation of the last gametocyte, the soma dies off. It appears that at this evolutionary stage sexual undifferentiation leads unavoidably to death.

There is a certain confusion in the picture presented by the protists. It is only in the next group that there is some clarity again. Here we find the soma already developed, but still asexual. It seems still to possess the same capacity of eternal life as the vegetative cells of the protists. In the coelenterates non-sexual propagation by division or budding is practically general, and it is also fairly frequent in worms. In the higher groups, however, it is rather the exception, as in the molluscs and tunicates. The same is true of the regenerative powers; these are practically unlimited in the coelenterates, still very marked in the worms, and disappear in the higher groups apart from a few traces. Pieces cut from hydra, planaria or an oligochaete can reproduce the entire animal. Crabs and lizards, to take a couple of well-known examples, are only capable of replacing lost extremities, and these often only in stunted form. More highly evolved animals are capable, at the best, of not more than closing large wounds with cicatricial tissue. This means that the bonds between the single cells or parts of the body are comparatively lax in the lower groups and only become strong among the higher species. *Individuality becomes firm*

[1] Quoted by Kniep: *Die Sexualität der niederen Pflanzen*, p. 91, footnote. Jena, 1928.

only during phylogenesis. A very interesting parallel exists between these individuality attributes and the formation of colonies. In general it is the asexual, self-propagating species which form colonies; while these attributes are less frequently found in those that live independently. This division, while not completely hard-and-fast, is, all the same, fairly comprehensive. Thus, for example, non-sexual propagation can be observed among the molluscs in the colony-forming endo- and ecto-procta, but not among the brachiopods which live independently. We find the same division in the case of the tunicates; the individually existing copelates reproduce themselves sexually, whereas the ascidians and salps form colonies and propagate asexually. We know that the forming of colonies can only take place where individuality is weakly developed.

Individuality, however, connotes indivisibility, and therefore inevitable death. And, in fact, we frequently find, especially among insects, animals that mate only once during their lifetime and then die. Attention has often been drawn to the fact that animals such as butterflies, beetles, etc., that are prevented from mating, live longer than those used as controls. Death and mating are not so inseparably connected in the vertebrates; although we often hear from patients, as well as from poets, that the greatest rapture contains an admixture of a sense of passing away, of dying. Lovers are also dominated by another feeling, that of merging into each other, of giving up their own individuality. The mind can only recapture what has already once existed, and so here, too, we must look for prototypes. These are most obvious among the worms. In the case of some parasitic species the male and female are permanently linked to each other, as, for instance, the bilharziae and didymozoeae. Here the couples form the individuals.

We have found the first true individuals in the gametes. Correspondingly, we find already among the colony-forming coelenterates—the most primitive metazoa—that the sexually differentiated individuals, the medusae, strive towards individualisation. As I have pointed out in the biological part, it is among the medusae that the first sexual differentiation of the soma in the phylogenesis becomes observable. This parallel runs right through the animal kingdom, with very few exceptions. A strongly marked individuality, that is to say one in which there is no forming of colonies, no asexual propagation, and only reduced powers of regeneration, is almost always linked to a sexually differentiated soma, to sexual dimorphism, well-developed mating function, and to intense orgastic phenomena; and, of course, vice versa.

The state of affairs now appears somewhat complicated. Under compulsion from Eros the soma is not only forced to eroticise itself but must at the same time individualise, as we have seen the gametes do, in order then to die. In the living world mating and mortality form an inseparable unity. The orgasm is not only at the same time a lure and a reward for the taking over of the mating functions, but also a consolation for the immortality lost thereby. By this metaphor I wish to emphasise the dynamic element in the relationship between soma and germ cells. An everlasting struggle goes on between them. The soma wants to be an autonomous individual, independent and self-contained, obeying only its own laws. It is forced, however, to carry out the commands of Eros, which it does only unwillingly, in a reluctant submission to the foreign power, the conqueror. The gametes, and perhaps also the gametocytes, ever remain a strange element within the soma, essentially foreign (the body cells are diploid, the gametes haploid) and independent individuals with their own life and aims. Perhaps we can push the comparison farther: the conqueror gametes live apart; only on special occasions, on great festivals, do they allow the vulgar soma to share their joy as a spectator. And even this is not so much their intention, rather they make wise use of the fact that the rabble finds such an intense pleasure and enjoyment in merely looking at them. This is one aspect of the relationship. The other is that in which the soma seeks to rid itself of its rulers, eliminating them like its excrements (cf. Ferenczi, op. cit., p. 67). In this it succeeds to some extent while still in the sea, but to a far smaller extent on dry land, and also here in the case of the male better than in that of the female. This biological difference is certainly one of the reasons for women being more neurotic than men.

We have not yet enough biological material to elucidate these complex phenomena. Nor is there sufficient psychological material to hand, either. We are therefore forced to content ourselves for the moment with the only certain conclusions arrived at, namely that individuality, mating, orgasm and death are interconnected and must be explained together.

3. Reduction and New Beginning

So far we have only observed the cells up to their union; now we want to see what happens afterwards. A puzzling phenomenon follows: the reduction of the nucleus. The nuclear material is divided into several particles, mostly into four; the cell then divides into as many daughter cells as there are new nuclei, or the greater part of the nuclei are absorbed by the plasma.[1]

[1] The already complex generation relationships are further complicated by taking the reduction into account. We have to do with a new factor that must not be neglected, namely whether or not the nuclear material is single or double. Or, to put it more scientifically: whether the generation is haploid or diploid. (I am leaving out of account the rare phenomena of total or partial polyploidy.) *A priori* there are two possibilities, and cases of each can be shown. If the vegetative form is haploid (naturally, the gametes are always haploid), through the union a diploid zygote results, from which through reduction the haploid individuals arise (example A in diagram). Or else the vegetative individuals are diploid, the reduction introduces the formation of the gametes and, after the union of the haploid gametes, the diploid vegetative individuals result from the diploid zygotes (example B).

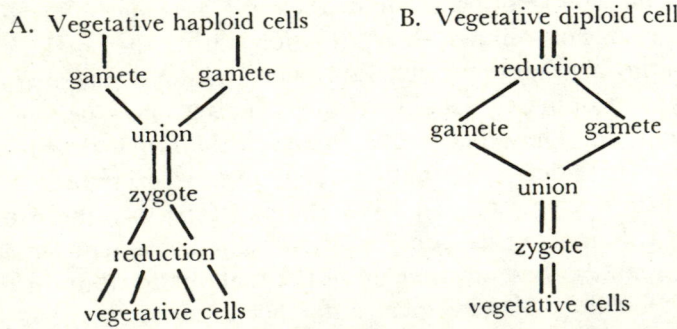

A. Vegetative haploid cells

gamete   gamete

union

zygote

reduction

vegetative cells

Example: chlorophyceae.

B. Vegetative diploid cells

reduction

gamete   gamete

union

zygote

vegetative cells

Example: Infusoria, amoeba diploidea.

Here another phenomenon crops up which is highly important for my thesis. During the formation of the gametes, or at least after union, the organisation of the cells becomes very often, one may say almost always, considerably simplified. Most of the cell organs are cast off or absorbed, so that even highly developed cells appear at this stage extremely primitive. Another result is that the marked sexual differentiation in the gametes often disappears. One cannot rid oneself of the impression that the organism regresses to an earlier stage of evolution, returning to long-abandoned life-forms, in order to begin its existence anew from there.[1]

This *new beginning* [2] plays a very important part in the living world. The development of each fertilised ovum represents a new beginning. And the potential immortality of some forms of life has been shown by the latest experiments to be based on their capacity for continually making this new beginning. When the environment is unfavourable, the result is almost always the formation of gametes, and their subsequent union. In order to suppress these sexual 'epidemics' the research worker must cultivate the organisms under optimal conditions, and even then he does not always succeed in checking all sexual phenomena. An instructive example was the unsuccessful attempts, lasting over decades, to achieve an asexual culture of Paramecia. The result, as is well known, was the discovery by Woodruff and Erdmann of the so-called parthenogenesis as an

Gametes are always haploid; vegetative individuals, on the other hand, occur both in the haplo- and in the diplo-phase. Thus among the higher animals the individual is itself diploid, but is made up actually of two generations: the gametocyte-carriers and the gametocytes. The haplo-phase is limited to a single cell, the gamete, which, however, represents a completely independent individual. Among plants and a few exceptional animals the situation is even more complex. Reproduction can take place at several points, several independent individuals can emerge in the generation cycle and these can be either haploid or diploid, and so on.

[1] Many biologists have expressed similar ideas Schaudinn (*Verh. d. dtsch. Zool. Ges.* (1906), **15,** 16, and M. Hartmann (for instance: *Biol. Sol.* (1922), **42,** 364), in particular.

[2] I should like to have another opportunity of speaking about the connection between these concepts and the well-known ones of regression and repetition, as well as about some technical inferences for character analysis.

essential stage in the life-cycle of Paramecia. The fertilising function can, however, be replaced by other revolutions in the cells, amongst them, but only under the most favourable conditions, by the common cell division. If this too is prevented, if only assimilation and growth can take place, and no reduction of the system is possible, all the cells slowly die, as was shown by the experiments of Hartmann on stephanosphaera, gonium, stentor and yeast.[1] The reduction of the system need not necessarily take place through division; it is possible to secure continual existence for some organisms—through ever-new regeneration—by repeated operative mutilation. In this way Hartmann kept alive for months an infusorium (stentor), a turbellaria (stenostoma) [2] and finally also the amoeba proteus,[3] without fertilisation or division. Most interesting in this connection are the experiments made by Goetsch.[4] Among other organisms, he worked with flatworms, the most primitive of worms. He let them grow until the commencement of sexual maturity and then cut down their food. As they began to starve their body substance was absorbed, starting with the gonads. When they were emaciated to about a tenth of their former size they again received normal supplies of food. This alternation was repeated. In this way it was shown that the same individual scould be kept alive for a year and three-quarters, that is to say, for a practically unlimited time. It thus appears that not only in the protists but also among the metazoa potential immortality is dependent on this capacity to make a new beginning.

The lowest stage of regression, the farthest starting-point for the new beginning, is always the cell. This fits in with the fact that we know of no living substance not organised into cells. We know nothing of whatever may lie beyond the cells. Nor do we know if this most primitive cell, which forms the ever new starting-point of all life, is sexually differentiated or is to be thought of as asexual. The most primitive life forms, according to the botanical researches of Pascher,[5] are the flagellates,

---

[1] M. Hartmann: *Arch. f. Protistenkde* (1921), **43**, 223.
[2] *Id.*, for instance: *Biol. Zbl.* (1922), **42**, 364.
[3] *Id.: Zool. Jb., Abtl. f. allg. Zool.* (1928), **45**, 973.
[4] Goetsch: *Biol. Zbl.* (1923), **43**, 481.
[5] *Arch. f. Protistenkde* (1918), **38**, 1.

which must be considered as the source of all later evolution. The theory of the new beginning is content with this discovery, as the flagellates are sexually differentiated in fundamentally the same way as the gametes among the multicellular organisms. Thus the first step towards ontogenesis would be a regression to the most primitive form of life.

The fertilised egg-cell, the zygote, is not, however, sexually differentiated. (I am leaving out of account the Mendelian sexual determination by heterochromosomes, as this only holds true at a much later stage in evolution.) It still remains an open question as to whether the zygote is bisexual or asexual. Equally important is the question whether such a thing as sexually undifferentiated life is possible. There are some phylogenetically very puzzling groups of organisms, such as the cyanophyceae and bacteria, in which, till now, no sexual activity has been observed. (Schaudinn alone [1] has found in the case of two bacteria phenomena which he classified as sexual, but both his observations and conclusions are still isolated and unconfirmed.) These species are generally considered not as primitive but as involuted or atrophied. This granted, we must remember, however, that any such retrogression can only follow a form that already once existed. Must we then assume that life was at first asexual? Now, these asexual species exist completely isolated, without connecting links to any others; the direct evolution begins in all probability in the flagellates. Perhaps these intruders are, after all, no relatives of ours at all, but the remnants of an unsuccessful asexual experiment of nature. Science can give no answer to any of these questions at the moment. What we have found in our study of individuality may perhaps serve here to carry us a step farther. The gametes are almost always individuals. They are at pains to renounce their individuality, to amalgamate and then to divide. We have seen the same thing in the protists. Only the most favourable external circumstances, the optimal conditions of existence, can, for a time, restrain them from this striving towards union. Now, the resulting zygote is, in all protists and in many groups of metazoa, no longer an individual. One is reminded of the so-called regulatory ova which—similarly to the above-mentioned

[1] *Arch. f. Protistenkde* (1902), **1**, 306; and (1903), **2**, 421.

organisms—develop, if cut into two, into two complete embryos. These observations point rather to an original life-form which was sexually not yet differentiated. But so far we have no absolute proof.

To escape from death and to continue their existence all organisms must ever begin anew. But what, we may ask, is gained by this new beginning? What is its meaning? Biology is not in a position to give us an answer. Ferenczi has suggested enlisting the help of analogies from a quite different branch of science. This he calls the utraquistic method (*Thalassa*, Chap. VI). We are familiar with a kind of new beginning, that made in psycho-analytic treatment, when we try to help the patient to make a fresh start in a life that has become unendurable. How do we achieve this? Is it not by freeing him from his rigid forms of reaction, and thus making him capable of a new adaptation to life? Probably something similar occurs at the biological new beginning. Biologists have very often indicated the nucleus as the organising centre of the cell and ascribed to it the control of the metabolic processes, of the motor and sexual activities. The nucleus reduction and the simplification of the cell organisation, which are closely connected with fertilisation, may be regarded also as a liberation from rigid forms of reaction. In this respect a new beginning by means of nuclear reduction, and one achieved by psycho-analytic treatment, would be similar processes. There is, however, a fundamental difference between the two, and this consists in the consciousness, one can say the premeditation, present in psycho-analytic treatment.

Up to here we have followed only well-founded scientific facts in our explorations. What now comes is fantasy. The transformation of living beings during phylogenesis proceeded in an autoplastic way. When there was a change of environment which prevented the further satisfaction of certain instincts, the species in question adapted themselves to the new conditions by altering the structure of their bodies. As a model for such changes we can take hysteria. In this case, just as with the phylogenetic adaptation to a changed reality, it is strong unsatisfied id desires which alter the body. Man has, however, another, a better way of dealing with reality. He has in the course of phylogenesis created another organ, physically, the brain, mentally, the preconscious, with the help of which he can transform his environment more or less as he wishes. Thus the step from autoplastic to alloplastic methods was taken. We are now experiencing a new evolutionary step, which, as usual, leads us forward by way of a regression. The human preconscious not only feels itself capable of adapting its environment to its desires but seeks to do the same with its own mind, as happens in psycho-analytic treatment. For this, though, it needs external help—that of the analyst.

Psycho-analytic treatment is thus a hybrid, autoplastic and alloplastic at the same time. It does not require too great a stretch of imagination to foresee a time when man will no longer be in need of external help. Then he will, with full consciousness and intention, reform body and mind as seems good to him. This idea is not my own; I am only quoting Bernard Shaw. In one of his plays, *Back to Methusela*, he described such persons in detail. He called them 'Ancients'. They are very old, very wise, are still sexually differentiated but have no longer any sexual desires. And they could transform themselves, '*if they really wanted to*'. It is interesting that even in poetic fantasy this knowledge and ability can be gained only by a far-reaching regression. These ancients live like hermits; they neglect their clothing, do not associate with one another, are silent, have, in fact, partially forgotten how to speak, and simply sit and meditate.

I do not believe it is necessary to paint such a pessimistic picture of our future. While it is true that very often, perhaps always, further development must be paid for by a regression, we have seen that this regression does not necessarily impoverish the world. Eros, it is true, forced the gametocyte-carriers to regress to the most primitive sexual function: to the union, but then bestowed love on us in all its multiplicity of forms. It is possible that the exquisite wisdom and ability, of which Shaw had a glimpse, must be paid for by a deep regression, but those who come after us need not remain at that stage. Starting from there they can begin a new life, which in spite of increased knowledge and capabilities can be still richer, more colourful, and more intense than the present one.

II
TWO NOTES ON THE EROTIC COMPONENT
OF THE EGO-INSTINCTS [1]
(1933)

1. *Adaptation and Educability*

To introduce some order into the vast domain of the ego-instincts, their erotic component appears to provide a suitable basis of classification. At one end of the line would come ego-functions which cause little or no erotic pleasure; at the other end such functions as one would hesitate to count as ego rather than as sexual functions. Such a line could be constructed as follows: heartbeat . . . breathing . . . muscular activity . . . intake of fluids . . . of solids . . . the diverse excretory functions . . . the considerably erotised 'herd instincts', such as ambition, domination, submissiveness, etc. . . . and lastly one could include the various character traits which in an adult certainly appear to be of a libidinal nature, but which doubtless contain also a strong ego-component, such as: obstinacy, steadiness, envy, but also magnanimity, generosity, cold-bloodedness, imperturbability, etc. Such a series could be continued farther in both directions, and many more items could be inserted; for the purpose of this paper, however, it will serve in its present preliminary form.

It is important to note that one gets the identical sequence if one orders the instinctual functions with regard to their educability. Heartbeat is not, as far as I know, trained anywhere (to be sure, there are a few people who can change the rhythm of their heart intentionally, but they are so rare that they can earn their living by it); respiration is trained in some diver tribes and in our athletes; drinking is often linked by education to certain set times, and eating practically everywhere; the training of the excretory function is obligatory among practically every tribe and nation on earth. One is

[1] First published in German in *Int. Z. f. Psa.* (1933), **19**, 428–33.

perhaps justified in assuming that it is just this erotic component that makes the ego-instincts educable. It is this component that makes an attachment to the educator possible. The satisfaction of the erotic component in the transference love compensates the individual under education for the frustration of the original instinctual urge, and thereby enables him to endure education.

If we consider our series from the point of view of biology we see that at its beginning stand functions which happen almost automatically, i.e. which are most *adapted*, while at the end of the series we find functions that *must be trained for their adaptation*, which in their original form are not yet completely adapted. In this connection it does not matter whether this incomplete adaptation is caused by the (because of civilisation) changed external conditions; the instinctual functions in question have not yet been fully adapted to those (changed) conditions, they are in the process of adjustment. Accordingly, the first items (heartbeat, partly also muscular activity) function already in intra-uterine life, or (breathing) immediately after birth, and they function without any period of learning; all the others must be learned. This discrimination is not quite strict; some children must learn how to breathe (asphyxia may occur without the mother's fault), others, on the other hand, get their fingers into their mouth, so to speak, while they are being born.

To sum up: the pre-condition of adaptation is the erotisation of the ego-instincts! [1] Such erotisation is continued as long as the work of adaptation lasts. Then the erotic component is gradually detached (probably in order to be used somewhere else), and parallel with it the ego-function in question loses its educability, it becomes rigid, automatic, like a reflex.

[1] An instructive example for this statement is the taming of wild animals, i.e. their adaptation to the whims of man. The tamers are in general (and especially in the phantasy of poets and novelists) stark, attractive people, and very often women choose male, and men female animals as partners. Scenes of jealousy (not only in fiction) are not uncommon; e.g. recently in the Budapest Zoo, the husband-to-be of a new female elephant badly maltreated her favourite keeper, a Hindu who had accompanied her from India.

Through this idea the so-hotly disputed orthogenesis becomes understandable, i.e. interpretable. If a tendency in the evolutionary process loses its erotic conponent which links it to the whole organism, and through it to reality, it will develop in a rigidly straight direction without any regard to reality, impelled only by its immanent forces. Such a development must lead to bizarre forms (cf. the always-quoted examples of Titanotherium and Ammonites). In extreme cases the loss of the erotic component, i.e. loss of love towards reality, may lead through the loss of capacity for adaptation to the extinction of the species.

This may explain why psycho-analysis has found an erotic component in all ego-instincts. This erotic component is the greater, the younger—in phylogenesis—the instinct is. It is possible that one way of development of reflexes has been the reducing of their erotic component practically to zero. If this is so, then the long-sought 'pure death instinct' may be found amongst the reflexes, and the well-known 'Totstellreflex' could be considered as a pointer towards it.

In principle it is possible that ego-instinct functions which are no more, or only very weakly sexualised, become recathected regressively with sexual libido. I presume that this is the mechanism at work in psychogenic organic diseases. Examples can be found without difficulty: the sudden changes of pulse rhythm in a highly emotional situation, extrasystoles, psychogenic asthma, the common 'organ neuroses' [1] in the field of the alimentary and excretory functions. Accordingly, such cases, and still more hysterical conversions, are the regressive forms of evolution. In a conversion, strong unsatisfied id urges cathect ego-functions which during phylogenesis had already been desexualised; in evolution, however, id-urges cathect ego-functions which until then had not yet been erotised.

During analytic treatment the erotic cathexis which led to a hysteric conversion is withdrawn and used elsewhere in a way better suited to reality. This may be one of the reasons why after a properly terminated analysis patients are generally unable to produce their symptoms again, while *a priori* there is no reason why they should not be able to produce their symp-

[1] Called today 'psychosomatic disorders' (Postscript, 1951).

toms at will, easily and safely, now that they have become fully conscious of their individual mechanisms of production.

But—no rule without exception. It is reported that there are people who are able to do so. Allegedly there exist prescriptions and training methods (Yoga, Buddhism, the exercises of St. Ignatius of Loyola, etc.) which aim at bringing under the sway of consciousness various functions of the body which are beyond the control of us common people. This happens prob- ably as Alexander has described,[1] by changing object libido into narcissistic libido, a procedure diametrically opposite to the goal of an analytic cure. This is the likely explanation of the two completely different final results.

Here I wish to refute a possible counter-argument. Almost certainly it will be pointed out that my train of thought does not take the important notion of narcissism sufficiently into account. It could be argued, for instance, that orthogenesis is not caused by the loss of the erotic component but, on the contrary, by the far-reaching change of object libido into narcissistic libido, as suggested by Freud in his explanation of malignant growth. Indeed, the phylogenetic phenomenon of orthogenesis has a good deal in common with the ontogenetic phenomenon of malignant growth. In both cases parts of the body start to grow without inhibition, without any regard to the well-being of the whole organism, and cause thereby the ruin of the individual or of the species. But even Freud [2] in this connection put the word 'narcissistic' between inverted commas, by which he obviously meant to call our attention to his use of the word in a metaphorical sense. Whether this striking metaphor describes the true reality, i.e. whether in the living cell processes of mutual cathexis with libido, or of abso- lutely narcissistic behaviour, really happen, is not at all proven. E.g. it is an easily ascertainable clinical fact that man nar- cissistically loves his own stomach or his own beauty (his lines and colours), but in my opinion the phrase that 'his stomach narcissistically loves itself' can have only a metaphorical meaning. But even if such a thing existed it would not influence my conclusions in any way. In practice it does not matter

---

[1] *Imago* (1923), **9**, 35.
[2] *Beyond the Pleasure Principle*, Int. PsA. Lib., London, 1950.

whether a function or a tendency pays no regard to reality and to the interests of the whole organism because it is no longer cathected erotically, or because it has used up all the cathexis by its narcissistic behaviour. In any case, my conclusions remain within the confines of psychology—and this is the firmer ground for the problems discussed here.

Thus in this contribution I am deliberately speaking only of the erotic cathexis of an organ, or of a part of the body, which cathexis has originated from the organised ego and can be again withdrawn into it. In this regard my ideas contain no new hypothetical elements at all. What I wanted to see was how far one could proceed in the field of the ego-instincts using our old, well-tried theoretical notions.

2. *Organogenic and Psychogenic Physical Illnesses*

There is, however, a third kind of phenomena which can be used to prove the erotisation of an ego-function as the prerequisite for its adaptation: the still hotly contested psychoanalytic therapy of organic illnesses. We know, ever since Ferenczi's pioneer work, that most organic illnesses—perhaps all of them—cause a great disturbance in the individual's balance of libido, the reason being that the diseased part of the body is strongly cathected by libido. The healing of a wound or, more generally, of an inflammation is a typical example of this process. It was Ferenczi who emphasised that the classic characteristics of inflammation: '*calor, dolor, rubor, tumor et functio laesa*', describe just as correctly genital excitement. This certainly suggests that inflammation is intimately linked, not only psychologically but also biologically, with erotisation of the part of the body in question. It is very probable that this erotisation is responsible for the first emergence into the consciousness of the existence of that internal organ. As long as we are well we know pretty little of our internal organs, especially as compared with the detailed information volunteered by patients. Inflammation, however, is the central problem of present-day pathology; with a little exaggeration it can be said: pathology is the theory of inflammation. It is worth noting that it is still not settled whether the several pathological processes—hyperaemia, stasis, oedema, atrophy, degeneration, metaplasia, hypertrophy, tumours, etc. —are truly independent phenomena or only extreme cases of inflammation which, only for the sake of systematisation and teaching, have been described as independent. In any case, it is safe to say that after some duration of any of these partial processes the other characteristics of inflammation become demonstrable. The various diseases—according to this idea— are differentiated less by the essence of the illness than by its localisation; and so our diagnosis too is primarily localisatory. If this is so, then most diseases are basically inflammations—and thus inseparably linked with erotisation.

The two kinds of diseases hitherto faithfully separated as organic and functional, regarded from this angle, are identical in nature. One main characteristic is common to both, the erotisation; what is different is the cause and the mechanism of such erotisation. In the case of a neurosis a man cannot satisfy some of his id impulses because of the prohibitive demands of his civilisation. He adapts himself to this situation by displacing those impulses, i.e. converting them into his symptoms. He cathects some of his ego-functions with libido, and creates thereby the illness which is at the same time an (unsuccessful) attempt at a cure.

As both the frustrating reality and the instinct work uninterruptedly, the process of adaptation must go on also. Something similar happens in extreme 'organic' illnesses, such as wounds or infections. Here, too, the first move towards new adaptation is the erotisation. The new adaptation has been made necessary by the new conditions created by the external force (in wounding) or by some infection. If the new adaptation proves successful the additional libido charge can be withdrawn, the illness heals off. If it is unsuccessful, the illness passes over into a chronic state, i.e. into a permanent cathexis of the 'diseased' part of the body. This outcome is almost the same as that of the production of a neurotic symptom. In both cases the tendency to new adaptation persists, in both cases one of the effective mechanisms is erotisation. What is different is the cause permanently disturbing the harmony and necessitating a new adaptation.

From another angle chronic illness can be compared to character. In both cases the starting-point is determined by the nature of the individual, i.e. by his present constitution; the external change which necessitates a new adaptation is created in the one case by the demands of education, in the other by the 'aetiological factor'. In both cases the individual proves to be unable to cope with the conflicts created, i.e. he cannot adapt himself harmoniously. How closely chronic illness and character are related to each other is shown by the old empirical fact that certain chronic illnesses are usually found in people with well-defined character traits. People suffering from stomach illnesses are often 'sour' or 'bitter', with lung diseases often over-active, erethic, with heart diseases often over-anxious, etc. I have not yet a wide enough experience in this field, and cannot therefore definitely state whether the character structure creates the disposition for the illness or, conversely, the illness shapes the character traits. In any case, I have the impression that a patient's illness and specific character structure are resolved by analytic treatment usually at about the same time.

III

CRITICAL NOTES ON THE THEORY OF THE PREGENITAL ORGANISATIONS OF THE LIBIDO [1]

(1935)

I

ACCORDING to our present theory, the first outline of which appeared only in the third edition of Freud's *Three Contributions* [2] in the year 1914, the two developments—that of sexual aims and that of sexual object-relations—run parallel to each other. It is not expressly said, thereby, but only tacitly assumed, that the biological nature of the leading component instinct, the gratification of which at the time is the most important because it causes the greatest pleasure, decides unequivocally the form of the child's object-relations. According to this the chief stress was laid on the changing instinctual aims and their respective sources, that is to say, on the biological aspect. The question of how and why these leading instincts succeed one another was never seriously raised by a psychologist, and consequently never investigated either. Here also our theory strove to shelve the problem and to await the explanation from biology. My Dresden paper [3] also originated from this tendency. Our colloquial usage is under the same influence: we not only speak of the primacy of the oral, anal, genital component instincts respectively, but also of oral, anal and genital love.

This parallel is somewhat broken up by the fact that still

[1] Paper read to the Vienna Psycho-Analytical Society on May 15th, 1935.

[2] Freud: *Drei Abhandlungen zur Sexualtheorie*, 1st edition, 1905; 2nd edition, 1910; 3rd edition, 1914. English edition: *Three Contributions to the Theory of Sex*, New York, 1910.

[3] M. Balint: 'Psychosexuelle Parallelen zum biogenetische Grundgesetz', *Imago* (1932), **18**. Reprinted in English ('Psychosexual Parallels to the Fundamental Law of Biogenetics') in this vol. p. 11.

another stage, called the polymorphous-perverse, is assumed to exist before this succession of development begins. But, according to theory, there is also a preliminary stage of object-relations, or rather two stages: auto-erotism, in which the child has as yet no object at all, and narcissism, in which he takes his own ego as first love-object. Only by the way is it then mentioned that oral object-relations can be observed very early, that, in fact, it is impossible to separate them in time from auto-erotism. I wish to emphasise that we shall often meet this kind of uncertainty in dating.

The above-mentioned tendency to strict and rigid parallelism is shown most clearly in Abraham's table. But it is important to know that the table in its original form, as Abraham presented it in Berlin in March 1923, contained three times as many (9 : 3) parallel series as appear in the later edition which was published in December of the same year.[1] Evidently Abraham felt—for even towards himself he was a severe critic—that he had forced this parallelism too far. Nevertheless, his tabulation influenced the psycho-analytic mode of thought fundamentally. Every infantile situation, every incident in childhood, was regarded as being conclusively defined only when an exact place in this step-ladder could be assigned to it. This is all the more remarkable because in the same year as Abraham's table there also appeared a paper by Freud: 'The Infantile Genital Organisation of the Libido', with the sub-title: 'A Supplement to the Theory of Sexuality'.[2] which invites us to insert a new, the phallic, phase hitherto overlooked. The position of this phase in Abraham's scheme is somewhat uncertain, it is mostly taken—in a rather Procrustean way—as being the last ambivalent phase. The overwhelming influence of Abraham's conception is also shown by the fact that even Ferenczi, who otherwise liked to go his own way, tried to make the development of the erotic sense of reality,[3] as he described it in *Thalassa*, correspond to Abra-

---

[1] Abraham: *Versuch einer Entwicklungsgeschichte der Libido auf Grund der Psychoanalyse seelischer Störungen*, Int. Psa. Verlag, Wien, 1924. In English in *Selected Papers*, Int. PsA. Lib., London, 1942.

[2] Freud: *Collected Papers* II, p. 244.

[3] Ferenczi: *Versuch einer Genitaltheorie*, Int. Psa. Verlag, Wien, 1924. In English: *Thalassa*, The PsA. Quarterly, Inc. New York, 1938.

ham's scheme, which could only be done by straining a point.

We know, further, that it raises considerable difficulties if one tries to date Abraham's individual phases according to years of life. The periods proposed in the beginning always proved to be too long, so that the individual phases had continually to be pushed back to still earlier periods of life. People tried to deceive themselves over this, in my opinion fundamental, uncertainty by putting the blame on the as yet incomplete state of our knowledge. In contradistinction to this there are a good many analysts who are rather reluctant to follow Mrs. Melanie Klein in assigning very early dates to these phases.

A further essential feature of the conception of the pregenital organisations is that it is based on only a few component instincts, and that all these instincts belong to a special class in that all of them possess well-known bodily sources, i.e. are bound to erotogenic zones. The other component instincts are hardly considered in this theory, as if they did not change in development, or as if their changes were of no importance; or again, they were considered as biologically necessary derivatives of the well-studied component instincts. I may remind you of the former attempts which aimed at conceiving sadism as a derivative of anal erotism, and of more recent attempts which tried to derive ambivalence from the biological nature of oral erotism.

After these considerations I think it is at least worth while attempting to examine these two developments separately. I am fully aware that the present theory of the pregenital organisations was derived from innumerable unbiased clinical observations. It is, however, not my intention to contest these observations, i.e. the basis of the theory. What I should like to propose is a re-formulation of our theory, integrating with the facts already considered some observations which, although well known, have till now been put on one side because it was thought that they could not contribute anything to the further development of our views, to the deepening of our theory.

One problem, then, is the development of object-relations, i.e. the development of love. This problem will be the subject of the present paper. The other allegedly parallel problem, the development of sexual aims, or, what comes to nearly the same thing, the development of the acquisition of pleasure, of erotism, I should like to deal with on another occasion.[1]

2

Let us begin with analytical practice. What does the analyst do if, in his therapeutic work, he comes up against phenomena which without doubt come under the diagnosis of autoerotism, or of pregenital love?

Let us take first the richest source, the analysis of neurotic people. The analysis of their symptoms shows that their object-relations are not wholly healthy. These people strive to reach normal relations with their love-objects, but instead are compelled to develop something else. In the symptoms either this 'something else' comes to light or the symptoms are determined by the defence against this 'something else'. This different relation, the substitute for genital love, or as I have called it, for active object-love, is regarded by analytic theory as either a regression or an arrest in development. As we have said, for our present investigation one kind of variation, that from the normal sexual aim, will be left out of account. The other kind of variation, the only one to be discussed in this paper, concerns the relations to the sexual object. They are twofold: either normally forbidden objects are loved (incest), or the mode of loving them is not normal. Now analytic work has proved in every case that all these abnormal phenomena can actually be traced back to earlier decisive situations. This empirical fact formed the basis of the theory of fixation, and further, it was just from the study of such object-relations, which in adults are certainly abnormal, that the theory of pregenital organisations of the libido arose.

Significantly, the term 'fixation' has too many meanings. In many cases the neurotic seems to be bound directly to the trauma that shattered his formerly undisturbed life. In such cases the analysis reveals that the person in question, unconsciously but deliberately, is always creating a similar trauma, apparently by fate. In other cases it can be shown quite clearly that the person is bound to the pre-traumatic happy situation, and his symptoms have the special purpose of protecting him

[1] See my paper 'Eros and Aphrodite', this vol. p. 73.

from a further development of his object-relation which might lead to a repetition of the trauma. There is still a third possibility, which could be described as a fixation to the adjustment of the trauma. These persons—mostly character-neurotics—are only capable of a certain kind of object-relation, nothing else seems possible for them. These relations to the objects are also explainable historically.

Now it is surely of no advantage if three such different phenomena—fixation to the trauma, fixation to the pre-traumatic situation, and fixation to the trauma adjustment—are thrown together and called by the same name, and I think the fact that we know so little about fixation, in spite of very thorough-going clinical investigation, is partly attributable to this very circumstance. Even today we still cannot really state in which system the fixation is to be found—in the ego, the id or the super-ego. Not only the topographic but also the economic and dynamic considerations leave us in the lurch here. Up to now analysis has not been able to form any idea as to what kind of change the process or the event of fixation means for the instincts.

For our problem, however, we do not need to clear up all these complicated issues. It is enough if we learn to distinguish the original infantile situation, in which the child lived before the trauma, and in which it encountered the trauma, from that which is later manifested clinically in the neurosis of the adult. The two can be analogous, even identical, but need not be so. Frequently they stand in the relation of cause and effect to each other. The fixated situation which appears in the picture of the illness can assume every form of sexual gratification and sexual object-relation, naturally also pregenital or even auto-erotic forms. On the other hand, the infantile situation, the origin of the fixation, belongs *without exception to object-erotism*. Moreover, the relation of the child to its object in this original situation, which at that time led to the trauma, is by no means as simple and unproblematical as one would expect from the present *biologically orientated* theory—even if this relation corresponds entirely to the classical picture of an oral, anal-sadistic or phallic love. The same is true of the so-called 'negative Oedipus complex'. If one goes a little deeper into the situation one inevitably gets the impression of a previous compromise, of an already accomplished adjustment. To heal a neurosis, or to put it more modestly, to remove the symptoms in question, it is not always necessary to deepen the analysis still further. I consider it, however, of the utmost importance that in every case there is always plenty of evidence that those fatal infantile situations which formed the basis of an illness still had complicated antecedents. If we aim at more than a superficial relief of symptoms, these antecedents too must be analysed.

As a single example I should like to cite the famous case of the Wolfman.[1] Not only the obsessional neurosis of his childhood but also most of his later object-relations and many traits of his character agree entirely with the classical picture of the anal-sadistic organisation of the libido. We know also the moment when these phenomena began. It was at the age of about $3\frac{1}{2}$. From Freud's description it is quite clear that just about this time the sexual development of the child received a violent blow. The primal scene and the scene with Gruscha had already taken place, but then there followed in rapid succession: the overhearing of the mother's complaints to the physician, the attempted seduction by his elder sister, and finally his unsuccessful attempt to approach Nanja; and that was more than the child could bear. What the sister, the father's favourite, might do without being punished, without even any evil effects, was in his case followed by the most serious consequences, the humiliation he had already once experienced (Gruscha) was repeated in the much more severe form of castration. The result was an enforced adjustment; he had to give up his genital strivings, and it was at this point that his 'anal-sadistic' relations began. The ever-returning 'fixated' situation in adult life showed the following characteristics: objects of socially inferior standing, wherever possible servants; prominent buttocks as the most important factor in his choice of objects; sexual intercourse *a tergo*, frequent valuable presents, strongly ambivalent feelings towards the object, a marked tendency to torment and unexplainable panicky attacks of mistrust, which necessitated continual changing of the love-object.

[1] Freud: *Collected Papers*, **3**; Mack-Brunswick, *Int. J. of PsA.* (1928), **9.**

The original situation in which the child encountered the trauma is of quite another kind. The child shows himself quite innocently playing with his genitals, when suddenly, like a bolt from the blue, the threat of castration from his beloved Nanja falls upon him. Freud expressly mentions in the case-history, that before these events the patient had been 'a very good-natured, tractable, and even quiet child'![1] In spite of this, as an explanation of the sudden change of character we read the phrase, which returns again and again like a refrain in psychoanalytic literature: '*His sexual life, therefore, which was beginning to come under the sway of the genital zone, gave way before an external obstacle and was thrown back by its influence into an earlier phase of pregenital organisation.*' [2] I wish to emphasise once more that neither in Freud's case-history nor in the Mack-Brunswick supplement is it mentioned anywhere that anal-sadistic object-relations had been observed before that fatal summer. I will return later to the question of why, nevertheless, this primary anal-sadistic organisation, which was neither observed nor remembered, is used as an explanation. At present I only want to point out that the scene with Nanja also had complicated antecedents. The case-history contains some essential parts of these, others one can only conjecture. It is important that here, also, the relation of the child to his love-object did not arise spontaneously, so to speak, on biological grounds, but was determined by his individual history. Certainly one has the impression that it would probably not have come to an outbreak of anal-sadistic object-relations if the child had been treated with more understanding.

As we have seen, the analytic work does not stop at such a situation; we inquire into the conditions which called forth just these particular circumstances. Although the relation revealed corresponds exactly to the theoretical picture, we are not satisfied and look for further explanations. This shows that our theory and practice are not in agreement. If 'anal object-love', 'narcissism', etc., are—as the theory demands—steps in a natural succession of development, why do we in practice analyse them further? And if in practice we succeed in analys-

[1] Freud: p. 482.
[2] op. cit., p. 494; italics of the original.

ing them and tracing them back to the individual history of the child, then the 'natural succession of development' postulated by the theory may not after all be so natural.

3

With all the greater interest we turn now to the second important source of our knowledge which has a bearing on this question, to child-analysis. After what has been mentioned above it will not surprise us how early children can become seriously neurotic. I mean not only primary states of anxiety, examined by Freud, with perhaps simpler mechanism but more complicated, more difficult cases of hysteria and obsessional neurosis, perhaps even something resembling schizophrenia. Such cases have really been observed and also described in all countries of the psycho-analytic world. The outbreak of these illnesses goes back to the age of four, even of two, or still earlier, therefore certainly to the period of pregenital object-relations.[1]

All these analyses show without any ambiguity that these infantile neuroses are not in any way less complex than the neuroses of adults. From this it follows that the object-relations of these children must in many respects resemble those of adults. This agrees again with our therapeutic procedure. I am convinced that no analyst in the world would allow a child who had been under analysis with him to leave off the treatment if symptoms of pregenital object-relations still held the field, e.g. if the child wanted exclusively or predominantly to torment, bully or domineer his love-objects, or if his interest remained exclusively or even only predominantly bound to the products of his own excretion, or if he insisted on clinging to the theories of oral conception and anal birth. The same is true of the phenomena of the phallic period: belief in the non-existence of the female genital organs, in the idea of the whole female sex being castrated, or in the existence of mothers with a phallus. All these phenomena, which our theory describes as 'anal-sadistic' or 'phallic object-relations', or 'negative Oedipus

---

[1] Berta Bornstein: *Int. Z.f. Psa.* (1931), **17**, 344. Fromm Reichmann: *Z.f. psa. Päd.* (1931), **5**, 460. Steff Bornstein: *Z.f. psa. Päd.* (1933), **1**, 253. E. Sterba: *Z.f. psa. Päd.* (1934), **8**, 197.

complex', and considers as natural phases in a normal mental development, are in our practice analysed, understood, interpreted and resolved.

Exactly the same takes place with the auto-erotic activities. These are also subjected to analysis, and here too it turns out regularly that these auto-erotisms are far from being objectless, but are to be understood and treated as stunted remnants of a fatally disappointing object-love.

I should like to call attention to the fact that in this respect our technique allows of no exception. There is no age at which, in an *analysed* child, these phenomena of *pregenital love* would be regarded as normal or not demanding further analysis. Especially not where they, so to speak, hold the field and *determine the child's reaction to his environment*. At best they can be tolerated as insignificant freaks which do not cause any trouble in the otherwise friendly relation to objects. All accounts of children's analyses end with almost the same final statements: the impulses of hate and aggression have nearly disappeared, the ambivalence of the feelings has been greatly eased, the child has acquired again, or for the first time in his life, the capacity for learning and for adjustment. What is generally not explicitly stated, only implied, is that *the reaction of the child to the persons of his environment has become conspicuously loving at the end of the analytic treatment*.

4

The observation of healthy children—our third source of experience—brings nothing which would contradict these findings. What we are able to see of the object-relations of such children in our society presents a rather variegated picture. First of all there are wishes for tenderness which play a very important rôle; these wishes, as far as one can see them, are always directed towards objects. Then the phenomena of hate and aggression, which can always be traced back to some event, have their explanation in the child's individual history. It is true they are sometimes carried to extremes, yet never without due reason. Finally auto-erotism, which if practised passionately and not in a free, playful way, always appears as an expression of defiance, of bitterly won independence; moreover, if regarded more closely it also reveals itself as a form of consolation. The all-important condition, however, is the existence of good, loving understanding between the child and the grown-ups around him; by the presence or absence of this one can, so to speak, gauge the success or failure of the up-bringing.

The importance of this good understanding can be traced far back, almost to the first extra-uterine days. A child who has been trained to cleanliness may temporarily lose this achieve-ment if he experiences a severe disappointment. Similarly, it can often be shown that little children, even infants, begin to whine and get disgruntled and troublesome if the good contact between them and their environment has been disturbed. Here, without doubt, it is a question of an object-relation, only until now, except for Ferenczi and his school, it has been almost entirely overlooked by the theory. Surely just because this rela-tion does not correspond to any stage of the theoretical pre-genital organisation of the libido. The theoretical objection that a child cannot have an object-relation in a very early period of extra-uterine life, when he knows nothing of the external world and has not yet learnt to distinguish between himself and his surroundings, has been dealt with by A. Balint in her paper 'Reality Sense and the Development of the Ability to Love', in the Ferenczi Memorial Volume.[1] I shall return to this work later. Here I can refer to a passage from Freud. He lays down in the Introductory Lectures,[2] that many component instincts (such as sadism) possess an object from the very first. He then continues: 'Others, more plainly connected with particular erotogenic areas in the body, only have an object in the beginning so long as they are still dependent upon the non-sexual functions, and give it up when they become detached from these latter.' The reference is to oral erotism. Freud then continues: 'The oral impulse becomes auto-erotic. . . . Further development has, to put it as concisely as possible, two aims: first to renounce auto-erotism, to give up *again* the object found

---

[1] A. Balint: in Hungarian *Lélekelemzési Tanulmányok*, Budapest, 1933. In English: 'Love for the Mother and Mother Love', *Int. J. PsA.* (1949), **30**, 251–9. Reprinted in this vol., p. 109.

[2] Freud: *Introductory Lectures*, p. 270. George Allen & Unwin Ltd. (London, 1936. Fifth imp.)

in the child's own body in exchange *again* for an external one . . .'[1] Here it is quite clearly expressed that even oral erotism, which till now has served as the classic example of auto-erotism in theoretical considerations, originally exists as an object-relation. But this generally known fact was never taken into consideration because it did not fit in with present views.

5

To sum up. However deeply we are able to penetrate with our analytic technique and observations into the history of a man's life, we have always, without exception, found object-relations. Auto-erotic forms of gratification were either harmless play, or they already represented compromise formations. They were revealed in analysis as mechanisms of consolation for, or of defiance against, objects which had been lost or had led the child into severe conflicts. The same is true of the phenomena of so-called pregenital love, such as 'anal-sadistic' or 'phallic' love, and also of the 'negative Oedipus complex'. They are either unimportant and harmless or, if of importance, then to be analysed and resolved. As has already been said, this paper is intended to deal only with the development of object-relations. For this reason, here as well as elsewhere in the discussion, the investigation of the changing instinctual sexual aims has been left on one side. Therefore, intentionally, I do not inquire why oral, anal, urethral, genital, etc., forms of gratification appear in the development and what they signify, but confine my problem to the question *why the attitude of the individual to his environment and especially to his love-objects changes*, and what are the causes of the various forms of object-relations which we describe as oral, anal, phallic, genital, narcissistic, etc., love.

These clinical facts are incompatible with the fundamental conceptions of the present theory of development of the libido. During the last few years secondary or supplementary hypotheses had to be developed which, though not defined as such, yet aimed at reconciling theory and clinical findings. Naturally, one could not question the accuracy of the above-

---

[1] op. cit., 270–1. [Italics are mine.]

mentioned clinical facts, therefore they were declared to be products of regression from a higher position of the libido, made untenable for the individual by a trauma, to some old modes of gratification and to old forms of object-relation. What we can observe in children and what we can bring back to memory in the analysis of adults are considered as phenomena of regression, which means that they already have antecedents, and it is for this reason that we find in them signs of 'genital' object-relations. A necessary consequence of this way of thinking is that we could never complete our theory. The theory was forced to accept ever earlier dates, and so some research workers from a single false premise, but otherwise quite logically, came to assume for example super-ego formation, genital tendencies of full value, complicated Oedipus situations, quite serious castration conflicts, etc., to be present, as a rule, already in the first year of life, or even earlier. From this derives the perpetual uncertainty of the theory in dating any event in the infantile development.

Another way out was to have recourse to the constitution. The curious thing is that the school that has made the greatest use of this at the same time was the boldest in pre-dating. According to this conception one or more component instincts of the child, especially that of aggression, are so strongly developed that even the slightest frustration entirely justified by reality may be followed by fateful consequences. The reality of quite early object-relations is not wholly denied by this assumption, but is also not fully accepted. It asserts that in reality these environmental influences were not in any way as serious and devastating as the analytic work shows them to us later, magnified out of proportion by the distortion caused by this instinctual constitution.

It is true that none of these lines of thought has been able to win full recognition in psycho-analytical literature, though in recent years their adherents have considerably increased. But the critics should not deny that this conception has the merit of courage; for a long time it formed the only attempt to explain the clearly recognised difficulties enumerated above. We others have quietly tolerated the existence of this discrepancy long enough without being much troubled by it.

6

Clinical experience may guide us out of this dilemma between theory and practice. We must finally take seriously what we have all found and what Ferenczi was the first to describe in *Thalassa*, namely that object-relations predominate even in the deepest layers of the mind, which can only just be reached by analysis. It is they that mainly decide the weal or woe of the individual. It is not easy, however, to describe them more exactly, i.e. to express the experiences in words. I recognised them first in analyses in which I had to deepen the analytic work, in the real sense of the word, because of specially obstinate character disturbances. In the end phase of such treatments, which I have called the 'new beginning',[1] the nature of this first object-relation is expressed quite clearly. It is almost entirely passive. *The person in question does not love, but wishes to be loved. This passive wish is certainly sexual, libidinous.* The demand that these wishes shall be gratified by the environment is absolutely unproblematical and is often expressed quite vehemently with great display of energy, almost as if it were a matter of life and death. The aim of all these wishes does not, however, correspond to what one generally means by sensual or erotic, but rather what Freud has called tender, aim-inhibited. Non-gratification calls forth passionate reactions; gratification, on the other hand, only a quiet, tranquil sense of well-being. Ferenczi described this difference in his last paper at the Wiesbaden Congress.[2] Hermann[3] recognised other properties of this passive object-love, above all the tendency to cling. From this tendency, too, derives the fear of being dropped, recently described by A. Balint.[4]

[1] M. Balint: 'Charakteranalyse und Neubeginn', *Int. Z. f. Psa.* (1934), **20**; 'Das Endziel der Psychoanalytischen Behandlung', *Int. Z. f. Psa.* (1935), **21**. English versions: 'Character Analysis and New Beginning' and 'The Final Goal of Psycho-analytic Treatment', reprinted in this vol., pp. 159 and 188.

[2] 'Confusion of Tongues between the Child and the Adults', *Int. J. PsA.* (1949), **30**, 225 (the German original appeared in 1933).

[3] I. Hermann: 'Zum Triebleben der Primaten', *Imago* (1933), **19** (there also further references to literature).

[4] A. Balint: 'Über eine besondere Form der infantilen Angst', *Ztschr. f. psa. Päd.* (1933), **8**.

Educators but also psycho-analysts have alike misunderstood these phenomena in a double sense. First of all the child's passionate way of demanding was regarded as primary, and was interpreted as a sign of aggression, of inborn sadism. This conception led directly to constitution: one forgot the etymology of 'passion', namely, that it derives from 'suffering'; but forgot also the clinical experience, namely that we have never really seen a congenitally wicked or evil person, nor a real sadist. Ill-nature, malice, wickedness, even sadism can be analysed, cured, or what comes ultimately to the same thing: they have their antecedents. It is suffering that makes one wicked. Grown-ups as well as children, if they are wicked, spiteful, aggressive, sadistic, have a reason for being so. And if one removes the cause, this trait, the sadistic object-love (but not the playful aggressive mode of gratification), disappears. I can hardly believe that there is any analyst who would contradict this assertion.

The second misunderstanding has also to do with passionateness. One confused the manner of appearance with the aim of the instinct, and thought that what was so passionately desired must also produce passionate pleasure or sensual orgasm. Hence it was inferred that children at a very tender age can exhibit voluptuous genital tendencies and so forth. I also became a victim of this deception until I recognised that wishes passionately demonstrated in the new beginning period are to be regarded as normal; but passionate aims, on the contrary, as warning signals. The same is true of the child. Wishes whose fulfilments are on occasion passionately demanded point to a healthy, vigorous instinctual life; but passionate instinctual aims point to a considerably disturbed development, to a longstanding misunderstanding, or, in Ferenczi's words, to a 'confusion of tongues between the adults and the child'.

In my opinion these ideas supplement the present theory. Freud called this first period of the child polymorphousperverse on the one hand, and auto-erotic or narcissistic on the other. Both names are certainly correct and describe the real condition, but seen only from a particular point of view. A baby is certainly polymorphously perverse; his whole body and all his functions are pleasurably toned. This term is therefore purely descriptive; it has, however, exclusive regard to the sphere of the instincts, to biology. It is just as true that the child's world is not yet separated into the ego and the external world. It is therefore narcissistic if one looks at it from the point of view of the sense of reality, or reality testing (cf. A. Balint [1]). Even external objects which are necessary to life, e.g. the mother's breast, are not yet separated off mentally from the ego. But libidinally the child is completely dependent on care from the external world, and without it would simply die.

Now this primary tendency: *I shall be loved always, everywhere, in every way, my whole body, my whole being—without any criticism, without the slightest effort on my part—is the final aim of all erotic striving.* This is also retained throughout life and is quite openly admitted by many people. Others, however—and they form the vast majority—can reach this aim of the 'passive object-love' only by roundabout ways. Education enforces, even devises, these by-paths. If the child is offered too little, it invests its auto-erotism, hitherto practised in a playful way, with its whole libido, becomes narcissistic or aggressive or both. If it gets something it becomes, as it were, moulded by the gratification received. The successive stages of development so frequently and regularly found—anal-sadistic, phallic and finally genital object-relations—have not a biological but a cultural basis. As you see I have left out the oral relation. Purposely, for I cannot make culture, i.e. education, solely responsible for this.

7

One by-path to the attainment of the primal and ultimate aim—to be loved, to be gratified—is narcissism: *if the world does not love me enough, I have to love and gratify myself.* Consequently, libidinous narcissism is always of a secondary nature. In this connection it is very instructive to note the way in which the meaning of the term 'narcissism' has altered in the course of a few years. Originally this word was coined by Naecke to designate a certain perversion of grown-ups. Sadger [2] found similar phenomena among homosexuals; according to his

---

[1] 'Love for the Mother and Mother Love.' This vol., p. 109.
[2] Sadger: *Jahrbuch f. psa. u. psychopathol. Forschungen* (1910), **2**, 112.

definition in 1910 'narcissism is a necessary stage of development in the transition from auto-erotism to subsequent object-love'. Rank [1] in 1912 sees in narcissism also 'a normal stage of development, which precedes puberty and is designed to effect the necessary transition from pure auto-erotism to object-love'. Both of these papers—especially Rank's—date narcissism too late for our present views. So far as I know, Ferenczi created the term 'secondary narcissism', having found it in the study of organically ill persons. Freud [2] in his fundamental work *On Narcissism: an Introduction* (1914), still oscillates between two points of view. According to one conception only the auto-erotic instincts are primary, 'so there must be something added to auto-erotism—some new operation in the mind —in order that narcissism may come into being'.[3] The other conception first introduces primary narcissism; according to this: 'wären alle psychischen Energien zunächst im Zustande des Narzissmus beisammen und für unsere grobe Analyse ununterscheidbar'.[3] (The English translation is not quite so explicit: 'at first in the narcissistic state they [the energies operating in the mind] exist side by side and our analysis is not a fine enough instrument to distinguish them'). As an illustration of this conception appears, for the first time, the picture (which later became so famous) of the amoeba with the pseudopodia. This wavering is still to be felt in the next work referring to the question, in *Beyond the Pleasure Principle* (1920). Only in *The Ego and the Id* (1923) is this question decided in favour of primary narcissism—it is true without any discussion. This development provides a typical example of the pre-dating tendency mentioned in the beginning, which, on principle, can only be brought to rest if the date is pushed back to birth, or even to intra-uterine existence. This is all the more noteworthy here, since Freud himself expressly pointed out that 'der primäre Narzissmus des Kindes, der eine der Voraussetzungen unserer Libidotheorien enthält, weniger leicht durch direkte Beobachtungen zu erfassen, als durch Rückschluss von einem anderen Punkte her zu bestätigen ist'. (Here, too, the

[1] Rank: *Jahrbuch f. psa. u. psychopathol. Forschungen* (1912), **3**, 401.
[2] Freud: *Collected Papers*, IV.
[3] op. cit., p. 33–4.

English is less forceful: 'The primary narcissism of the child assumed by us, which forms one of the hypotheses in our theories of the libido, is less easy to grasp by direct observation than to confirm by deduction from another consideration'.) [1] The controversy between the two conceptions here cited has never been decided; on the contrary, psycho-analytical research has sought rather to hush it up. The above-mentioned paper of A. Balint is the only exception. She comes to the conclusion that we should give preference to the first conception, according to which libidinal narcissism must develop during the course of life. But the disquieting problem remains unresolved as to how the other conception came up at all and, what is more, was able to hold the field for so many years.

I believe the reason for this is to be found in inexact colloquial usage and in the absence of fine enough distinctions. Several concepts were thrown together under the term 'narcissism' which are certainly related to one another but yet describe different experiences. First, auto-erotism, which, as we have seen, was originally a simple instinct-psychological description, almost purely biological. It denotes the phenomenon of self-gratification and nothing more, and does not state anything about object-relation. One can be head over heels in love and still gratify oneself auto-erotically, as was not infrequently the case with prisoners of war, for instance. By narcissism in its narrowest sense one understands at least two different things. First a kind of investment of the libido, i.e. the fact that the person in question loves himself; secondly, that relation to the external world in which the person does not take any or enough cognisance of reality. Since facts which build up two of these three interpretations can certainly be observed in new-born babies, namely auto-erotism and the narcissistic behaviour towards reality, one later came to regard the third interpretation, narcissistic love or self-love, also as primary, as inborn. In my opinion this is not correct. At least it is to be wished that in future it should be stated exactly which conception is meant when speaking of narcissism.

[1] Freud: *Collected Papers*, IV, p. 48.

8

One *détour* by which the primal aim of erotism, that of being loved, can be reached is libidinous narcissism, self-love. The other *détour* is active object-love. *We love and gratify our partner in order to be loved and gratified by him in return.* This active love always means a sacrifice, an effort, and is accompanied by a temporary increase of tension. One takes this privation on oneself and bears this tension in the hope of reaching in this way the aim of being loved as one was loved in the beginning. The kind of sacrifice one takes upon oneself depends on what is demanded of one, and on how one was brought up. Looked at in this way, the pregenital object-relations, the pregenital forms of love, appear in another light. They can no longer be explained biologically, but must be considered, to use perhaps a rather strong expression, as artefacts, i.e. we must make society in general, or the individual educator in question, responsible for them. Moreover—as I think I have shown—our clinical therapy has always acted as if this were an acknowledged fact.

One of the best witnesses for or against this view is anthropology. Unfortunately our knowledge in this respect is far too incomplete. But this much can be already established, that where children grow up without much 'upbringing' adult society is less given to reaction formation. In this connection Roheim [1] often quotes his experiences with the Australians and the Papuans. According to him, phenomena of oral and anal love are to be found among adults only when they are, so to speak, enforced by society, and therefore hardly exist among the Australians. Margaret Mead has been able to establish a similar difference among the inhabitants of Samoa and New Guinea. Also her reports in her latest work, *Sex and Temperament*, are important here. [2]

Not only pregenital love, however, but also so-called postambivalent genital love, which I should like to call in Ferenczi's sense 'active object-love', originates in passive object-

[1] G. Roheim: 'Psycho-Analysis of Primitive Cultural Types', *Int. J. of PsA.* (1932), **13**, 1.

[2] M. Mead: *Coming of Age in Samoa*, London, 1929. *Growing up in New Guinea*, 1930. *Sex and Temperament*, 1935.

love. This is also an artefact, or, to give it a finer-sounding name, *a product of civilisation*. It must also be learnt—sometimes very painfully. I should like to emphasise once more that this assertion is true only for 'genital love', and not for the genital mode of gratification. Here also I can call our clinical experience as witness. People who are not capable of loving, although they are genitally potent, can acquire this capacity in the course of analytic treatment. Another proof that genitality and active object-love are not identical is given us in the love of elderly, even of quite old people. It is not at all so rare that even after the complete loss of genital functions the capacity for love remains. May I refer here to Goethe's poem, 'Dem aufgehenden Vollmond', written in his seventy-ninth year, one of the most glowing love poems in the literature of the world.

The same error was committed with the term 'genitality' as with that of narcissism. Here also a biologico-instinctual concept and a psycho-sexual one were confused with each other. Genitality should really mean a certain form of erotism, of gaining pleasure. Genital potency and the capacity for genital pleasure respectively are—as practice teaches us—far from being identical with love. What has till now been called 'genital love' should, on the strength of this description, be more correctly called 'active object-love'.

In my opinion a straight line could lead from passive object-love straight to active love. Let us bear in mind that the period of passive object-love is rightly called polymorphous-perverse. In it are potentially present all modes of gratification, every possible kind of object-relation. Which of these are developed, which gain the upper hand over the others, depends upon which of these help most quickly and surely to reach the primal aim—that of being gratified—therefore upon the influence of the environment. Thus, and I mean it quite seriously, if children could be properly brought up, they would not have to struggle through the complicated forms of pregenital object-relations which are only forced upon them. Certainly their difficult task could be considerably lightened if the grown-ups were healthier, i.e. more sincere. But today I cannot visualise clearly this development from passive object-love with its tender sexual aim, to active object-love with its genital sensual aim. All the less because the origin of passionateness, of sensual orgastic lust, is not clear to me. What I know about it I intend to discuss in another paper.[1]

9

Here I should like to show that the ideas developed above can be successfully employed as a working hypothesis on a number of problems.

First, the problem of tenderness. This was raised by Freud in his pioneering essay 'The Most Prevalent Form of Degradation in Erotic Life'. He writes: 'Of these two currents—the sensual and the tender are meant—affection is the older. It springs from the very earliest years of childhood. . . . This tender feeling represents the earliest childish choice of object. [In the German original the last phrase is italicised and runs thus: '*primäre kindliche Objectwahl*'.] These fixations of the child's feelings of affection are maintained through childhood continually absorbing erotic elements. . . .' [2] The source of this 'absorbed' erotism is also given. It originates partly from the so-called tenderness of the parents with its hardly disguised erotism, which then awakes the erotism of the child, and partly from the powerful sensual stream at puberty. What I have done in this lecture was, following Ferenczi's lead, to take these ideas seriously and to work them out in detail.

Psycho-analytical research has paid attention to only one side of the question of tenderness. Perhaps just because Freud, in the work mentioned above, only needed this side to solve his problem. Tenderness was conceived as aim-inhibited erotism, i.e. the adult would really like to love sensually, but cannot allow himself the full attainment of his instinctual aim if he wants to retain his original love-object. This description only fits the facts as regards active tenderness of adults, but does not settle the question why and how this aim-inhibited mode of loving is demanded and even enjoyed by the recipient, the partner. The ideas discussed here give the natural answer to this, that such demands, such forms of gratification existed throughout the whole of life, that since very early childhood

---

[1] cf. 'Eros and Aphrodite', reprinted in this vol., p. 73.
[2] Freud: *Collected Papers*, 4, pp. 204–5.

they were always an important aim of any love-relation. As a matter of fact, every tender lover is inclined to give his partner nicknames, really childish names, to treat her in every respect as a child, even to speak to her in baby language. She usually meets him half-way by behaving as a child, and acting as if she were helpless, talking like a baby, etc. Very frequently, however, the relations are reversed, the man behaving as a child so that he may receive this kind of tenderness.

It is interesting that in some languages there are special phrases for expressing this tender form of love. In German: 'ich bin dir gut', 'ich hab' dich lieb', 'ich hab' dich gern', etc. Also in English, such as: 'I am fond of you', 'I care for you', and so forth. On the other hand, in Hungarian there is only one expression: 'szeretlek', i.e. 'I love you', as also in French: 'je t'aime'. It is noteworthy that parallel with this respective richness and poverty goes another characteristic of these languages as far as I know them. This is the presence or absence of a special literature in the language of children. English seems to me the richest language in this respect: the many Nursery Rhymes (such as the well-known verses of 'Mother Goose'), then, for example, *Alice in Wonderland*, such figures as Mickey Mouse and those of the Silly Symphonies by Walt Disney, and many others. All these speak in their own language, which is certainly droll but not unpleasantly so. German comes next. French, on the contrary, has no children's language acceptable in literature, e.g. the 'Big Bad Wolf' and 'The Three Little Pigs' in the French edition speak in a style which is as elegant, refined and grown-up as that of a member of Parliament. It is nearly the same with Hungarian. It seems, therefore, that tenderness and childishness are treated more or less alike by the different cultures; some allow the participators of the culture in question to speak openly of such things in words reserved for such use, and others do not.

In one respect, however, all European languages are the same—again as far as I know them. They are all so poor that they cannot distinguish between the two kinds of object-love, active and passive. Thus, for instance, the pain, distress and grief which one partner feels at parting may be a source of joy to the other, for it is shown by this that he is still, and very intensely, loved. Another on such occasion will seek to console the sad partner and to hide his own pain, in order to spare the other and make the parting easier. For both relations the languages have at their disposal only one word—love—though the psychological situation is essentially different. What is pain to the one is joy to the other. The one is already in the stage of active object-love, the other is still partly in the passive stage.

In general, love—as our Western culture understands it—is strongly intermixed with tenderness. It is hard to say whether this is healthy or not, whether egoistic love, which looks only for the gratification of its own wishes and considers the partner only in so far as it needs him for this purpose, is not more natural than the considerate, altruistic love which puts the gratification of the partner first.

Our present line of thought, however, gives a decided answer to the question as to why narcissistic love can never be fully satisfying. Narcissistic love reaches the primal aim of all erotism, 'I shall be loved', not in external reality but only inwardly in phantasy. Something in the nature of an incomplete substitute, the feeling 'for want of something better', always adheres to it. With this another question is settled, which Freud came to ask quite consequently in *On Narcissism: An Introduction*: 'Whence does that necessity arise that urges our mental life to pass on beyond the limits of narcissism and to attach the libido to objects?'[1] On the basis of the hypothesis of primary narcissism he had to be satisfied with an answer which, though clinically correct, theoretically begs the question. 'We are so impelled when the cathexis of the ego with libido exceeds a certain degree. A strong egoism is a protection against disease, but in the last resort we must begin to love in order that we may not fall ill, and must fall ill if, in consequence of frustration, we cannot love.'[2] Only the conception of passive object-love provides an explanation of this precise clinical description. As I described it, narcissistic love can never reach the primal aim of all sexual striving; in order to be loved, i.e. to be able to remain healthy, one must come into contact with the world and invest the objects with libido.

[1] *Collected Papers*, **4**, p. 42.
[2] op. cit., p. 42.

10

A word more on our technique. We know how often it happens that our patients complain that they can never be free, that they must always take care of themselves, that they can never succeed in reaching complete surrender, either in love or in the treatment. Following mainly the lead by Otto Rank, psycho-analysis has till now seen in the wish for this surrender a regression to the mother's womb, and the trauma of birth as the hindrance in attaining this. Ferenczi was struck by the readiness with which our patients accepted this interpretation —clearly because this idea hardly touched them emotionally. I believe we were on the right path, but we skipped an important step. For what were the characteristics on which we based this so-called 'regression to the mother's womb'? Warmth, quiet, darkness, comforting monotonous sounds, absence of desires, ceasing of the compulsion to constant testing of reality, the putting aside of all suspicion, etc. I believe that all these are rather to be explained as deriving from the condition of passive love. In my experience this interpretation calls forth much stronger affects than the colourless 'regression to the mother's womb'. Especially as the latter is unreal, phantastic, while, on the contrary, surrender to passive object-love, or as expressed in the language of grown-ups, the giving up of the many conditions on which the patient's trust depends can, and in fact must, be achieved in the course of the treatment.

The main result at which we have arrived is something like this: until now we have regarded the development of the genital functions and the development of object-relations as two aspects of the same process. We spoke, e.g., of an anal-sadistic phase, and meant by this a particular kind of object-relation as well as experiencing a special kind of gratification. It was tacitly assumed that the sequence of these phases is determined biologically, taking place, as it were, spontaneously, without being influenced in any way by the environment. Now I believe that these two developments—though frequently intertwined—are nevertheless two different processes; further, that the different object-relations do not succeed one another according to biological conditions, but are to be conceived as reactions to actual influence of the world of objects—above all, to methods of upbringing. Our therapy is the best proof of this. Where we are able to observe in an object-relation phenomena which, for example, were built up on the pattern of the 'anal-sadistic' phase, we analyse and resolve them. In other words, we have searched for the explanation of this phenomenon in the patient's individual history since we regarded it as abnormal, i.e. unhealthy. Our therapeutic attitude is the same as regards the 'phallic phase' and the 'negative Oedipus complex', etc.

If instead of the former parallelism one assumes an independent development of love, and chooses as the point of departure —as suggested first by Ferenczi—passive object-love, these experiences can be explained quite naturally. At the end of my paper I should like to quote a sentence from Freud's *Three Contributions to the Theory of Sex* in the non-attenuated form as it appeared in the first edition: 'Die Objektfindung ist eigentlich eine Wiederfindung' (*The finding of an object is really a re-finding*[1]). This sentence could serve as a motto for my paper.

[1] First edition (1905), p. 64.

IV

EROS AND APHRODITE [1]

(1936)

In classical antiquity there are two sovereign deities of Love, figures which are no mere doublets but separate and distinct beings. The one, Aphrodite, probably belongs to the same group of goddesses as Istar, Astarte and Isis; that is to say, she was originally a mother-goddess. In the more highly developed conception of the classical period, however, she is represented as a young, enchantingly beautiful woman, who kindles love on all sides and is herself in love as a rule. She is subject to no moral law and has many lovers, amongst them Adonis and Anchises. She has also several husbands, Hephaestus, Ares and Hermes. She leads, indeed, a mature sexual life, though not always with the same partner, and when she loves anyone she gives herself up to her love. The other love-deity is Eros, a mighty god and yet a child, a mischievous, wanton, impudent rogue. Ethnologists will, of course, prove that he really symbolises the penis, but we need not at the moment trouble about this. The important point for us is that Eros is never conceived of as a grown man; he is the constant companion of Aphrodite, but never her sexual partner. He only plays, yet in his play he performs most difficult tasks. He is a child and yet mightier than the major gods. A favourite subject for plastic representation is the Triumph of Eros, in which Zeus himself is led behind the triumphal chariot, smiling but in chains. Or again, the Loves are represented as playing with the insignia of the high gods or taming wild beasts. Eros is indeed a child, but his arrows spare no one. First of all the gods, he issued forth directly from Chaos, and Plato wrote the finest of his dialogues in his honour.

Thus the Greeks divided the phenomena of love into two

[1] Ferenczi Memorial Lecture, Budapest, May 23rd, 1936. German translation in *Int. Z. f. Psa.* (1936), **22**, 453–65, in English in *Int. J. of PsA.* (1938), **19**, 199–213.

groups, which they then embodied in two ideas, two deities. A similar duality of libidinal experience was described by Freud in the *Drei Abhandlungen*. In sexual gratification we have to distinguish fore-pleasure and end-pleasure, and of the latter infantile sexuality as yet knows nothing. All the writings on the theory of instincts which have appeared since Freud's work was published begin by postulating these facts, but their full implication has never been adequately worked out. End-pleasure has been tacitly assumed to be a more highly developed, somewhat more complicated, let us say an adult form, of pleasure, not fundamentally different from fore-pleasure. Even Ferenczi, who emphasised the exceptional position of genitality amongst the other component instincts, treats end-pleasure in his amphimixis theory [1] simply as the sum-total of the mechanisms of fore-pleasure. This assumption seems to me doubtful, and I would suggest that fore-pleasure and end-pleasure are two separate modes of experiencing pleasure, akin but fundamentally different. This distinction is, I think, brought out in the contrast between Eros and Aphrodite.

This hypothesis is supported by the universally recognised fact that there is a close connection between end-pleasure and anxiety: it looks as though end-pleasure were designed to make adult human beings immune from anxiety. In proportion as a man's capacity to tolerate orgasm is small and his opportunities for periodically experiencing end-pleasure are limited from within and from without, he will readily succumb to anxiety. This fact, also, is noted in Freud's earliest works. We may recollect the familiar example of an anxiety-neurosis, in which anxiety constantly recurs as long as unconsummated excitations continue, while the anxiety attacks cease as soon as complete gratification, end-pleasure, has been secured. We know, too, that a child, who as yet has no knowledge of orgasm, is much more subject to anxiety than an adult. It seems then that one condition of anxiety is the disproportion between the actual excitations on the one hand and, on the other, the opportunities which are provided for gratification.

[1] *Versuch einer Genitaltheorie*, 1924, Chap. I. (English version: *Thalassa*, New York, 1938.

If the excitation passes a certain point of intensity, orgasm—end-pleasure—is the only adequate means of discharge.

There is in this connection an important clinical observation to which Ferenczi called my attention in 1925. Sadger was the first to describe it, some years later.[1] Curiously enough he alluded to it only as it were in parenthesis, in a footnote, and since then no more attention has been paid to the subject. The point was this. We learn from genuine perverts that they derive no gratification from their actual perverse activity: it merely produces a state of tremendously strong excitation. They find ultimate relief only subsequently, through genital masturbation or coitus. This applies equally to active and passive scopophilia, fetishism, sadism, masochism, or whatever form the perversion may take.

I will give two examples out of many. A man of about forty was exclusively homosexual, and had only tried relations with a girl once or twice, out of curiosity, to see how he would get on. On no such occasion, however, did he feel the least excitement. Throughout life he played a passive part in the sexual act, which nearly always took the form of coitus *per anum*, and for long periods at a time he earned his living as a male prostitute, generally dressed as a woman. He came to the Policlinic on account of obsessional masturbation. Even when he had an opportunity of performing the sexual act with a suitable partner, possibly several times over, it resulted merely in excitation, which had finally to be discharged by means of repeated masturbation. The only form of gratification of which he was capable was masturbation during paedicatio.

The second patient was a young man of about thirty, who exhibited a motley collection of perversions—various methods of handling the anus, which resembled masturbation, scopophilia, the objects being young lads in tight-fitting shorts (Boy Scouts, athletes and so on), a compulsion which he found pleasurable, to get and put on shorts himself, various homosexual practices, both active and passive, but also attempts at heterosexual relations with prostitutes. In his pursuit of gratification he often combined several of these activities, but

[1] 'Genital and Extragenital Libido', *Int. J. of PsA.* (1929) **10**, 350, footnote.

the result of it all was merely a state of the most intense excitation, never satisfaction. He could attain the latter only by means of masturbation, whether performed by himself or by someone else.

I must defer to a future occasion the attempt to show the bearing of these observations on the general theory of perversion. At the moment I will merely say that we have been accustomed to think that in the perversions one or other of the component instincts has usurped the hegemony of genitality, and that the whole of the individual's sexuality has become organised under the primacy of this component instinct. But that is only part of the truth. It is true that in perverts some component instinct occupies the foreground and that its excitation preponderates over all the rest, but ultimately it finds discharge by the genital method of end-pleasure, even though it be almost in secret. Thus the perversion is only a means of stimulation, an indirect way to genital end-pleasure, a way often very circuitous and sometimes actually dangerous to the subject himself, but a way which he must tread, because all other paths are blocked by repressions. The mechanism of perversion, like that of dreams, is displacement of affect. The accent is displaced from the primary to the secondary—i.e. to the component instinct—in order that subsequently genital gratification may, at this price, be after all attained. The gross symptoms of the perversions are really only a blind, or even a piece of deception, a fraud, and indeed this is entirely in accordance with the general character of these unhappy people.

We have an allusion to this fact in the old joke about two men who had a bet as to which of them knew more ways of sexual enjoyment. The one mentioned normal intercourse as the first way, whereupon the other—generally represented as an old roué—declared that he had lost his bet, for he had never thought of that method. Now this may have been true; but he certainly had many other devices for getting pleasure at his command. Why did he not disclose them? No doubt because all of them, taken together, did not, even in his eyes, tip the scale against normal intercourse.

If we thus accord an exceptional position in the libidinal economy to genital end-pleasure, we answer at the same time the old question of why genitality is not a perversion. This question arose logically out of the theory of the libido, according to which genitality was only a component instinct, not in any way distinguished from the other component instincts. So long as only the fore-pleasure mechanisms function, genitality has actually no preferential position. But the whole situation changes as soon as end-pleasure can be regularly experienced, for it seems to be somehow bound up with genitality. On the other hand perversions, i.e. roundabout methods, can be formed only from fore-pleasure mechanisms.

There is another distinction which is equally important but does not seem to be so universally valid. We know that fore-pleasure erotism is neither masculine nor feminine but is experienced by both the sexes in the same way, their aims and often their objects being the same. It is, in fact, actually sexless. It is true that we call some of these activities and modes of behaviour masculine or feminine, but this description is to a large extent arbitrary and, besides, nearly all these interpretations are based on the two more than doubtful equations 'active = masculine', 'passive = feminine'.[1] All this applies equally to the fore-pleasure associated with genitality. As I have already shown, this kind of fore-pleasure is actually no more important than the other component instincts, until the experience of end-pleasure has been secured. If we bear this in mind, we shall perhaps be able to give a simpler account of the much discussed phallic phase. Above all, we shall have more insight into the very remarkable observation that in that phase the two sexes are still not yet differentiated. On the other hand, the end-pleasure function is always sexually differentiated. It is quite plain that, in contrast to the mechanisms of fore-pleasure, end-pleasure—and end-pleasure alone—has two forms: masculine and feminine.

The mechanism which produces fore-pleasure is very simple: it generally takes the form of stroking, tickling, licking or sucking. In adults the corresponding reaction may be smiling, giggling, laughing, or even screaming and crying out, etc. The whole thing is akin to jokes and the comic. Hence fore-pleasure

[1] Hermann: 'The Use of the Term "Active" in the Definition of Masculinity,' *Int. J. of PsA.* (1935), **16**.

erotism is, for adults, a kind of game, something quite simple without any very definite aim, and consequently disjointed and incoherent. It is, in fact, a sort of pastime. The end-pleasure function, on the contrary, is serious, dramatic, if not tragic. It is often even a matter of deadly earnest, for the animals of many species die during the first orgasm. Even the facial expression conveys this meaning, for it becomes almost gloomy. We think, for example, of Michelangelo's Leda. Above all, coitus is something very definitely in pursuit of an aim: it is not a pastime but a process with a precise intention, a task to be performed. But anyone who knows how to make ample and skilful use in coitus of a number of the mechanisms of fore-pleasure will be dubbed a pervert not only by strict Catholic or Puritan theologians but by the laity in general. This is entirely in accordance with what I said earlier; for here again it is a matter of taking a longer way round, with the aim of heightening excitation in the greatest possible degree. We see then that, especially in adults, fore-pleasure is related to end-pleasure as play is to earnest. We are not surprised at this, for it is only when orgasm follows surely upon excitation that the youth becomes a man and the girl a woman.

Finally, fore-pleasure erotism is manifested by children from the beginning, while there is no doubt that the end-pleasure function is subject to limitations of time. It is not possible to state with any precision when it begins or ends, but the division of human life into childhood, puberty, maturity, the climacteric and old age is based on the phases of the function of end-pleasure. The capacity for such pleasure is not originally present but probably develops during or immediately before puberty, and is then slowly and gradually established. In old age it becomes weaker and finally disappears, or at most makes quite sporadic appearances. Fore-pleasure erotism on the contrary is perennial; it begins with birth and ceases only with death. This difference is finely expressed in the figures of the two Greek love-deities: Eros issues out of Chaos as a child and never becomes an adult, while Aphrodite was never a child but, according to the myth, rose from the sea as an adult woman, Anadyomene, and remains eternally young.

I will now summarise in tabular form some further differences between fore-pleasure and end-pleasure. There is the less need for me to describe them at length since Sadger [1] has dealt with them in some detail.

Fore-pleasure	End-pleasure
From birth on.	Developed later, probably about the time of puberty.
Always ready to function.	Marked periodicity.
Persists till death.	Is invariably subject to limits. The limits vary with the individual.
A relatively simple mechanism.	Very complicated (erection, friction, ejaculation, secretion of viscous mucus, contractions).
No executive organ of its own.	An organ of its own.
Always attached to ego-functions.	Independent system closely associated with reproduction.
Both organ and function are only secondarily designed to secure gratification.	The organ is specially adapted to secure gratification.
Strictly speaking, sexless.	Two distinct forms according to sex.
No definite termination; can be continued indefinitely.	When successful, terminates in orgasm, cannot be prolonged, insusceptible of further stimulus.
May turn into a perversion.	Is a final act.
?	Renders the subject immune from anxiety.
Play.	A serious task.

We have now arrived at our main problem. Has the function of end-pleasure been evolved from fore-pleasure erotism, or has it developed quite separately? It is very remarkable that the question of origin has never been raised in relation to fore-pleasure erotism. Fore-pleasure issues—apparently like Eros

[1] op. cit.

himself—directly out of Chaos. On the other hand, throughout the ages there have been many who have racked their brains in the effort to discover why, whence and how end-pleasure has come to us. In myths, in legends, in fairy-tales, in jests and in philosophical and scientific theories, attempts have been made to solve this problem. In psycho-analytical literature the accepted view—accepted, indeed, without discussion—has been that which Rank [1] formulated most exactly as follows: 'It is certain that genitality has developed from pre-genital erotism, through displacement of libido.' Most of the psycho-analytical literature on this subject appeared between 1924 and 1930 and was no doubt inspired by Ferenczi's genital theory. The writers unanimously adopted his standpoint. In *Thalassa* Ferenczi gives a detailed account of the physiology of genital end-pleasure. He holds that in the history of the race genitality, like Aphrodite Anadyomene, rose from the sea. It is quite clear that he would have liked to give it a special position, but he was far too much under the influence of the general view for our present question even to occur to him. In spite of the title of his paper 'Zur Genese der Genitalität' Rank deals only with the genesis of genital object-relations. Sadger's fine study [2] is an exemplary piece of clinical description but it does not deal with the genesis of orgasm. In *Die Funktion des Orgasmus* [3] Reich comes to the conclusion that genitality is made up of the three following fundamental elements: (1) local erotogenicity of the genital zone (genital susceptibility to stimulus), (2) somatic libido centred in the genitals (genital impulsion), (3) psychogenital libido (genital desire). Under the second heading Ferenczi's amphimixis theory is reproduced. The third point, genital desire or, more correctly, active love, does not really come within the scope of this paper and, besides, I have recently stated in a concise form all that I know on that subject.[4] The first point, genital susceptibility to stimulus, i.e. the question of why the genital organ in particular

---

[1] 'Zur Genese der Genitalität', *Int. Z. f. Psa.* (1925), **11**.

[2] Ibid.

[3] Vienna, 1927. See especially Chapter VI.

[4] 'Zur Kritik der Lehre von den prägenitalen Libidoorganisationen', *Int. Z. f. Psa.* (1935), **21**. (Critical Notes on the Theory of the Progenital Organisations of the Libido'). Reprinted in this vol., p. 49.

is adapted to produce orgasm, leads directly to our problem. Reich, however, went no farther, but referred his readers to physiology: 'The explanation of the fact that the genital apparatus is the sole instrument of orgastic gratification must lie in the physiological structure of the different erotogenic zones.'[1] This is certainly true, but let us not give up the attempt to advance at any rate a step farther in the field of psychology.

First, however, we must make an excursion into biology. As we have seen, fore-pleasure lasts as long as human life itself; it arises continually and is inseparably connected with all somatic functions (e.g. nutrition, digestion, excretion, sense-perception, muscular activity, etc.). So it is probably one of the primal functions of our body, the soma. End-pleasure—orgasm —on the other hand, seems to be a relatively recent acquisition. Throughout life there is an alien element in it; it acts upon the soma in an intoxicating or even in a stupefying manner. Also, in contradistinction to fore-pleasure, end-pleasure can be done without for quite a long time and, moreover, the capacity for it does not endure throughout life. We even hear frequently that old people are quite glad when they can feel free at last from its demands.[2] It might therefore be concluded that the soma, i.e. our body, was originally asexual, incapable of orgasm but not of eroticism, and that at first it knew only fore-pleasure but later, in the course of phylogenesis, became subject to sexual differentiation and capable of end-pleasure. We know that we, like all vertebrates, are made up of two different systems, the diploid body-cells and the haploid germ-cells, and there must, after all, be some significance in the fact that the period of end-pleasure roughly coincides with that in which mature haploid germ-cells are present in the body. I once made an attempt[3] to work out these relations, but I only succeeded in arriving at the conclusion that copulation, orgasm, individualisation, and death make their appearance together

[1] op. cit., S. 150.

[2] Cf. Cicero, *De senectute*; Schopenhauer, *Vom Unterschiede der Lebensalter*; Wells, *William Clissold*; and many others.

[3] 'Psychosexuelle Parallelen zum biogenetischen Grundgesetz', *Imago* (1932), **18**, 28 ff. ('Psychosexual parallels to the Fundamental Law of Biogenetics'). Reprinted in this vol., p. 11.

in the history of the race, and that they develop on parallel lines and probably must have a common explanation, since none of these functions is a primal attribute of life or of the soma.

In the psychic life also a strong genital wish, the longing for end-pleasure (and sometimes that experience itself) involve considerable disturbance. This impulse leads, much more often than any other, to conflicts, and then the solution is often the familiar one of regression: end-pleasure is prohibited and gratification in a 'pregenital' form, that is to say fore-pleasure, is substituted for it. To the psyche as well as to the soma the function of fore-pleasure seems much more akin and less dangerous, as though the source of end-pleasure were remote and lay in some other system. This is in accordance with the fact that end-pleasure, in contrast to all forms of fore-pleasure, which are almost continuous, is obviously intermittent. So in this respect too it may be said to occupy an intermediate position between the genuinely somatic instinctual stimuli and those which originate in the external world. This biological argument suggests that fore-pleasure and end-pleasure are two separate functions, i.e. that end-pleasure has not been evolved from the mechanisms of fore-pleasure.

Now let us turn to psychology. With the exception of Ferenczi,[1] most psycho-analytical writers have discussed the orgastic function from the dynamic standpoint. Let us consider its economic aspect. Our first idea would probably be that fore-pleasure is associated with a lesser and end-pleasure with a greater degree of excitation, but this does not correspond to the facts. As we have seen in the case of perversions and the subtleties of the *ars amandi*, the fore-pleasure mechanisms are capable of producing intense excitation. True they can produce it, but they cannot discharge it. It seems as though any considerable quantity of excitation could be discharged only by means of genital end-pleasure. If this outlet is blocked by the resistances due to repression and the only way open to the individual is that of fore-pleasure, the result is either an

---

[1] *Versuch einer Genitaltheorie*, op. cit.; 'Sprachverwirrung zwischen den Erwachsenen und dem Kind', *Int. Z. f. Psa.* (1933), **19**. In English, *Int. J. of PsA.* (1949), **30**, 225 *et seq.*

anxiety-neurosis or some form of morbid craving. From the economic point of view the anxiety-neurosis would correspond to an ever-increasing tension, while the craving would represent a forced discharge *in refracta dosi*—the tension being in this case constant and painfully great, as is the case in *ischuria paradoxa*.

The genital organ, on the other hand, is not adapted to producing such excessive tension, for the culminating gratification is easily induced and is followed by a refractory phase. Coquetry is coquetry only so long as it does not lead to end-pleasure; its weapons are the mechanisms of fore-pleasure, and end-pleasure is fatal to it. On the other hand, if there has been no preparatory fore-pleasure, the gratification afforded by coitus is less complete, as Ferenczi showed in 1912, in his contribution to the discussion on masturbation in the Vienna Psycho-Analytical Society.[1] One of the essential conditions of satisfactory end-pleasure is that it should be preceded by an appreciable heightening of tension, but fore-pleasure in no way depends on this.

To some extent this heightening of tension is brought about by the objective situation. If a man is to obtain genital gratification, he must first secure the compliance of his love-object. This is not an indispensable condition in the case of every instinct: it is far less necessary where the oral and the anal instincts are concerned but somewhat more so in active or passive scopophilia. In many perversions, e.g. kleptomania and fetishism, the love-object is something inanimate. Genitality (like sado-masochism) demands the greatest degree of compliance in the love-object. If our object does not yield or fall in with our wishes and feel itself one with us, genital gratification is scarcely possible. Something must be done therefore to convert the object into a genital partner.[2]

Thus the objective situation does in part explain the necessity for a heightening of tension before end-pleasure. But this explanation is very inadequate. The clinical phenomena which precede and accompany the act of coitus are certainly of much

[1] 'On Onanism', *Contributions to Psycho-Analysis*, Chap. VI.

[2] This compliance is brought about by means of fore-pleasure mechanisms: it is as though the two partners must first become children together, in order to develop together to the adult capacity for orgasm. (Note by Alice Balint.)

too violent a character to be explained simply as the process of securing the compliance of the love-object. The movements can hardly be said to be co-ordinated any longer and consciousness is in some degree clouded. If we look for similar phenomena, we shall note first epileptic attacks, then outbreaks of affect, as in rage and panic, and finally traumatic neuroses. All of these are characterised by intolerable tension, which irresistibly produces movements of a particular type. These are almost or entirely uncontrollable, in the nature of reflexes and yet rhythmical, and have to be continued for a certain length of time in order to cause the tension to disappear. Freud holds [1] that in these situations the individual has experienced some excessively strong stimulus and that the resulting excitation is so intense that he cannot discharge it all at once. The dominance of the pleasure-principle is for the time being suspended; that is to say, the crucial point is no longer whether the excitation is pleasurable or painful; it must be reduced at all costs. The effort so to reduce it always takes the form of movement. Freud deduced this archaic mode of functioning of the psychic apparatus from traumatic neuroses, certain children's games and the phenomena of transference. A fourth object of study in this connection might well be the function of end-pleasure, for in it, I think, we can observe a traumatic situation *in statu nascendi*. Unfortunately nearly everything that our analysands tell us on this subject relates to the body. We can learn very little of the mental processes, perhaps just because they take place in archaic strata to which it is hard to gain access. The meagre material which patients produce has some such content as this: They feel increasing tension, which produces an impulsion towards rhythmical movement; the tension becomes even greater . . . they want to be relieved of it at all costs, even if it involves suffering . . . they can hardly bear it . . . they often groan, sob, cry out or even curse and swear; sometimes they even commit acts of aggression or violence against their sexual partner . . . they describe the feeling before the excitation reaches its climax as an inability to contain themselves, a sense of bursting, dissolving or disintegration . . . and it is only at the end that sets in a tranquil, quiet sense of well-being. This latter

[1] *Beyond the Pleasure Principle.*

feeling seems to be the primal form of pleasure. It is certain that all the fore-pleasure functions have this for their direct aim and, even if they cannot by themselves compass it, this state is nevertheless striven after and finally attained by the roundabout way of increasing excitation and end-pleasure.

What I have just said throws light on one particular disturbance of the sexual function. When the stimulus is excessive —as may frequently be observed in the case of men who have been abstinent for a long time—the tendency to relieve the tension becomes so powerful that the pleasure of gratification is considerably reduced or may even disappear altogether. Some men make a regular system of this; the first coitus is of this traumatic character and produces nothing but relief and not until the second is there any pleasure. When the amount of excitation can be exactly regulated, so that a man is quite sure that it will not exceed what he himself desires and knows himself capable of tolerating, then and then only is gratification— end-pleasure—satisfactory.

From the economic point of view end-pleasure is the integration of two conflicting tendencies. The one is the more archaic and may almost be called biological. It dates from the period before the pleasure-principle asserted itself; its aim is to relieve tension at all costs and it is not necessarily pleasurable. The tendency to autotomy, described by Ferenczi,[1] may serve as the prototype of this tendency. The second is of much more recent origin and is undoubtedly mental. Its aim is to keep the excitation at a certain level which has been found safe, and to submit consciously and deliberately to this degree of excitation with the assurance of being able to discharge it. This function, which might almost be called an accomplishment, is eminently pleasurable.

S. Pfeifer [2] pursues a similar line of thought. He too distinguishes two types of discharge. The more primitive an instinct, the smaller will be the increase in tension which can be tolerated, and the more care must be taken to contrive that 'stimulus and gratification shall coincide as nearly as may be

[1] *Versuch einer Genitaltheorie*, 1924, Chap. IV. (English version: *Thalassa*.)
[2] 'Die neurotische Dauerlust', *Int. Z. f. Psa.* (1928), **14**.

in time'. Pfeifer holds that the difference between this mode of discharge and genitality lies in a certain 'catastrophic' element which has been imported into the process.

If we follow out this train of thought, it leads us straight to the psychology of the ego. The concept of the 'strength of the ego' is one which we have frequently employed, especially of late years. It has not yet been exactly defined, but it is clearly based on a quantitative idea. I would now suggest that the strength of the ego at a given moment may be measured by the maximum tension or excitation which it can tolerate without disturbance. Where conditions are fairly normal, the only excitation which approximates to this maximum in adults is the excitation before and during orgasm. Even supposing that it were not the only one, it is certainly the most frequent, for it is one of the normal conditions of adult life. Here we have a simple explanation of what sounds somewhat mystical—the dictum that the sexual life is the pattern of all life. The first signs of a latent disturbance or defect in the ego become perceptible when it is subjected to a heavier strain of excitation, i.e. precisely in the 'orgastic function'. On the other hand, people who can safely expose themselves periodically to orgasm have a sufficiently strong ego, which can stand strains of other kinds.

Broadly speaking, all those who bring up the young have only two methods. On the one hand, children are treated lovingly; that is to say, they are subjected to a libidinal strain, from the economic point of view. (I am thinking of such things as caressing, rocking, embracing and kissing a child, or taking him on one's knee.) On the other hand, certain channels of fore-pleasure are closed to the child; that is to say, when he is weaned, when pleasure-sucking is forbidden, or when he is trained in habits of cleanliness and regularity. Thus education menaces the already unstable libidinal balance of the child simultaneously from both sides: actual excitation is increased and opportunities of discharge are restricted.

When the strain is too great, the child has two ways of recovering his balance. Either his ego may be overwhelmed by the growing excitation and a state of panic set in, which then finds relief in an outbreak of affect and unco-ordinated movements. Or else it will do its utmost and call up all his energies to stem the excitation. The first method resembles a clonic, and the second a tonic spasm. Now there is no doubt that these two modes of reaction are the ego's primal forms of defence; and I think that the later forms, of which Anna Freud was the first to give a systematic account in her recent book,[1] are derived from these and are, as it were, psychic superstructures based on these two almost physical modes of defence.

Clearly education is in favour of tolerating excitation: it regards with horror any outbreak of affect. Sometimes it succeeds only too well in its purpose: children do indeed learn to tolerate everything—but they pay for it with a chronically spastic condition. They react to every stimulus with an increased spasm, especially if they are uncertain whether the stimulus may not become more powerful. Ferenczi[2] was the first to draw attention to these physical forms of defence (especially chronic muscular tension). People with this spastic disposition can give themselves up to free association only in the face of great resistance and can never abandon themselves in love and hardly ever relax in enjoyment. We have a return of repressed material when women suffering from spastic frigidity laugh or weep convulsively instead of experiencing orgasm. The tonic spasm has here, after all, given way to the clonic outbreak of affect.

In the function of end-pleasure also we find these two tendencies: the more biological, clonic tendency to relieve tension and the more psychological tendency, which has a greater affinity with the ego, to tolerate or even to increase excitation. We can now understand that the undisturbed co-operation of these two tendencies demands a certain strength in the ego (and the instincts). Probably this can be achieved only after the biological upheavals of puberty; but even then, at least in our modern civilisation, the discovery of end-pleasure has a traumatic effect. Kovács[3] was the first to show that, when end-pleasure is experienced for the first time, it often arouses fear

[1] *The Ego and the Mechanisms of Defence*, 1937.

[2] 'Technical Difficulties in the Analysis of a Case of Hysteria' (1919), *Further Contributions*, Chap. XV. Int. PsA. Library; 'Psycho-analysis of Sexual Habits' (1925), *ibid.*, Chap. XXXII.

[3] 'Das Erbe des Fortunatus', *Imago* (1926), **12**.

and anxiety. In men this occurs on the occasion of the first ejaculation, in women of the first orgasm, whether these be induced by masturbation or coitus (defloration). It is very seldom that these processes take place without any disturbance. The 'spontaneous cure of pregenitality', described by Anna Freud,[1] takes place only very gradually, and the first acts are almost never pleasurable in tone. It is true that they relieve tension, but it is long before they are enjoyable. Thus there is much to be said in defence of the apparent paradox that coitus, the prototype of pleasure, is originally entirely devoid of pleasure and merely serves the tendency to autotomy; only later, when erotisation has taken place, does it become pleasurable and a source of enjoyment.

The many people who suffer from disturbances in potency or from frigidity are not really ill but merely inhibited in their development. Their ego is not yet strong enough to bear so high a degree of tension: either it relieves itself in a kind of short circuit (e.g. *ejaculatio praecox*) or it loses itself in convulsive attempts to force the excitation to an even higher pitch (frigidity). Sometimes this is successful up to a point, but the spasm itself prevents end-pleasure and there is nothing left but to stop from exhaustion. Patients of this type always describe the progress of their analysis in the same terms. They say such things as 'I was able to go further', 'I managed to get higher', 'I was able to bear more', etc.

The train of thought which I have been pursuing in this paper would lead us to a number of interesting problems, such as the difference between masculine and feminine, the phenomenon of primary anxiety in the face of instinctual danger, the economic differences between the instinctual life of children and that of adults, and other similar points. On the present occasion, however, I cannot deal with these, so I will merely summarise the principal conclusions at which we have arrived.

The difference between fore-pleasure and end-pleasure is much more fundamental than has hitherto been supposed. The function of fore-pleasure is comparatively simple and it seems to be a primal attribute of living beings. The function of end-pleasure, on the contrary, is a new acquisition in the

[1] op. cit., p. 162.

history of the race and so complicated that each individual has to learn it afresh. It comprises two opposite tendencies, and the integration of the two to an orgasm may be called an accomplishment and depends on the ability to tolerate a degree of excitation which is all but traumatic. I have tried to show the bearing of these observations upon the theory of libido and the psychology of the ego.

V

EARLY DEVELOPMENTAL STATES OF THE EGO. PRIMARY OBJECT-LOVE [1]

(1937)

THE genetic approach is the principal method we use in our science of psycho-analysis; a mental phenomenon observed in the present is explained by tracing it back to a previous one, and by demonstrating how far and by what external and internal influences the previous process was changed into the present one. This crab-like thinking must, however, come to a halt somewhere, i.e. where the previous earlier phenomenon, the original one, can no longer be observed but must be inferred from what can be observed. In the early years of psycho-analysis theoretical research reached as far as the Oedipus situation, i.e. to the third to fifth year of life. The theoretical gains thus achieved led to greater power of observation and in turn the better-trained observers could verify all the theoretical assumptions.

Naturally research has not come to a standstill, and time and again attempts have been made to infer still earlier mental states from observations. This new situation, however, is utterly different from the previous one. Then only one theory, or, more correctly, two complementary theories—that of the classic Oedipus situation and that of the polymorph-perverse nature of infantile sexuality—were under discussion, today we have to deal with several theories that often contradict one another. Slight differences in theoretical constructions are understandable, but we hear and read of theories which diverge considerably and are often diametrically opposed. These differences somehow seem to depend on geography in a way that justifies one in speaking of regional opinions. Probably each one of us

---

[1] Shortened version of a contribution to the First Symposium of the Second 'Four Countries' Conference' in Budapest, May 1937. Published in German in *Imago* (1937), **23**, 270–88. In English in *Int. J. of PsA.* (1939), **30**, 265–73.

will protest against his ideas being submerged in a regional opinion and will quote sharp controversies within his own group; still the results of his work appear to a distant observer as one or more notes in a regional harmony. Such 'regional'— not quite identical but consonant—opinions have been formed during the last years[1] in London, in Vienna and in Budapest.

The word 'opinion' is used intentionally. We must not forget that we are arguing here about theoretical constructions. For we all agree that the earliest state of the human mind is not essentially different in London from what it is in Vienna or in Budapest. These unpleasantly diverging opinions originate very likely from the fact that the various research workers start from different points of observation and use somewhat different terms. In this paper I shall try to trace back the differences in the theoretical constructions to the different points of view, the different expectations and the different terms used. This, however, does not mean that each point of view and each terminology is equally advantageous. On the contrary, I wish to show that some points of view are linked with certain disadvantages.

I have said that the material from which we have come to such dissimilar conclusions is the same for all of us. To start with I have to choose a description of the infantile mind which will be acceptable to everyone. We need for this purpose a reliable observer who at the same time must be a precise reporter. I quote him: [2] 'Childish love knows no bounds, it demands exclusive possession, is satisfied with nothing less than all. But it has a second characteristic: It has, besides, no real aim; it is incapable of complete satisfaction and this is the principal reason why it is doomed to end in disappointment and to give place to a hostile attitude' (p. 286). Hence the reproach: 'that the mother gave the child too little milk and did not suckle her long enough. Under the conditions of modern civilisation this may very often be quite true, but certainly not so often as is maintained in analysis. It would seem rather that this complaint expresses the general dissatisfaction of children . . . as if our children remained for ever unappeased, as if they had never been suckled long enough. So great is the greed of

[1] Written in 1937.
[2] Freud: 'Female Sexuality', *Int. J. of PsA.* (1932), **13**.

the childish libido' (pp. 288–9). 'In the first phases of the love life ambivalence is evidently the rule' (p. 289). And further: 'Those first impulses of libido have an intensity of their own which is greater than anything that comes later and may indeed be said to be incommensurable with any other force' (p. 296). This description by Freud will be acceptable to all of us; it gives only the facts without any theoretical evaluation or attempted explanation.

The Londoners will certainly see in this description nothing but a confirmation of their opinion. The described features of the infant's mental life, such as extravagance, hostility, general discontent, insatiable greed, obvious ambivalence, etc., are the phenomena always emphasised by them. Thus Joan Riviere started her representative lecture in Vienna with the sentence: [1] 'My object in this paper is to attempt a short general formulation of the earliest psychical developmental processes in the child, i.e. of the problems of oral sadistic impulses and their attendant anxieties . . .' (p. 395). According to the Londoners: 'The baby's mental life in its first weeks is narcissistic in character . . .' (p. 397). Further they assume 'that oral and cannibalistic impulses . . . are formed during the actual exercise of the oral function as an object-relation' [2] (p. 396). This development has two sources. Sadistic instinctual impulses may arise spontaneously, i.e. without the influence of the external world, as manifestations of the death instinct turned outward. These impulses use mainly, but not exclusively, the oral zone; in addition the muscles, the eyes, breathing, the excretory function, etc., also come into their service. The second—also unavoidable—source of these sadistic impulses is the delaying of gratification. Such a delay causes the child to experience the increased tension as a 'traumatic situation' in Freud's sense; he is compelled to give up gradually the security of his narcissistic omnipotence, feels helpless and powerless, at the mercy of evil

[1] Riviere, J.: 'On the Genesis of Psychical Conflict in Earliest Infancy', *Int. J. PsA.* (1936), **17**.

[2] I noticed only while preparing this translation that the German text of Mrs. Riviere's paper omits the words 'as an object-relation' which are in the original English. The German sentence runs: 'dass orale und kannibalistische Triebregungen . . . primär in der Säugeperiode entwickelt werden' (*Int. Z. f. Psa.* (1936), **22**, 488).

powers, and reacts to all this with hate and aggressiveness. These affects are, either from the very beginning or very soon after, directed towards objects as well as towards the self; as they are intolerable to the weak and undeveloped ego, they are felt as originating from the objects, they are projected on to them. Thus a kind of paranoia (op. cit., 405) develops, the infant becomes oversensitive and reacts vehemently to all—however small or unimportant—signs of a negative, careless or only indifferent, attitude in his environment: everywhere and in everything he sees bad objects. These bad objects engender fear in the infant, who then will be afraid of their vengeance. But: 'guilt and remorse will also be present to some extent along with these persecutory feelings and will greatly increase the conflict of ambivalence' (op. cit., 405).[1] Here the struggle begins between the earlier aggressive and the somewhat later developing impulses of tender love which, however, are ultimately based on the original acquisitive impulses with all their tendencies to greed and sadism. Both forms of 'love' employ the mechanisms of introjection and projection (as also does hate); mental content in the earliest months consists mainly of phantasies of various physical methods of absorbing, or of expelling (or restoring) good and bad objects (i.e. good and bad aspects of the original object split into two); in addition all other defensive mechanisms, including repression, are already at work in the first months of life. (M. Schmideberg, quoted by Riviere, op. cit., p. 398.) Two important tendencies are to be mentioned here: the one is an almost spastic effort to keep the good objects apart from the bad ones, for fear the good helpful ones might be destroyed by the bad ones; the other is the tendency to repair the effects of one's own sadistic impulses, to change the bad and therefore maltreated objects into good ones.

The subsequent development need not concern us here. I now wish to sum up the most important suppositions which are fundamental for the English point or view: (1) The infant is

---

[1] At this point the German translation again deviates from the English original: 'Zugleich mit diesen Verfolgungsängsten treten auch schon ansatzweise Schuldgefühle und Sorge für das Objekt auf sobald sich die Liebe zur Brust und zur Mutter geltend macht' (op. cit., p. 497). Reference to an early object-relation is omitted here from the English version.

born in the state of primary narcissism. (2) Vehement sadistic and aggressive impulses appear very early; it remains undecided how much of them is attributable to the archaic death instinct turned towards the external world, and how much to the reactions of hatred caused by the influence of the environment. It seems, however, that the loving impulses appear later and are weaker. (3) The Londoners seem to be uncertain as to when and how reality testing begins [1]; the uncertainty is so great that authors occasionally contradict each other. One instance may be quoted here: J. Riviere asks us to 'keep in mind that this narcissistic world of the psyche is . . . entirely autistic, not only lacking in objectivity, but at first without objects'. In the following sentence, however, Glover is quoted who 'has emphasised that even babies have a sense of reality of a kind' (op. cit., pp. 398–9). (4) Further it is assumed that the infant deals with his primary experiences above all with the help of introjection and projection.

Here the Viennese criticism begins. I am in the fortunate position—as I was with regard to London—to be able to quote a representative paper of this school, and so to be very brief [2] Wälder doubts the ubiquity and intensity of the oral sadistic manifestations as described by the Londoners and consequently the validity of the conclusions which were arrived at by generalisation from these alleged observations. Further, he criticises the inexact, unorthodox use of the concepts of introjection and projection as causing confusion. Equally confusing, according to him, is the way in which the Londoners describe phantasy and reality, or perhaps more correctly, external and psychic reality. Finally he doubts whether the experiences of the very first developmental stages of the human mind can ever be consciously recollected and even less expressed in words.

Although these objections are very weighty and Wälder's argumentation appears to be convincing, the problem still remains. If one abandons the Londoners' point of view and accepts the Viennese, one remains perplexed in face of the

---

[1] Apparently the same is true of the beginning of object-relations. Cf. the divergences in the English and German versions of Mrs. Riviere's paper.

[2] Wälder, R.: 'The Problem of the Genesis of Psychical Conflict in Earliest Infancy', *Int. J. PsA.* (1937), **18**, 416–73).

infantile phenomena as described by Freud. Why are infants so extravagant, greedy, insatiable, why does hostility appear unavoidably, whence the reproach that mother never fed them rightly, never treated them lovingly? We cannot side with Wälder, i.e. the Viennese, without having first found some explanation for the infantile phenomena described by Freud. For it must be admitted, if one accepts the Londoners' assumptions, all these phenomena, observed by all of us, can be explained easily.

The situation is very embarrassing: on the one hand we have a theory which can make understandable very many of the most important phenomena of the infantile mind, the fundamental assumptions of which, however, can hardly stand up to a perfectly justified criticism; on the other hand we have a criticism the conclusions of which can hardly be contradicted, but which can teach us almost nothing about the field we are interested in.

The obvious conclusion is that the present material is insufficient to allow of a decision in this issue of paramount importance. But where can we find new material? I have mentioned that according to Wälder it is hardly to be expected that the experiences of the very early age can ever be recollected consciously. But it is at least equally certain that the experiences of this time are of paramount importance and essentially influence the whole later life of the individual. On this we all agree; but the question arises how can one get reliable data about these experiences? In principle there are—as emphasised by Wälder—two possible ways: direct observation of the infant and reconstruction of infantile behaviour from the data of adult life. If I understood Wälder rightly, the difficulties that stand in the way of a reliable verification are so great that the Viennese consider any assumption in this field with extreme scepticism.

This brings me to Budapest. We have only recently, it is true, become [1] somewhat less sceptical on this point. Three different trains of thought, independently begun from different angles of approach, have recently led A. Balint, I. Hermann and myself to such converging conclusions that we are practically convinced at least to be moving in the right direction. The

[1] Written in 1937

common principal stimulus to our trains of thought can be traced back to Ferenczi [1] and beyond him to Freud. Our common starting-point was to consider the formal elements of the analytical situation, more than was hitherto customary, as phenomena of transference, hoping that in this way we might obtain valuable data about the individual history of our patients. This hope has been realised; we have even found more, namely that certain features of the analytical situation appear monotonously in every treatment, nay, that they can be observed more and more clearly and frequently as, in the process of analysis, the patient becomes liberated from the defensive mechanisms that he can remember having acquired. Thus we have come to the conclusion that these ever-recurring features must be considered as a general human quality. There remained, however, to be decided whether these features are determined by the biological nature of man or are precipitates of the earliest psychic experiences.

Independently from each other and without having formulated it explicitly all three of us chose the latter of these possibilities as a working hypothesis. We asked ourselves *how many of these observable, monotonously recurring features of the analytical situation could be traced back to early infantile experiences* or more correctly *how much of the early infantile mental processes can be inferred from these easily verifiable observations?* We tried, in addition, to support our conclusions by further material. Here each of us went a different way. Hermann's second source of material was comparative psychology, above all the study of the primates; Alice Balint's a just developing science, comparative pedagogics, while I collected data from the theory of sexuality.

I wish to review the results briefly and shall start with my own investigations.[2] I found that at times, when the analytic

---

[1] *Stages in the Development of the Sense of Reality* (1913); *Thalassa: A Theory of Genitality* (1924); *Confusion of Tongues between the Adults and the Child* (1933).

[2] 'The Final Goal of Psychoanalytic Treatment', *Int. J. PsA.* (1936), **17**, 206–16. (The German original appeared in 1935.) 'Zur. Kritik der Lehre von den prägenitalen Libidoorganisationen', *Int. Z. f. Psa.* (1935), **21**, 525–43. 'Eros and Aphrodite', *Int. J. PsA.* (1938), **19**, 199–213. (The German original appeared in 1936.) Reprinted in this vol., pp. 49, 73 and 188.

work had advanced fairly deeply, my patients expected and often even demanded certain primitive gratifications, mainly from their analyst but also from their environment. If I kept strictly to the rule of analytic passivity, i.e. if these desires for gratification were frustrated automatically by my passivity, phenomena appeared which corresponded in all their essential features to the conception of the infant as put forward by the London analysts. Loss of security, the feeling of being worthless, despair, deeply bitter disappointment, the feeling that one would never be able to trust anyone, etc. Mixed with these came most venomous aggression, wildest sadistic phantasies and orgies depicting the most cunning tortures and humiliations for the analyst. Then again fear of retaliation, the most complete contriteness, because one had spoilt for ever the hope of being loved by the analyst or even merely to be treated by him with interest and kindness; never more could one expect to deserve a good word from him.

If, however—warned by the experiences I have quoted—I later permitted the satisfaction of those modest wishes, we simply went from the frying pan into the fire. An almost manic state broke out. The patients became overblissful; they wanted nothing but to experience again and again the satisfaction of these wishes. All the symptoms disappeared; the patients felt super-healthy as long as they felt secure of obtaining immediately on demand the satisfaction of those extremely important wishes; at such times it was very difficult indeed to keep them at the analytical work. This state very closely resembles that of an addiction or of a severe perversion, even in its lability. At the first serious dissatisfaction or considerable delay of the gratification the whole structure of this enraptured blissfulness breaks down and abruptly the mood changes into the form described previously of despair, hatred and fear of retaliation.

Let us go one step farther. What are these dangerous wishes in reality? Rather innocent, naïve one would say. A kind word from the analyst, the permission to call him by his first name or be called by him by one's first name; to be able to see him also outside the analytical session, to borrow something or to get a present from him, even if it be quite insignificant, etc. Very often these wishes do not go farther than to be able to touch the analyst, to cling to him, or to be touched or stroked by him. (The latter will lead us into the field of the phenomena of clinging about which more later.)

I must confess that it took me a long time to notice two essential qualities of these wishes. Firstly *without exception they are directed towards an object*, and secondly *they never go beyond the level of fore-pleasure*. That means: firstly, that it is only the external world, the environment, that can satisfy them; auto-erotic narcissistic satisfaction is never sufficient. Secondly: if the satisfaction arrives at the right moment, and with the right intensity, it causes reactions that are observable only with difficulty because the experience of gratification happens so quietly. Properly this feeling of pleasure could be described as a *tranquil quiet sense of well-being*. If, however, these wishes must remain unsatisfied, their gratification will be demanded very vehemently and an eventual frustration will call forth the most stormy reactions.

Now at last I could explain how the noisy and passionate experiences of satisfaction which perplexed me so much in the beginning came about. They are not naïve primary reactions but have already a history; they are reactions to frustrations in a similar way as, e.g., compulsory masturbation often luxuriates for quite a long while after some events in the environment—interpreted by the child as a threat of castration. This knowledge enabled me to evaluate these phenomena of the *new beginning* more correctly and to treat them properly. I shall return to these experiences later.

Now it was but a step from here to surmise that our patients have brought these ever-recurring forms of reactions from their early infantile stages. I am afraid I shall meet some opposition at this point. It may be admitted that these phenomena repeat certain infantile situations, but why should these be the most primitive ones? I shall deal with this question later when discussing the concept of primary narcissism; for the present, however, I must follow the thread of my argument. In my opinion a very early, most likely the earliest, phase of the extra-uterine mental life is not narcissistic: it is directed towards objects, but this early object-relation is a passive one. Its aim is briefly this: *I shall be loved and satisfied, without being under any obligation to give anything in return.* This is and remains for ever the final goal of all erotic striving. It is reality that forces us to circuitous ways. One *détour* is narcissism: if I am not loved sufficiently by the world, not given enough gratification, I must love and gratify myself. The clinically observable narcissism is, therefore, always a protection against the bad or only reluctant object. The other *détour* is active object-love. We love and gratify our partner, i.e. we conform to his wishes in order to be loved and gratified by him in return.

These observations are well supported by the results of I. Hermann.[1] As just mentioned, during the period called by me the 'new beginning' desires appeared that took the form of being permitted to touch the analyst or of being touched by him. This instinctual desire for physical contact has occupied Hermann—independently from me—for more than ten years. I can only give here that part of his results which refers to our topic. His theory starts from two observations: (*a*) The infant of the primates spends the first few months of extra-uterine life clinging to its mother's body; (*b*) the human infant is forcibly separated from the maternal body much too early. The human child has the wish to continue living as a component part of the mother-child unit (a dual unit); as this is frustrated—at least in our civilisation—by reality, it develops a number of instinctual substitutive symptoms, such as its sleeping position, a number of reflexes (Moro, etc.), many phenomena of sucking and hand erotism and, last but not least, the general tendency to cling to something in moments of threatening danger.

In all these instances we are faced with active behaviour on the part of the infant, even with an activity directed towards an object. The fact must also be mentioned that, contrary to common parlance, the child is not suckled, indeed it sucks actively.

Sequelae of this tendency are naturally to be observed in the adult also, in his sexual life, in his neuroses, in his way of associating and in the phenomena of the period of new beginning quoted above. Further, I wish to mention the innumerable

---

[1] Hermann, I.: 'Zum Triebleben der Primaten', *Imago* (1933), **19**, 113, 325; 'Sich-Anklammern—Auf-Suche-Gehen', *Int. Z. f. Psa.* (1936), **22**, 349–70.

magic, mystic, or symbolic acts, such as hand-shaking, laying on of hands, touching, clinging, etc., all of which have this tendency as their basis, and show the conscious aim of identifying oneself with the object or asking help from it.

Moreover, Hermann has proved that clinging is the common precursor of a large number of object-relations. By attenuating this tendency to touching, stroking, caressing, tenderness develops; in the same way it is possible that frustrations followed by regressive reinforcement may bring forth sadism. Further masochistic tendencies can be traced back to primitive clinging. The importance of clinging in normal sensual sexuality, e.g. embracing, pressing, etc., needs no further proofs.

This theory obtained a still firmer foundation through the research carried out by A. Balint.[1] Hermann and I examined these phenomena only from the point of view of the patient, i.e. of the child. A woman was needed to illuminate this dual unit also from the other side, i.e. from the side of the mother. The most important though not at all unexpected result is that the two parties of this relation are libidinously equal. Libidinally the mother is receiver and giver to the same extent as her child; she experiences her child as part of her own body and yet as something strange and hostile in the same way as the child regards the body of its mother. Often only in phantasy, but not so seldom also in reality, she does as she likes with her child as if it had no life, no interests of its own. And it is almost with the same words that our Londoner colleagues describe the behaviour of the child *vis-à-vis* its parents.

This primitive—egoistic—form of love works according to the principle: what is good for me, is right for you, i.e. it does not recognise any difference between one's own interests and the interests of the object; it assumes as a matter of fact that the partner's desires are identical with one's own. Claims of the object which go beyond this harmony are intolerable, and call forth anxiety or aggressiveness. The same attitude develops

---

[1] 'Handhabung der Übertragung auf Grund der Ferenczi'schen Versuche', *Int. Z. f. Psa.* (1937), **22**, 47–58. 'Love for the Mother and Mother Love'. (Originally appeared in German in 1939.) Reprinted in this vol. pp. 105–127.

regularly in the course of analytic treatment. Here, in addition to unscrupulous egoism, another quality of this object-relation can be observed: paranoid sensitivity. The patient is the pivot of everything, he draws far-reaching conclusions from the minutest details as to whether he is loved, and whether or not he is sufficiently taken into consideration.

It is a commonplace that the ultimate goal of all instincts is the union with the object, the recovery of the ego-object-identity. The adult arrives nearest to this ultimate goal in the orgasm. Coitus, it is true, begins as an altruistic act, but the higher one's excitement grows the less regard is paid to the partner until finally immediately before and during orgasm the partner's interests are completely forgotten, and thus in the safe belief of being united with him (her) in perfect harmony one is able to enjoy together the highest pleasure.

In all these cases we have to do with a faulty or even absent sense of reality with regard to the partner, or the analyst; he is treated as if his desires were truly identical with one's own. His existence, however, is never in doubt. It is legitimate to assume the same primitive form of love in the child. A. Balint was able to support this conclusion by data from comparative peda-gogics, especially from the different forms of education in primitive tribes.

The results of these three researches can be summed up as follows:

(1) The phase of object-relation described by all three of us, which could be called primary or primitive object-love, must occur very early in life.

(2) This phase is unavoidable, a necessary stage of mental development. All later object-relations can be traced back to it, i.e. vestiges and remnants of this primitive phase can be demonstrated in all the later ones.

(3) This form of object-relation is not linked to any of the erotogenic zones; it is not oral, oral-sucking, anal, genital, etc., love, but is something on its own, as are the other forms of love, such as auto-erotism, narcissism, object-love. In my opinion this fact is of paramount importance and I hope that through this strict discrimination it will be possible to disentangle the hopeless confusion brought about by equating both in our

theory and in our terminology the development of instinctual aims with the development of instinctual object-relations.

(4) The biological basis of this primary object-relation is the instinctual interdependence of mother and child; the two are dependent on each other but at the same time they are tuned to each other; each of them satisfies himself by the other without the compulsion of paying regard to the other. Indeed, what is good for the one is right for the other. This biological interdependence in the dual unit has been considered hitherto only very superficially; e.g. we thought we had explained it, from the mother's side, by a narcissistic identification with her child.

(5) This intimate relation is severed by our civilisation much too early. Consequences of this early severance are, among others, the well-known tendency to cling, and the general discontent, the insatiable greed of our children.

(6) If the instinctual desire is satisfied in time, the pleasure experience never goes beyond the level of fore-pleasure, i.e. the tranquil, quiet sense of well-being. On the other hand, frustration calls forth extremely vehement reactions, and possibly only such misunderstood and consequently misinterpreted environmental influences can cause reactively in the child insatiable cravings, reminiscent of addiction and perhaps also of orgasm-like conditions.

These assumptions perhaps make it possible to understand the disagreement between Vienna and London. Both parties are right and wrong at the same time. The Londoners studied only the vehement reactions after frustration, but the experience of the tranquil, quiet sense of well-being after proper satisfaction escaped their attention altogether or has not been appreciated according to its economic importance. The form of appearance drowned the essence: *what presented itself as loud, forceful or vehement, has been valued as important, what happened quietly, as unimportant.* This incomplete description has given rise to a one-sided theory; everything in it is correct, except the proportions. The Viennese recognised this fault clearly, and duly emphasised the incompleteness of the London views; but they were either unable to explain satisfactorily the correctly observed phenomena of the infantile period, such as greed, insatiability, strong ambivalence, etc., or had to resort to *ad hoc* hypotheses, such as the primary fear of the strength of an instinct.

Thus developed a hopeless polemic. The English felt that they were right in emphasising the insatiability of the children. However, their thinking got arrested here and they could not go on to view the infantile situation as an instinctual inter-dependence of mother and child. And the reason for this in-ability is the fact that they—in the same way as the Viennese—clung desperately to the hypothesis of primary narcissism. This hypothesis bars the assumption of any relation to external objects. This argument from the theory was in fact quoted time and again by the Viennese. To counter it the Londoners could do nothing but stress time and again their rather one-sided clinical material about the aggressive phenomena showing the infantile dissatisfaction: a typical example of talking at cross purposes despite real goodwill on both sides.

In my opinion it is the hypothesis of primary narcissism that mainly causes the confusion of tongues between Vienna and London. Primary narcissism is a very curious notion, full of meaning and yet very poor. If we accept it, the very earliest state of the extra-uterine mental life can be characterised as follows: the infant has no knowledge as yet of the external world, does not yet even perceive it; it has subjectively no relation to the objects and persons of its environment and thus no desires orientated towards the world; it experiences only increase and disappearance of its needs, but does not yet con-nect them with the external world; the observable emotional phenomena, such as crying, whining, scratching, gripping, fidgeting on the one side, smiling, tranquillity on the other, are merely abreactions; as the infant does not yet perceive any external objects, it can have no libidinous object-relations as yet; of its libido nothing has yet been turned outwards.

Two objections are to be raised here. One is methodological: all the characteristics of the notion 'primary narcissism' are negative, and in addition all of them contain the restrictive adverb 'as yet'. Primary narcissism is, thus, a negative notion; moreover, it gives a description of the real situation only during a very short period. It is extremely difficult to discuss such negative notions as they do not contain anything one can get hold of; they are as slippery as eels. In addition there is that adverb 'as yet'. Everything and anything that can be stated as counter-argument can be dealt with schematically without thinking: whatever contradicts the assumption is *already* a product of development, originally it was not *yet* there.

This is a clear case of extrapolation. It means that primary narcissism is not an observable fact but a hypothesis based on theoretical extrapolation, a point which was time and again duly stressed by Freud himself, e.g.: 'The primary narcissism of the child assumed by us, which forms one of the hypotheses in our theory of the libido, is less easy to grasp by direct observation than *to confirm by deduction from another consideration.*' [1]

The other objection is this: The two states which come nearest to this assumption and which ever since Freud's basic papers have been quoted as arguments, are the catatonic and that of the new-born infant. I have not had much experience with psychotics, but experienced and analytically trained psychiatrists have often stated that no catatonic is absolutely unresponsive. With sufficient perseverance proper reactions can be elicited from them, i.e. a proper object-relation can be demonstrated.[2] According to Petö's observations,[3] reactions of infants to libidinous environmental influences can be demonstrated indisputably as early as the first week of their life and certainly in the first month. I am certain that to weaken the force of these observations the two adverbs 'already' and 'as yet' will be invoked. These observable phenomena are *already* results of development; primary narcissism describes *still* earlier phases, *still* deeper regressions.

To strengthen my thesis I shall quote a few facts about narcissistic states. These facts have been well known for quite a long time, but as they were uncomfortable for our theory one pushed them on one side and tried hard not to notice them in their true significance:

(1) Already Freud has emphasised that absolute narcissism in itself is impossible because a living being in this state is not

---

[1] Freud: *Collected Papers*, Fourth impression (1948), **4**, 48. (Italics by me.)

[2] Written in 1937. Cf. the new attempts at a psychothery of catatonics by J. Rosen.

[3] 'Infant and Mother,' *Int. J. of PsA.* (1949), **30**, 260. German original appeared 1937.

viable. Ever since, following his example, we quote in this connection the nursing environment. It is quite correct to do so. This primary state is only possible in the form of the mother-child unit.

(2) A narcissistic attitude should make one independent of the world. Experience teaches us, however, that this state can be reached only very seldom. (As is well known, Buddha himself did not succeed completely.) In general, narcissistic peoples are almost paranoid-hypersensitive, irritable, the slightest unpleasant stimulus may provoke vehement outbursts—they give the impression of an anxiously and painfully counterbalanced enormous lability. The same is true of children's behaviour from the very beginning. This everyday experience can hardly be made to agree with the theory of primary narcissism; on the other hand it follows naturally from our theory of primary object-relations.

(3) The fact that narcissistic people are so difficult to satisfy also belongs here. Whatever one tries to do for them, however considerate one tries to be, it is always wrong, they never have enough. According to the theory of primary narcissism one would expect a sort of indifference towards the world. These people, however, behave as infants. Freud's description quoted at the beginning of this paper is valid for them too.

(4) It is generally known that newly born babies cry much more in their first weeks than later. Wälder, too, quotes this observation (op. cit., p. 412) although it goes against his thesis. If one picks up such a child—which, however, according to most paediatricians one should not do—it happens fairly regularly, although not always, that it stops crying. To explain this everyday happening the oddest *ad hoc* hypotheses were invented, such as that the mother serves as defence against a possible increase of instinctual excitement, etc., but one would not accept the naïve fact that the crying is the expression of the desire for simple physical contact. The acceptance of such a desire would mean the acceptance of a demonstrable object-relation and with it a serious challenge to primary narcissism.

(5) Again it is generally known that the state of primary narcissism cannot ever be observed in a pure form, i.e. without

easily demonstrable phenomena of 'oral' or 'oral-sadistic love'. This too follows as self-evident from our theory: oral erotism is in fact one of the most important forms of expression of the primary object-love. For the old theory primary narcissism is by definition without any object, therefore all the observed forms of object-relation had to be ascribed to oral erotism, most pregnantly by Abraham in his paper on 'The Influence of Oral-erotism on Character Formation' [1] which has fundamentally influenced the development of theory (not only in England). Freud was much more cautious: in his description of 1931, quoted above, 'oral love' is not even mentioned; he speaks of the insatiability, greed, dissatisfaction, etc., as of *qualities of the infant*. I wish to add that these are just the features of the primary object-love assumed by us. Oral erotism develops under its domination, but so also do other erotic tendencies, e.g. clinging, the need for physical contact, etc., all of which can be insatiable, greedy, in the same way as oral erotism.

Two objections can be expected here. Firstly it will very likely be argued against the assumption of primary object-love that the infant does not know of any external world and still less can discriminate objects in the external world; accordingly it is nonsensical to think that he can build up any relation to such objects not yet existing in his mind. As far as I know it is the first time in the history of psycho-analysis that the possibility of an experience (perhaps) not being conscious is used as an argument against its psychological existence. Moreover, how do we know for certain that the infant does not know anything at all of the external world? Certainly not from unchallengeable observations but from theoretical assumptions about the mental life of the infant, i.e. from the assumption of primary narcissism, while it is just this theory that ought first to be proved. And it is remarkable that the very authors who doubt even the possibility of any verifiable assumption about the earliest phases of the mind, claim to know absolutely firmly and safely what *cannot* exist in the infantile mind.

It will then be said, and that is the second objection, that the phenomena quoted above have been known for a long time and

[1] Abraham, K.: *Selected Papers*. pp. 393–406, London, 1942

have nothing to do with the mind, they are simply phenomena of physiological adaptation. Here again the thesis which stands to discussion is used as an argument. Doubtlessly all these are phenomena of adaptation, but this statement proves nothing for or against their psychic nature. The infant's sucking is certainly adaptation, but I do not think anyone will deny that sucking plays a very important rôle in the mind also.

It only shows the overwhelming power of the hypothesis that the whole mind, and with it the id, could only be thought of as originally narcissistic. It is true, a mind that maintains no relation to the external world is logically the simplest proposition. But does it follow that the logically simplest form must be in reality the most primitive one? This is a fallacy of which we psycho-analysts are not the only victims. In the same way the economists, for quite a long time, put the so-called Robinson Crusoe situation at the beginning of economic development; in the same way it was assumed that the history of civilisation started with logically simple conditions *à la* Rousseau, and in biology the apparently simplest living being, the amoeba, was presented as *primum vivens*. The psychological content of all these assumptions is the narcissistic state totally cut off on all sides, obviously a wish-fulfilment in a sublimated form. More exact research has cleaned up all these assumptions. Thus biology, for instance, had to learn that the logically so-simple amoeba is in fact a secondary form: in its individual (not phylogenetic) youth it shows forms which swim freely about like flagellata, have a rather complicated structure, and above all are sexually dimorphous, which means that they develop proper object-relations to each other.

I think we find ourselves before a similar change in psycho-analysis. Certainly the logically simplest form of the mind is primary narcissism. This never-observed form was inferred from the clinically easily observable condition of so-called secondary narcissism by extrapolation. This assumption was eminently useful as long as analysis could not go considerably deeper than the Oedipus situation. Early analyses of children, the recent studies of psychotics, and above all the essential improvements of our technical ability, and with it the deeper understanding of the transference, have brought more and more material of the pre-oedipal time to light. For the explanation of these new data the theory of primary narcissism proved to be less and less useful.

It must be admitted that the theory of primary object-relations, as proposed here, is also based on extrapolation. But firstly we extrapolate to states much nearer, and secondly our theory is anything but a negative notion. Some features of the assumed primary object-love were enumerated in this paper, others are to be found in the originals quoted. All of them are verifiable. A further methodological advantage of our theory is that it has no such way of escape as—for the theory of primary narcissism—the play with the adverbs 'not yet' and 'already'. What we ask for is that our theory be examined, above all in the study of the infant and the psychotic. Whether, beyond the primary object-relations, the way will lead to primary narcissism or not, must remain undecided for the time being. I, for one, do not think so. In my opinion the time has come for us psycho-analysts to follow the biologists in facing the end of the amoeba myth.

VI

LOVE FOR THE MOTHER AND MOTHER LOVE [1]

By Alice Balint [2]

(1939)

The mother-child relation has been at the centre of psycho-analytic interest right from the beginning. Its importance became even greater when, in the exploration of our cases, it was found necessary to go back regularly into pre-oedipal times. As this is the earliest object-relation, the beginnings of which reach into the nebulous times where the frontiers of ego and external world merge into each other, it is of paramount importance both theoretically and practically. Thus it is quite understandable that each of us has tried his mettle on the mother-child relation. My contribution to this problem is mainly an attempt at a résumé, and I can only claim originality for the point of view from which the summing up was carried out.

I

Clinical examples may serve as a starting-point. I begin with a case in which love for the mother was expressed in a particularly peculiar way. This was the case of a woman patient whose main symptom was that she had to be the slave of her mother. Her unsuccessful attempts at liberation soon became revealed as reactions to disappointments, for in reality she loved her mother and made enormous sacrifices in order to try to satisfy her, which, however, she never succeeded in doing. It was astonishing that the daughter was absolutely helpless in face of

---

[1] Parts of this paper were first published under the title 'Reality Sense and the Development of the Ability to Love' in the S. Ferenczi Memorial volume: *Lélekelemzési tanulmányok*, Budapest, 1933. The final version appeared in German under the title 'Liebe zur Mutter und Mutterliebe' in *Int. Z. f. Psa. u. Imago* (1939), **24**, 33–48, in English in: *Int. J. of PsA.* (1949), **30**, 251.

[2] See Preface, p. 6.

the unreasonable reproaches of her mother and reacted to them with guilt feelings which were quite incomprehensible to her. An extraordinarily strong masculinity complex gave the first explanation of these guilt feelings. Right from the beginning of the analysis it stood out clearly that she wanted to replace her father (and a generous lover) *vis-à-vis* her widowed mother. The first years of the analysis were almost completely taken up with a working through of her masculinity complex. By the end of this phase, her relation to her mother had improved considerably. She had attained an almost normal freedom of movement, could come and go as she liked and had a private life as befits an adult. In her sexual life, too, there was a change for the better. A capacity for orgasm developed, although somewhat labile, in place of an absolute frigidity, and repeated, though interrupted, pregnancies pointed also in the direction of accepting the feminine rôle. But despite all these improvements, her feelings of anxiety and guilt towards her mother remained in unmitigated strength. It was the analysis of her death wishes against the mother that led to the discovery of the deep roots of the guilt feelings. It came to light that the death wishes did not originate in any hatred against her mother. This hatred served only as a secondary rationalisation of a much more primitive attitude, according to which the patient simply demanded that her mother 'should be there' or 'should not be there', according to the patient's needs. The thought of her mother's death filled the patient with the warmest feelings, the meaning of which was not repentance but something like 'How kind of you that you did die, how much I love you for that.' The patient's guilt feeling proved to be well founded in reality, i.e. in the type of love she felt towards her mother. This was a kind of love of which one would indeed be afraid and which explained fully why the patient never wanted to have children. We discovered in it the deep conviction that it belongs to the duties of a loving mother to let herself be killed for the well-being of her children, should an occasion demanding it arise. In other words we discovered in this 'daughter of a bad mother' that deep down she demanded *absolute unselfishness* from her mother. She loved her mother as the only human being who—at least for her unconscious—allowed for the possibility of such a demand. Both the attempts at liberating herself and the exertions made in the attempt to satisfy her mother now gained a new significance. They were obviously also counter-cathexes with the help of which she maintained the repression of her primitive form of love. Also the significance of the identification with the husband (lover) of the mother could be clearly recognised. In the first layer this identification, as previously stated, served as a gratification of her masculine desires. In the deeper layer, however, it was the expression of the patient's demand for love in the reversed form. Just as the mother was loved by her lovers, so did the daughter want to be loved by her mother. And just as the mother unscrupulously exploited the men and then dropped them when they became useless (old or sick), so did the daughter want to use her mother and then get rid of her according to her whims. While the patient let herself be exploited by her mother, she tried secondarily to *gain from hatred the strength necessary for that unscrupulous ruthlessness which in her mother she envied so much.*

This, the deepest layer of the attitude towards the mother, cannot be regarded as ambivalence proper (just as we cannot say that a huntsman hates the game he intends to kill). When children, with the most innocent face in the world, speak of the desirable death of a loved person, it would be quite erroneous to explain this by hatred, especially if the wish concerns the mother or one of her substitutes. The little daughter who is of the opinion that mummy should peacefully die in order that she (the daughter) might marry daddy does not necessarily hate her mother; she only finds it quite natural that the nice mummy should disappear at the right moment. The ideal mother has no interests of her own. True hate [1] and with it true ambivalence can develop much more easily in relation to the father whom the child gets to know right from the beginning as a being who has interests of his own.

The next case concerns a homosexual patient of twenty-one who complained above all of his incapacity to find and to win someone who would love him. Gradually it came to light that it was he who could not love (in the social sense). We learn how

---

[1] True hate is *pure aggressiveness*; pseudo-hate is originally always a demand for unselfishness from the mother.

little he knows of the men with whom he has homosexual relations and from whom he demands excessive tenderness. His lack of interest in other people becomes clear and with it the tendency to claim from anyone and everyone the same gratuitous love that the infant claims from his mother. At this level it becomes clear that he does not want at all to love and to be loved in the sense common to adults. Through his claims the partner who loves him (the patient) causes him anxiety, makes him frightened. Eventually the patient becomes aware that he really wishes to find someone who, not out of love—for lovers are egotistic—but out of chivalry, would heap presents on him. We soon learn that the 'chivalrous duty' really stands for 'parental duty'. The essence of the parental duty is that parents make no demands upon their children because they do only their duty—yielding to the pressure of public opinion—in providing for their children irrespective of whether the children are brave or naughty. These are the comfortable 'lovers'. It is not difficult to discover that underlying this disguise is the primitive way of loving of the infant who does not yet know of his mother as a separate entity having her own interests and who has not yet been compelled to make this discovery. Later, when the mother demands a return for her love she will be felt to be a nuisance and her demands will be refused. 'I do not want to be loved at all', the child appears to say defiantly. In reality it ought to be 'Why am I not loved in the same way (i.e. unselfishly) as I was before?'

The same fear of being loved, or to express it more correctly, fear of the demands of the (love) partner, is shown in the third case. The patient, while in analysis, told the following dream: 'As he enters his flat he sees a large tube in the middle of the room; he lies down on it as if on a bed. It changes in fact into a bed (or couch), but soon it becomes an old woman who makes lewd, grunting sounds. He feels disgust and descends from her although she tries to hold him back.' The immediate cause of the dream was his having seen how his mother was spoiling her grandchild whom she wanted to have completely to herself. With great misgiving he recognises the repressed erotism in her action and at the same time feels ashamed of his own jealousy. Beneath the jealousy there is also a sympathy with his little nephew who, apparently, has to face the same fate as he (the patient) himself. The time will come when the nephew, too, will try to get out of the grandmother's clutches, and she will hold him back in just the same way as she held him, her son. The dream contains many layers, among others several indications of the patient's castration anxiety. From our point of view, the most important feature is the indignation which the patient experienced on discovering the erotism in the (grand)mother love. Until then, when criticising his mother's attitude, he had thought of lack of understanding and not of selfishness. Now she had changed into that grunting old thing who uses her son for her own lust. In fact, *he* has the same attitude towards all women. The sexual desires of the woman he feels to be painful and frightening. The women must be willing but not demanding. He likes best to approach them as a cry-baby who wants to be pitied and comforted. Marriage is prohibited, for then the woman gains something and because of that he cannot believe in the purity of her love. Reciprocity of demands is as incomprehensible to him as to an infant who lives as an ecto-parasite on his mother. One of his main symptoms is his predilection for quite little girls who, however, can be represented by obscene pictures of children. The children, whom he treats as dolls and for whose feelings he need not care, signify in fact the mother. They are the true, unselfish objects of love.

In these three cases the attitude towards the love-object was interpreted in the course of analysis in various ways: as an oral tendency to incorporation, as a narcissistic attitude, as a need to be loved, as egoism, etc., as suggested by the material at the particular time of the interpretation. Yet, ultimately, the version that seemed most adequate was that which I used when describing the case material. The oral tendency to incorporate appeared as only one special form of expression of this kind of love which could be present in a more or less clearly marked form. The conception of narcissism did not do justice to the fact that this kind of love was always firmly directed towards an object, the concept of passive object-love (the wish to be loved) was least satisfactory, especially because of the essentially active quality of this kind of love. We come nearest to it with the conception of egoism. It is in fact an *archaic, egotistic* way of loving, originally directed exclusively to the mother; its main characteristic is the complete lack of reality sense in regard to the interests [1] of the love-object. I shall call this egoism—which in fact is only the consequence of the lack of reality sense— naïve egoism, to differentiate it from the conscious neglect of the interests of the object.

A particularly clear picture of this love, directed especially towards the mother, emerges, in my opinion, from certain quite general phenomena of the transference which appear in each case independent of age, sex and form of illness, and are also to be found in training analyses, i.e. in practically healthy people. I have described these transference phenomena in a paper [2] on the handling of the transference as a paranoically over-sensitive and yet inconsiderate egocentric attitude, the maintenance of which is made possible by a characteristic blindness concerning the person of the analyst; for during treatment the analyst is not a man who has his own interests as other men have. The insight necessary to change this attitude is attained, as a rule, only during the period of growing detachment from the analysis, and even then only very gradually. I would add yet another example to this general description.

A patient asks for one more session per week. His wish is justified in so far as he comes only four times a week because of the lack of time. In spite of this I preserve my passivity and restrict myself to the analysis of this wish which helps us to gain insight into the emotional life of the patient. The wish for one more session each week revealed itself as a declaration of love of the affectively very inhibited patient. At the same time, however, it was the defence against his becoming conscious of the emotional urge. He wanted to have one more session in order to avoid feeling the longing by which his love betrayed itself. Really he wanted the extra session in order not to be compelled to love me—as he explained it to me in detail on this occasion. The most painful thought for him was that possibly I might not have time for him, i.e. that our interests

---

[1] I mean here both the libidinal and the ego-interests of the object.

[2] Balint, A.: 'Handhabung der Übertragung auf Grund der Ferenczi-schen Versuche'. *Int. Z. f. Psa* (1936), **22**.

might clash. *He wished to be with me but, if possible, in such a way as not to be compelled to take notice of me.* It would have been easy to attribute this attitude to narcissistic withdrawal of libido at a moment when the tension created by the longing had passed a certain point. On the other hand, his wish was undeniably a declaration of love. The correct way is to assume that here we have to deal with love, that archaic love, the fundamental condition of which is the complete harmony of interests.[1] For this love the recognition of the *actual* love-object is superfluous, i.e. 'anyway, it wants the same as I do'. This apparently insignificant observation is in my opinion important, for it may possibly explain something of the essence of that subjective self-sufficiency which we assume the satisfied infant possesses.

Another characteristic of archaic love is pseudo-ambivalence. In the case of primitive object-relation an alteration in the behaviour towards the object is not necessarily the consequence of an altered emotional attitude (love, hate), but originates in the child's naïve egoism. In this naïve egoism the antagonism that exists between self-interest and the interest of the object is not perceived at all, e.g. when a little child, or the patient in this particular state of transference, feels that the mother (or the analyst) must not be ill, then it does not mean concern for the well-being of the other, but for one's own well-being which might possibly be endangered by the other's illness. That this is really so is shown by the very unfriendly way in which the child—or the patient—reacts to the actual occurrence of the dreaded illness. Must we then doubt the love-character of this behaviour? After an illness of several months I had a good opportunity for studying the question. My patients, without exception, were angry with me because they felt wronged by the fact that I had been ill, a feeling that was, in a way, justified by the real situation. Their anger was the most forceful expression of their infantile love and attachment. I want to draw attention to the fact that the expressions 'attachment', 'clinging' as well as the German 'Anhänglichkeit' and the Hungarian 'ragaszkodás' (adhesiveness, stickiness),

[1] Another patient equally inhibited in his emotions said once, towards the end of the session, '*Es geht zu Ende mit uns*' (We are nearing our end).

describing this kind of infantile love, are beautiful examples of unconscious knowledge.

Although I do not doubt that everyone will recognise in this description the kind of love that is directed especially towards the mother (I have only repeated what is generally known), I wish to emphasise the observation that most men (and women)—even when otherwise quite normal and capable of an 'adult', altruistic form of love which acknowledges the interests of the partner—retain towards their own mothers this naïve egotistic attitude throughout their lives. For all of us it remains self-evident that the interests of mother and child are identical, and it is the generally acknowledged measure of the goodness or badness of the mother how far she really feels this identity of interests.

Before leaving this subject and turning to discussion of maternal love, I wish to return for a moment to a remark of mine on the love towards the father.[1] Although the *pater-familias* has assumed many maternal traits and is, therefore, treated by the child in many ways like the mother, yet that archaic tie linking mother and child is missing. The child's learning to know the father is governed by the reality principle. Such general observations as, for instance, that children are usually more obedient with their fathers than with their mothers cannot be wholly explained by the fact that the father may be more strict than the mother. The child behaves towards the father more in accordance with reality because the archaic foundations of an original, natural identity of interests has never existed in its relation to the father. The mother, however, must not want anything that might run contrary to the wishes of the child. The same explanation holds true for the greater pedagogical effectiveness of strangers. Folk tales seem to confirm this, the wicked mother is always the stepmother, while the wicked father is not necessarily the stepfather; and this is true for both son and daughter. (It is, in fact, a further argument for the archaic nature of the kind of love described above; it is revealed in similar form in both sexes, and is therefore likely to be of pre-oedipal origin.) Hence: *love for the mother is originally a love without a sense of reality, while love and*

[1] Balint, A.: 'Der Familienvater', *Imago* (1926), **12**, 292–304.

hate for the father—including the oedipus situation—is under the sway of reality.

2

Turning now to mother love, I will again start with an example. A young mother told me her opinion of a lecture on criminal psychology which she had heard on the previous day. The lecturer spoke about the case of a woman who was unhappily married and in her despair murdered her two daughters, and then tried to commit suicide. She did not die, however, and was condemned to fifteen years' imprisonment. The lecturer considered this sentence to be unjust, and my patient agreed with him. The explanation added by her was, however, very remarkable. She thought the sentence was unjust because the woman could not be considered a 'public danger'—she had killed only her own children. In the ensuing discussion it became increasingly clear that the idea of the children having any right to express their opinion did not even enter her mind. She considered the whole occurrence as the internal affair of the mother because *one's own child is indeed not the external world.*

I do not need to emphasise how strange the woman felt after the voicing of these, to her, quite natural thoughts. What she said was a piece of archaic reality which—in our civilisation—is expressed only under various disguises. Primitive people, however, regard infanticide as something that is in no way connected with murder. It is a domestic, internal affair of the family, and society has nothing to do with it.

Roheim wrote that the Central Australian mothers, when under the domination of 'meat hunger', bring about an abortion with their fingers and eat the foetus. He does not mention any feelings of guilt or remorse. The foetus appears to these women to be, in the strictest sense of the word, their own property with which they may do as they like. One can even think of the rule whereby every second child is eaten by the family as a restriction of sovereignty, because by this means life is safeguarded for a certain number of children. But we must not think that the Australian women are in general 'bad' mothers. On the contrary, they give a full measure of maternal care to their living children. They are even capable of great sacrifice, spending nights on their knees and elbows crouching over their babies in order to protect them from the cold with their own bodies.

Some reports of the Esquimaux show a transitional stage between those Australian mothers who unconcernedly eat their children and our conscious attitude. (I say 'conscious attitude' because cannibalistic desires towards children are by no means rare in dreams, etc.) For example, it has been reported that an Esquimaux woman who ate her child during a period of famine is now paralysed and cannot hold her urine. The inhabitants of the village consider that this state was brought about because she 'ate a part of herself'.[1] It happens even more frequently that during a famine children would be left behind to die of cold. On such occasions the Esquimaux show a harshness as well as a resoluteness which amazed the author who reported on this matter, for he was well aware of the love and tenderness usually felt by the Esquimaux for their children. It is under the pressure of a terrible emergency that the children are thus abandoned, just as we ourselves would sacrifice our most precious possessions when shipwrecked in order to save our own lives. An additional important detail which is quite familiar to the people of more primitive ways of thought than our own, and appears strange to us only because of our high regard for any individual, is the fact that children can be produced at will, just like any other chattels.

The eating of children, which for the Australian woman is a simple satisfaction of an instinctual need free from any burden of guilt and is for the Esquimaux woman a desperate action undertaken only in a desperate emergency which may have dire consequences but is something to be pitied rather than condemned, appears in Hungarian folklore as the punishment in hell for those women who bring about a miscarriage.[2]

The institution of abortion is a paramount factor in the relation between mother and child. Women all over the world know of artificial abortion, so that it is women who have the final say about the existence or non-existence of a child. (This fact is undoubtedly one of the reasons why the mother appears sometimes so weird and gruesome to the child whose life

[1] Rasmussen: *Thulefahrt* (1926), p. 358.
[2] *A magyarság néprajza* (Folklore of the Magyars), **4**, 156.

depends in the truest sense of the word on whether it pleases her or not.) The undeniable fact of psychogenic sterility points to another fact, namely that *the child who is born is always the child who was wanted by the mother*. Moralising condemnation or penal prosecution of artificial abortion are probably only defensive measures against the dangerous, absolute power of the woman. It is another defensive measure that the right over the child's life which originally was maternal was transferred to the *paterfamilias*. It argues for the primordiality of the maternal right that it is an informal and private affair of the woman. The paternal right, however, is a social institution.

In spite of these limitations on the archaic maternal rights which have been imposed by civilisation, it probably remains true of most children born that they are born as the realisation of the instinctual wishes of their mothers. Pregnancy, giving birth, suckling and fondling are instinctual urges to a woman, and these she satisfies with the help of her baby.[1] Physical proximity lasting as long as possible is pleasurable to both mother and child. In fact, I believe—turning again to anthropology—that those rules which separate man and wife after the birth of a child, often for many months, have their origin in the desire of the woman to enjoy without disturbance the new relationship with her infant. The unlimited confidence of the child in the love of his mother grows from this mutuality, and later it will be badly shaken by the foreboding or by the actual experience of the mother's being able to dissolve this link at will, and by her power to substitute one child by another.

Maternal love is intended—according to its instinctual sources—only for the very young child, the infant depending upon the mother's body. That is why we so often see mothers who—influenced by their cultural patterns—continue to nurse and fondle their children far beyond infancy even until they are quite grown up and still think of them as their 'little ones', however big and tall they may be, a sentiment often openly expressed both in words and behaviour. For the mother the

[1] See Ferenczi's notion of 'parental eroticism' in *Thalassa*, New York (1938) (German original: *Versuch einer Genitaltheorie*. Int. *Psa.* Verlag (Vienna, 1924.)

child is never grown up, for when grown up he is no longer her child. Is not this yet another proof of the remoteness of maternal love from reality, just as the child's love is remote because he never imagines his mother as a being with divergent, that is to say, self-interests? *Maternal love is the almost perfect counterpart to the love for the mother.*

Thus, just as the mother is to the child, so is the child to the mother—an object of gratification. And just as the child does not recognise the separate identity of the mother, so the mother looks upon her child as a part of herself whose interests are identical with her own. *The relation between mother and child* is built upon *the interdependence of the reciprocal instinctual aims.* What Ferenczi said about the relation of man and woman in coitus holds true for this mother-infant relation. He meant that in coitus there can be no question of egoism or altruism, there is only mutuality, i.e. what is good for one is right for the other also. *In consequence of the natural interdependence of the reciprocal instinctual aims there is no need to be concerned about the partner's well-being.*

This behaviour I call *instinctive maternity* in contradistinction to *civilised maternity.*[1] This can be studied best in animals, or with quite primitive people. In it naïve egoism plays the same rôle as in the child's love for the mother. But, if we consider both partners (mother and child) simultaneously, we can speak with Ferenczi of mutuality. The mutuality is the biological, the naïve egoism the psychological aspect. *The biological interdependence makes the naïve egoism psychologically possible.* Every disturbance of this interdependence calls forth a development beyond the naïve egoism.

If in man, as is the case with animals, the mother-child unity were replaced without any gap by mature sexuality, i.e. by the man-woman unity, naïve egoism could perhaps suffice for the whole of life as a method of loving. The interval, characteristic for man, between the infantile and the adult period, i.e. the two phases of life in which a mutual interdependence of two beings is naturally given—leads to a discord which must be resolved. This discord, increasing parallel with the develop-

---

[1] For 'civilised maternity' see Alice Balint: 'Die Grundlagen unseres Erziehungssystems', *Z. f. psa. Päd.* (1937), **11**, 98–101.

ment of civilisation, is resolved to a great extent by the *progressive strengthening of the power of the reality sense over the emotional life.*

Tact, insight, consideration, sympathy, gratitude, tenderness (in the sense of inhibited sensuality) are signs and consequences of the extending strength of the reality sense in the sphere of emotions. The real capacity for loving in the social sense is a secondary formation created by an external disturbance. It has nothing to do directly with genitality. The genital act is really the situation in which the reciprocal interdependence as experienced in early childhood is re-created. Everything learnt in the meantime may play an important rôle in wooing, but must be forgotten during the act. Too much reality sense (tact), a too precise delimitation of one partner from the other, is disturbing, causes coldness, may even lead to impotence, for example the anxiety of some neurotics—originating from training in cleanliness—that they might disturb or even disgust their partner by their body odour or by some involuntary sound or movement.

The first disturbance of the naïve egoism is caused by the mother's turning away from her growing child. This turning away may be expressed either directly as true estrangement or indirectly in the mother trying to delay in some way the development of the child. I think there is no need to give examples here. For the child it would be quite natural if the mother were to remain his (or her) sexual partner even after the period of infancy. Her reluctance can only be attributed by the child to the disturbing influence of some external power. In fact this is true with animals where the infantile period is followed immediately by sexual maturity. It is the strength of the father animal which is the only obstacle to the sexual union of mother and child. With man it is different: the sexual significance of the child for the mother ceases to exist much earlier than the time of the child's attaining sexual maturity, i.e. the time when he could be a sexual partner in adult form to the mother. The instinctual attachment to the mother is replaced by instinctual rejection by the mother. From this it becomes clear what is the essential difference—in spite of many corresponding traits—between maternal love and love for the mother. The mother is unique and irreplaceable, the child can be replaced by another. We experience the repetition of this conflict in every transference neurosis. Each patient is more or less concerned at some time or another with the relative irreplaceability of the analyst as compared to the real or assumed ease with which the analyst can fill the time vacated by any of his patients. The detachment from the mother, in the sense of the dissolution of the primitive attachment based on mutuality, means the reconciliation with the fact that the mother is a separate being with her own interests. Hatred of the mother is no solution, because it means the preservation of the attachment but with the negative sign. One hates the mother because she is no longer what she used to be. (In analytical practice we have long known that hatred of the analyst after the end of an analysis is a sign of undissolved transference.)

To sum up: the child who has outgrown his infancy is no longer so agreeable to the mother (thinking still in terms of instinctual maternity), nevertheless he clings to her and does not know any other form of love but that of his naïve egoism. This naïve egoism, however, becomes untenable, because now there is no mutuality, which was its basis. Thus the child is faced with the task of adapting himself to the wishes of those whose love he needs.[1] It is at this point that the rule of the reality sense starts in the emotional life of man.[2]

3

In this connection I would like to discuss briefly the problem of auto-erotism. We know that auto-erotism is archaic. Its most important quality from the point of view of adaptation to reality is its far-reaching independence of the external world. The auto-erotic activity need not be learned by the child, and for its practice there is no need for help from the environment;

[1] Protracted infantilism may itself be adaptation of a sort.

[2] I wish to point out that this rule of the reality sense over the emotional life is not identical with Ferenczi's notion of the erotic reality sense. The concept of the erotic sense of reality relates exclusively to the erotic functions whose development is thought of as a quest for the most perfect way of discharging erotic tensions.

it may, however, be disturbed or even inhibited by the external world. Moreover, it is not independent of internal processes. As is well known, several auto-erotisms may supplant each other when one or the other method of discharge has become impossible. But the dissolution of the instinctual interdependence of mother and child also influences the auto-erotic function. One could even say that it is here that the psychological rôle of auto-erotism really begins. In the next period, rich in relative love-frustrations, auto-erotism assumes the significance of a substitute gratification. In this way it becomes the biological foundation of secondary narcissism, the psychological pre-condition of which is the identification with the faithless object. The earlier the infantile harmony disappears, the earlier auto-erotism assumes this role in the mental life of man. Contrary to the opinion of the majority of analysts, I do not think that this is a regression to the auto-erotic phase; moreover I think that auto-erotism and archaic attachment to the mother exist simultaneously, maintaining a balance, but that from the beginning they are two different factors, their difference becoming apparent only after the original harmony has been disturbed. In my opinion there is no phase of life that is dominated solely by auto-erotism. When man fails to obtain sufficient gratification from the world of objects, auto-erotism offers itself as a means of obtaining comfort. If the frustration is not too great, all this happens without much ado. The overburdening of the auto-erotic function, however, soon leads to pathological phenomena; the auto-erotic activity degenerates into addiction. But, inversely, we may observe that an all too successful pedagogical suppression of auto-erotism is followed by an overburdening of object-relations which usually appears as an abnormal dependence on and pathological clinging to the mother (or her representatives). On the other hand, a not too exaggerated inhibition of auto-erotism reinforces the object-attachments to the extent desirable for the educability of the child. Apparently there is for each age an optimal proportion between auto-erotism and object-attachment. This equilibrium is elastic, i.e. frustration may be equalised by gratification, but this cannot go beyond certain limits. This circumstance secures the development of the reality sense in the emotional life. Man cannot renounce object-love without suffering severe impairment.[1]

4

The different kinds of loving have been classified by psychoanalysis according to several principles: first as to their relation to aim-inhibition, secondly as to whether they belong to a component instinct or to genitality. Using the one principle the concepts of oral, anal and genital love were developed, using the other those of tender and of sensual love. A third principle of classification results from contrasting narcissistic with object-libido, leading to narcissistic and object-libidinal forms of love, which in some way are connected with the difference between egoism and altruism. And finally Ferenczi's differentiation must be mentioned, that of active and passive love, which he uses as often as not in place of the customary terms—narcissistic and object-libidinal love—but without exactly stating whether passive object-love is identical with narcissistic love or not. The principle I use in differentiating the several forms of love is their relation to the sense of reality. Object-love proper has two mainstays, (a) gratification of needs by their objects, (b) reality sense.

(a) exists from the beginning, especially if we accept the teachings of Ferenczi's Theory of Genitality according to which the whole of sexuality including the auto-erotic function, is founded on an object-orientated tendency.

(b) this is developed only gradually. On the basis of observations of a form of love, the most characteristic trait of which is the scanty development of the reality sense (the object is recognised but not its self-interests), I assume that along with a gradual development of the reality sense there is a gradual development of object-love. The parallel between these two developments is not quite complete. The extension of the rule of the reality sense over the object-relations is limited by two powerful factors: as is well known, one of these factors is the far-reaching independence from the external world which is

---

[1] cf. the observations by the analyst and pediatrician, E. Petö: 'Säugling und Mutter', *Z. f. psa. Päd.* (1937), **11**, 244. In English: *Int. J. of PsA.* (1949), **30**, 260.

made possible in the libidinal sphere by the auto-erotic (according to Ferenczi autoplastic) method of gratification. The second factor is the interdependence between mother and child (and later between man and woman in coitus). The instinctual interdependence of two beings creates a situation in which the recognition of the object's own interests is unnecessary. This is the basis of naïve egoism in the sphere of object-libido.

I arrive at the concept of primary *archaic object-relation without reality sense* through extrapolation. It is the last link in a series which is constructed from the various grades of adaptations to reality in the field of object-relationship. Accordingly there exists an archaic form of love of which the essential determinant is the lack of reality sense towards the love-object and not the prevalence of any component instinct. (To avoid a possible misunderstanding I wish to emphasise that one must differentiate strictly between forms of gratification, e.g. oral, anal, etc., and forms of love, e.g. naïvely egoistic, altruistic,[1] etc.). The development of the socially higher forms of love derives as a consequence of adaptation to reality. This classification is closely related to Freud's distinction between sensual and aim-inhibited love, for aim-inhibition is indeed the most important of the factors, originating in the influence of the external world, which bring about the development of emotional life; pure sensuality, on the other hand, knows solely 'the erotic reality sense' and can exist, in relation to the partner, fairly comfortably coupled with naïve egoism.

The point at which my train of thought deviates somewhat from that of Freud is the significance I attribute to the rôle of the libidinal object-relation in this connection. Freud, too, traces back the growth of object-love to the irreplaceability of the external world, but the basis of this irreplaceability according to him lies not in the erotic but in the self-preserving instincts. In dependence on the gratifications of the self-preserving instincts the first object-relations develop which,

---

[1] cf. M. Balint: 'Zur Kritik der Lehre von den prägenitalen Libidoorganisationen', *Int. Z. f. Psa.* (1935), **21**, 525–43. English version ('Critical Notes on the Theory of the Pregenital Organisations of the Libido') reprinted in this vol., p. 49.

however, are soon replaced by the auto-erotic investment of the libido. It is only by this *détour* via auto-erotism that the libido finds its way back—in the course of further development—to the world of objects. Freud assumes that 'certain of the component impulses of the sexual instinct have an object from the very beginning and hold fast to it; such are the impulse to mastery (sadism), to gazing and curiosity'.[1, 2] After the completion of the theory of the libido by the theory of narcissism it then appeared 'that auto-erotism was the sexual activity of the narcissistic phase of directions of the libido',[3] whereby this narcissistic phase is assumed, as is well known, to be the primary phase.

I have tried, from observable phenomena, to represent this early phase as an archaic object-relation lacking any sense of reality, but from which what we are wont to call love develops directly under the influence of reality.

My assumption can easily be described in terms of ego and id. The archaic love without reality sense is the form of the love of the id, which persists as such throughout life, while the social reality-based form of love represents the manner of loving of the ego.[4]

[1] Freud: *Introductory Lectures*, Fifth ed. (1936), p. 276. London: Allen & Unwin.

[2] Since the recent researches of I. Hermann the number of the components of the sexual instincts directed towards an external object from the beginning must be increased by the instinct to cling.

[3] Freud: op. cit., p. 347.

[4] Papers of recent years which follow a similar theme:

Balint, M.: 'Zur Kritik der Lehre von den prägenitalen Libidoorganisationen', *Int. Z. f. Psa.* (1935), **21**. English version ('Critical Notes on the Theory of the Pregenital Organisations of the Libido') reprinted in this vol., p. 49.

Balint, M.: 'Frühe Entwicklungsstadien des Ichs. Primäre Objektliebe', *Imago* (1937), **23**. (Early developmental States of the Ego. English version ('Early Developmental States of the Ego. Primary Object-love') reprinted in this vol., p. 90.

Hermann, I.: 'Sich-Anklammern—Auf-Suche-Gehen', *Int. Z. f. Psa.* (1936), **22**. (To cling—to go.)

Hoffmann, E. P.: 'Prokjektion und Ich-Entwicklung', *Int. Z. f. Psa.* (1935), **21**. (Projection and Ego development.)

Rotter-Kertész, L.: 'Der tiefenpesychologische Hintergrund der inzestuösen Fixierung', *Int. Z. f. Psa.* (1936), **22**. (The depth-psychological background of the incestuous fixation.)

Dual-unity and Primary (Archaic) Object-relation

In several contributions to the discussion of this paper it was suggested that I abandon the term primary object-relation in favour of the term 'dual unity'. I am of the opinion, however, that it is more helpful to use terms in such a way that emphasis is given to quite small deviations in theory, and thus to increase the general understanding. I. Hermann, E. P. Hoffman and L. Rotter-Kertész emphatically stress the fact that they do not want to think of dual unity as a form of object-relationship at all, whereas I, on the contrary, actually think of a possible, very primitive object-relation which already exists before one can assume an ability to distinguish between ego and object, i.e. already in the id, so to speak. The starting-point of these ideas is Ferenczi's well-known concept of *'passive object-love'*. In my paper on this subject—printed in the Ferenczi Memorial Volume—I used only this term. Later, under the influence of M. Balint's ideas on the 'new beginning' in which he emphasises the active features in early infantile behaviour, as well as partly under that of I. Hermann's work on the instinct to cling, I thought that the term *passive* was not a suitable description of a relation in which such markedly *active* tendencies as the instinct to cling play a paramount rôle. Since then I have used—as in the present paper—in place of *'passive object-love'* mainly the terms *'archaic'* or *'primary object-relation'* (*object-love*).

This latter term I could only change to 'dual unity' if those using it changed their views and accepted dual unity as a primitive kind of object-relation, or else if I, for my part, could relinquish the idea that object-relations are as old as their biological basis.

VII

ON GENITAL LOVE [1]
(1947)

IF one looks through psycho-analytical literature for references to genital love, to one's surprise two striking facts emerge: (a) much less has been written on genital love than on pre-genital love (e.g. 'genital love' is missing from the indices of Fenichel's new text-book [2] and of Nunberg's *Allgemeine Neurosenlehre* [3]); (b) almost everything that has been written on genital love is negative, like Abraham's description of his famous term 'postambivalent phase'. We know fairly well what an ambivalent love relation is—of postambivalent love we know hardly more than that it is, or at least ought to be, no longer ambivalent.

This emphasis on the negative qualities, i.e. on those which have, or ought to have been, superseded in the course of development, blurs the whole picture. It is not the presence of certain positive qualities that is accentuated, only the absence of certain others.

To avoid this pitfall let us imagine an ideal case of such postambivalent genital love that shows no traces of ambivalency nor of pregenital object-relationship:

(a) There should be no greediness, no insatiability, no wish to devour the object, to deny it any independent existence, etc., i.e. there should be no *oral* features;

(b) There should be no wish to hurt, to humiliate, to boss, to dominate the object, etc., i.e. no *sadistic* features;

(c) There should be no wish to defile the partner, to despise him (her) for his (her) sexual desires and pleasures; there should be no danger of being disgusted by the partner or being

[1] Paper read at the Conference of European Analysts in Amsterdam on May 26th, 1947. First published in *Int. J. of PsA.* (1948), **29**, 34–40.
[2] Fenichel, O.: *The Psycho-Analytic Theory of Neurosis*, New York, Norton, 1945.
[3] Nunberg, H.: *Allgemeine Neurosenlehre.*, Berne, H. Huber, 1932.

attracted only by some of his (her) unpleasant features, etc., i.e. there should be no remnants of *anal* traits;

(*d*) There should be no compulsion to boast about the possession of a penis, no fear of the partner's sexual organs, no fear for one's own sexual organs, no envy of the male or female genitalia, no feeling of being incomplete or of having a faulty sexual organ, or of the partner having a faulty one, etc., i.e. there should be no trace of the *phallic phase* or of the castration complex.

We know that such ideal cases do not exist in practice, but we have to get all this negative stuff out of our way before we can start with the proper examination.

What then is 'genital love' apart from the absence of all the enumerated 'pregenital' traits? Well, we love our partner

(1) because he or she can satisfy us;

(2) because we can satisfy him or her;

(3) because we can experience a full orgasm together, nearly or quite simultaneously.

This seems very plain sailing, but unfortunately it is not so. Let us take the first condition, that our partner can satisfy us. This condition may be, and very likely is, rather egotistical, or even completely narcissistic. It entails hardly any regard for the partner's happiness. Such types are well known, among men or women alike. Their only aim is their own satisfaction, which is truly *genital* and which obviously may or may not be coupled with love.

The same is true about the second condition, i.e. that we can satisfy our partner. This is certainly too altruistic, though not necessarily masochistic. Here only the object counts, and for this kind of love a more or less complete disregard for one's own needs, interests and happiness is characteristic. Again there are many examples of this type both among men and women. And again, although the satisfaction is truly genital, it may or may not be combined with love.

One could argue that these two types are not real love relations, but this argument is faulty. Relations based on these two types of genital satisfaction may be truly harmonious for very long periods—even for life—especially if the types of love of the two partners are supplementary to each other.

These two types seem to have led us into a blind alley. The investigation of the third type may be more promising. If two partners love each other because they can find happiness together in one mutual experience, this must truly be real love. But is that really so? There are many examples—in history, in the *chronique scandaleuse*, and in psycho-analytical practice—where two partners have perfect sexual experience, find real happiness in each other's arms, where they feel an absolute security that whenever they meet they can give each other happiness and still—even though they are called lovers—they do not love each other. Often quite the contrary is true, as in Shakespeare's famous 129th sonnet:

> '*All this the world well knows; yet none knows well*
> *To shun this heaven that leads men to this hell.*'

This attitude—irresistible desire for the partner before the act, inability to bear him after—is sometimes mutual, more frequently onesided. Often the partner is not quite unbearable after the orgasm, only indifferent. And there are many intermediate forms too.

We expected that this form of genital relation would give us some idea what true genital love is; the result was, however, disappointing. Genital satisfaction is apparently only a necessary and not a sufficient condition of genital love. What we have learned is that genital love is much more than gratitude for, or contentment about, the partner being available for genital satisfaction. Further, that it does not make any difference whether this gratitude or contentment is one-sided or mutual.

What is this 'more'? We find in addition to genital satisfaction in a true love relation:

(1) Idealisation;
(2) Tenderness;
(3) A special form of identification.

As Freud [1] dealt with the problem of idealisation, both of the object and of the instinct, I need only to repeat his findings. He showed convincingly first that idealisation is not absolutely necessary, that without any idealisation a good love relation is

[1] Freud, S.: 'The Most Prevalent Form of Degradation in Erotic Life'. *Collected Papers*, IV. London, Hogarth Press, 1925.

possible, and second that in many cases idealisation is not a help but a hindrance to the development of a satisfactory form of love. We may accordingly discard this condition too as not absolutely necessary.

It is different with the second phenomenon: tenderness (*Zärtlichkeit*). Since Freud first mentioned it, the whole of psycho-analytical literature has used this term in two different senses. According to the first [1] tenderness is the result of aim-inhibition. In fact tenderness is the most often quoted example of aim-inhibition: the original urge was directed towards a certain aim, but—for one reason or another—had to content itself with only partial satisfaction, i.e. with much less than the intended aim. According to this view tenderness is a secondary phenomenon, a faint representative only of the original aim; and because of this quality of *faute de mieux* it never leads to full satisfaction, i.e. it is always and inherently connected with some frustration.

According to the second view,[2] tenderness is an archaic quality which appears in conjunction with the ancient self-preserving instincts, and has no further aim but this quiet, not passionate gratification. Consequently passionate love must be a secondary phenomenon, superimposed on the archaic tender love.

This second idea can be supported by some suggestive data from anthropology. In general, different forms of civilisation may be grouped in two types. In the first type we find passionate love, idealisation of the object or the instinct, strict social enforcement of the latency, courting, abundant love-songs and love poetry, sexual hypocrisy, appreciation of tenderness, and usually a well-developed complicated *ars amandi*. In the second type the society does not seem to care much about enforcing a latency, in fact, there is hardly any social demand for sexual abstention at any age; there is hardly any courting, hardly any love-songs, and very poor love poetry, very little idealisation, not much tenderness; but there is simple, straightforward, uncomplicated genital sexuality. Perhaps both passion and

[1] Freud, S.: *Three Contributions to the Theory of Sexuality*. New York, 1910.
[2] Freud, S.: 'The Most Prevalent Form of Degradation in Erotic Life.' *Collected Papers*, IV. London, Hogarth Press, 1925.

excessive tenderness are 'artificial', products of civilisation, the result of systematic training by frustration during education. The apparent contradiction in Freud's two uses of the term 'tenderness' could thus be reconciled: tenderness is not a secondary aim-inhibition but an inhibited development.

Etymology, too, seems to support this idea. The German *zart*, the root of *Zärtlichkeit*, means not strong, delicate, young. The same is true of the French word *tendre*. Alix Strachey [1] translates *Zärtlichkeit* with 'affection', 'fondness', 'tenderness'. Of these 'affection' has a double meaning; apart from tenderness it means disease or weakness, as when we speak of an affected heart or affections of the kidney. 'Fond' has even a treble meaning. It is the past participle of the Middle English verb 'fonnen' which means to dote, to befool, of which the present-day words 'fun' and 'funny' are derivatives. The three meanings of 'fond' are (1) vain, inept (thus King Lear is described as 'a very foolish fond old man'); (2) credulous, as 'fond hope'; and (3) affectionate. 'Tender' means soft, not tough, as in 'tender meat'; easily touched, as in 'tender heart'; susceptible to pain, as in 'tender spot'; delicate, fragile, as in 'tender colour'; immature, young, as in 'tender buds', and only lastly, kind and loving.

Something is surely wrong here. How has genital love, the mature form of love, got mixed up with this doubtful company of disease, weakness, immaturity, etc.? And still more surprising: the pregenital forms of love—according to psycho-analytical literature—are not necessarily connected with tenderness, whereas genital love is genuine only if it has undergone a considerable fusion with tenderness.

Undoubtedly one task of all education, and certainly of education in our form of civilisation, is to teach the individual to love, i.e. to compel him to bring about this kind of fusion. What we call genital love has really very little to do with genitality; in fact it uses genital sexuality only as a stock on which to graft something essentially different. In short, we are expected to give, and ourselves expect to receive, kindness, regard, consideration, etc., even at times when there is no genital wish, no

[1] Strachey, A.: *A New German-English Psycho-analytical Vocabulary.* London, Baillière, Tindall and Cox, 1943.

genital satisfaction to be felt. This is contrary to the habits of most animals, which show interest for the other sex only during heat. Man, however, is supposed to show unfailing interest in, and regard for, his partner for ever.

A parallel phenomenon to this everlasting demand for regard is man's prolonged childhood. When animals reach sexual maturity they usually show no further filial or emotional attachment to their parents, only respect for strength and power. We, however, demand eternal gratitude and, in fact, man remains a child for as long as his parents live, if not to the end of his days. He is expected to, and usually does, pay love, regard, respect, fear, gratitude to his parents for ever. Something similar is demanded in love: a prolonged perpetual emotional tie, not only as long as the genital wish for satisfaction lasts but far beyond it, as long as the partner lives, or even after his death.

According to this view, what we call 'genital love' is an artefact of civilisation, like art or religion. It is enforced upon us, irrespective of our biological nature and needs, by the condition that mankind must live in socially organised groups. Genital love is even doubly artificial. Firstly, constant interference with free sexual gratification (both genital and pregenital) builds up external and later internal resistances against pleasure, and thereby causes passions to develop in order that man should be able to break down these resistances in odd moments. Secondly, the demand for prolonged, perpetual, regard and gratitude forces us to regress to, or even never to egress from, the archaic infantile form of tender love. Man can therefore be regarded as an animal which is retarded even in his 'mature' age at an infantile form of love.

It is interesting that anatomists discovered similar facts long before we did. The discovery was that anatomically man resembles the ape embryo rather than the adult ape. The verdict of the anatomists is that man is biologically retarded, structurally a foetus, is in fact *foetalised*, but in spite of that has attained full genital function.[1, 2] There are several more such

[1] Bolk, L.: *Das Problem der Menschwerdung*, 1926.
[2] Keith, Sir A.: 'The Evolution of the Human Races,' *J. Roy. Anthr. Soc.* (1928), **58**, 312.

instances in the animal kingdom, where an embryo acquires truly developed bisexual genital functions; these are called *neotenic* embryos. Genital love is an exact parallel to these forms. We find full genital function coupled with infantile behaviour, i.e. man is not only anatomically but also mentally a neotenic embryo.

This train of thought can explain a few of the peculiarities of genitality in man. It is well known how unstable genital love is, especially as compared with the eternal 'pregenital' forms. Being a phylogenetically 'new' function, it is not yet firmly established; man has not yet had enough time, so to speak, to adapt himself to this form of love, in fact he has to be trained anew in every generation. Obviously no such training is needed in *oral love* for example. Conversely, there is no danger of a breakdown of oral love, whereas genital love is much more precarious.

Another peculiarity is the contradictory attitude of society to genital love. On the one hand, society admires and worships the unscrupulous he-man or the glamour girl, though with suspicious awe; on the other hand, it pays due respect to a lasting genital love, notices and celebrates golden and diamond weddings, but often derides such faithful relations and calls them cautious, sentimental and sloppy.

The third phenomenon connected with genital love is a special form of identification which is totally different from the better studied oral identification, and should perhaps be called *genital identification*. Oral identification is based mainly on introjection: the ego assumes certain qualities of the object, without showing any consideration for it. A good example of this kind of identification is the rite of the holy communion, which the believer performs (with the help of a priest) for his own benefit. *He* wants to be similar to his God, and it is no problem for him if God wishes to be incorporated, to be assimilated; all that is taken for granted. The whole situation is different in genital identification, i.e. in a relation based not only on genital satisfaction but also on 'genital love'. Here interests, wishes, feelings, sensitivity, shortcomings of the partner attain—or are supposed to attain—about the same importance as our own. In a harmonious relation all these conflicting tendencies have to be balanced very carefully, which is anything but an easy task. In order to win a loving and lovable genital object and to keep it for good, nothing can be taken for granted as happens in oral love; a permanent, never-relaxing, exacting reality testing must be kept up all the time. This might be called *the work of conquest* (conversely for the subject this means an exacting piece of *adaptation to his object*). It is most exacting in the initial stages of a relation, but in a milder form must be maintained unwaveringly throughout the whole duration. In other words, the two partners must always be in harmony.

Again, animals are entirely different. If they are on heat both desire the sexual act and hardly any work of conquest is necessary; compared with man there is hardly any preliminary love-making. If they are not on heat, the most expert love-making is of no avail. Lasting harmony between the partners is not usually demanded. Man, on the other hand, is potentially always on heat, can always be interested; but potentially is always capable of rejecting any would-be partner. The condition of lasting harmony is of paramount importance.

It was Freud [1] who described the importance of fore-pleasure, i.e. of pregenital satisfaction, in the work of conquest. This could also be described [2] as a short recapitulation of one's own sexual development before every sexual act. This development, of course, is more or less individual, i.e. different for any two given partners. Harmonious love can only be established where these individual differences are not too great, where mutual identification between the two partners is possible without causing undue strain.

Thus harmonious genital love requires a constant testing of reality in order that the two partners may be able to discover, and to satisfy, as much as possible of each other's needs and wishes in the fore-pleasure. Further, we are not only expected to give our partner as much as we can bear, but even to enjoy giving it, while not suffering too much under the necessarily not quite complete satisfaction of our own wishes. All this

[1] Freud, S.: *Three Contributions to the Theory of Sexuality*, loc. cit.
[2] Balint, M.: 'Eros and Aphrodite', *Int. J. of PsA.* (1938), **19**, 199. Reprinted in this vol., p. 73.

must go on all the time both before and after genital gratification for as long as the love relation itself lasts. This work of conquest (and of adaptation) is therefore a mutual attempt by the two partners at satisfying each other's individual wishes and needs which were rendered individually different, i.e. distorted from the original primitive ones by the process of education. This work causes considerable strain on the mental apparatus, and only a healthy ego is able to bear it. Still, it cannot be relaxed, till just before the orgasm. Then, however, the happy confidence emerges that everything in the world is now all right, all individual needs are satisfied, all individual differences sunk, only one—identical—wish has remained in which the whole universe submerges, and both subject and partner become one in the 'mystical union'.

But one should never forget that this supreme happiness is to a very large extent an illusion, based on a regression to an infantile stage of reality testing. This primitive reality testing permits the individual to believe—for a short time—that all his needs have been satisfied, that the whole world, in particular everything good in the world, is the happy *Me*. This is the most primitive stage of object-relationship, called by Ferenczi [1] the passive object-love. Healthy people are elastic enough to experience this far-going regression without fear, and with complete confidence that they will be able to emerge from it again.

I wish to leave out all the interesting pathological consequences of this theory except one. The most important anxiety connected with this situation is that of losing the mature attitude, and once having lost it, of not being able to regain it. In these cases, maturity is mainly a defence against the wish of infantilism, which means conversely that these people had a very hard task to become mature, achieved maturity only with considerable difficulty, and therefore do not dare to let themselves go. For such people every pregenital pleasure is childish, disgusting, even despicable; they cannot give up their 'mature dignity', they do not dare to lose their heads in or before an orgasm.

[1] Ferenczi: *Thalassa. A Theory of Genitality*, Psycho-Anal. Quarterly Inc., New York, 1938.

As is well known, there are three common dangers for a weak ego: (a) psychosis, either transitory as in an acute anxiety state, or chronic as in paranoia or schizophrenic hallucinations; (b) intoxication, either acute as in drunkenness or chronic as in addiction; (c) falling in love. All the poets since the beginning of time have known that these three are closely related, and have often spoken of love as mad or intoxicating. The psychological basis of the similarity is the danger of a breakdown of the ego structure. It must be a strong ego that can face this danger with equanimity, proud in the confidence that it will be able to emerge from any danger unscathed or even thrilled and refreshed.

To sum up: 'genital love' in man is really a misnomer. We can find genital love in the true sense only in animals which develop in a straight, undistorted line from infantile ways of behaviour to mature genital sexuality—and then die. Man, that neotenic embryo, never reaches full maturity; he remains an embryo in his anatomical structure, in his emotional behaviour towards his elders and betters—and in his love life. What we call 'genital love' is a fusion of disagreeing elements: of genital satisfaction and pregenital tenderness. The expression of this fusion is 'genital identification', and the reward for bearing the strain of this fusion is the possibility of regressing periodically for some happy moments to a really infantile stage of *no* reality testing, to the short-lived re-establishment of the complete union of micro- and macrocosmos.

APPENDIX

1. *Homosexual Origins*

If we accept Freud's theory [1] about the beginnings of mankind, a very probable assumption emerges, according to which 'genital love'—this queer mixture of genital satisfaction and pregenital tenderness—first developed in a homosexual form. This is another startling paradox, 'genital love' the true form and quintessence of adult sexuality is in its original form homosexual, i.e. perverse, not fully mature. It is obvious, however,

[1] Freud, S.: *Totem and Tabu*. New York, Moffat Yard, 1918.

that in the 'primal horde', between the primal father and his women, there existed no genital love, only genital satisfaction. The same was true of the occasional furtive sexual acts between the sons and the women. The only relation in which 'genital love' could have developed was the sacred, friendly bond uniting the sons in homosexual love against their tyrant-father. As long as this homosexual love remained weak—to break down (after the killing of the father-tyrant) under the impact of the possibility of open heterosexual satisfaction—each of the sons grabbed as many women as his power, cunning and strength were able to secure for him, and founded a new father horde. When, however, true love developed linking the sons in perpetuity, regard for, and gratitude to, each other prevailed and the 'brother horde' was established. The main features of this new organisation were (a) respect for, and regard to, the fair rights, wishes, interests of every male member; (b) a periodical, complicated, sacred ceremony with strong, hardly aim-inhibited, genital-homosexual features again and again re-uniting all adult males; and (c) rather simple, straightforward heterosexual genitality, without much sentimental, romantic fuss.

Pending the final verdict of the anthropologists whether this idea is compatible with the available facts or otherwise, it will be permissible to use it as a working hypothesis and to follow up the spreading of 'genital love' from its original homosexual sphere into heterosexual genitality and into social life.

2. *Heterosexual Relations*

In every form of civilisation the trend is unmistakably towards curbing and limiting coarse, straightforward genital gratification and developing more and more complicated 'refined' forms of love. Conversely this means an ever-increasing intrusion of pregenital and therefore infantile, 'perverse' stimulations and gratifications into adult genitality, changing it into 'love making' in the sense of the various *artes amandi*.

As pointed out previously, the attitude of any human love-object is as a rule ambivalent: willing and reluctant at the same time. To change it into a 'genital partner' is a strenuous task, which I called 'work of conquest'. This begins with the acceptance of the fact that our object is a singular individual, because he too was subjected to a tortuous form of education, forcing upon him various likes and dislikes, different from ours. And further that our object will agree to the rôle of a genital partner only if in a fair compromise due regard will be given to a large number of his (her) individual peculiarities.

Thus, lasting genital relations are always based on a mixture of harmony and strain; an uncertain enough foundation, especially if we realise that individual developments continue throughout life. The often hypocritical demand for absolute monogamy is based on the assumption that once harmonious genital relations have been established between two partners, their individual developments will run parallel for ever. Unfortunately, as common experience shows, this assumption is correct in exceptional cases only.

A fairly frequent solution of the strain caused by diverging individual developments is the gradual change of the originally passionate, genital love-relation, into a less passionate, tender, more or less aim-inhibited, true and warm heterosexual friendship. Many a naughty comedy, and many a serious psychological novel, describes this kind of solution, showing this or that facet of its many complicated possibilities. What interests us, however, is the ontogenetic emergence of the phylogenetically original form of friendly love, out of the burnt-out passions of genital sexuality.

3. Social Implications.

Genital sexuality is highly exclusive, indeed it can be called egotistic and asocial. Nothing and nobody exists apart from the two partners, any outside event or stimulus is disturbing, even painful.

Pregenital sexuality has a much wider field ranging from lonely narcissism to wholesale group gratifications; *vide* the pleasures of the white table, smoking, football and boxing matches, royal pageants, theatres, etc. All these can be enjoyed by a single person as well as by a large group, organised or unorganised. The only condition of such a group enjoyment is that due regard must be paid by everyone to the interests and peculiarities of the average member, that each of the members should be content with a more or less 'average' share. This 'average' share may be more or may be less than would correspond to the wishes and individuality of any particular member, but he is still expected to enjoy his share.

This was certainly not true in the father horde. The first relation where the 'average share' idea developed was the homosexual love cementing the brother horde together. Since then, every social development can be regarded as a voluntary or enforced acceptance of the demand for an increased regard for the interests and wishes of the 'average' member. My present thesis is that the new demand is usually recognised first in the (homosexual) relation between men and men, and is only secondarily extended to women, thus repeating the early stages of man's social evolution.

One interesting phase of this process is the modern demand for equality in every respect for both sexes (franchise, legal rights, access to higher education and to the professions, equal pay and so forth). Such a demand goes certainly against the testimony of biology, which irrefutably proves that the two sexes are not equal. This, however, does not mean—as is generally assumed by the stronger sex and enforced throughout the social life—that man is superior to woman in every way. Psychologically, however, the demand for universal equality is the result of a consequent development. 'All males must be equal' was the homosexual phase of the brother horde described above; 'women must have equal rights to men' is the spreading of the homosexual love into the heterosexual sphere.

If this is true, civilisation means a gradual conquest of all relations between man and man by sublimated, aim-inhibited, homosexual love and only secondarily the transference of those new forms of love to the relation between man and woman. One has the impression—though it may be only an unjustified male slander against the gentle sex—that the relation between woman and woman is the sphere least civilised by this process of evolution.

VIII

ON LOVE AND HATE [1]
(1951)

IF one has to ask the reader to re-examine some old, very familiar concepts, it is advisable to quote as an illustration a quite simple example. So I wish to begin with one which is an almost commonplace event in psycho-analytic practice. A patient of mine, a woman in her middle forties, recently bought a house, the first settled home in her much-unsettled life. Of course, it was a great event; the house had to be altered, furnished and made just as she wanted it to be. I will not dwell on its obvious significance as a symbol of herself and, behind that, of her mother. Anyhow, it was a great thrill. Then she heard that a couple intended to visit her and to stay in the new house for about a fortnight. They were old, well-proved friends, and she was delighted that they were coming. They arrived, the house got ready just in time, and it was a great happiness. She could not repeat often enough how nice it was to have people one really loved as the first guests in a new house.

To our great surprise, within a few days, gradually, almost imperceptibly, feelings of irritation, tension and uneasiness arose in her. The irritation increased till it amounted to a fairly severe anxiety state which, however, could be kept under control, though only with some difficulty. Gradually she became impatient: for heaven's sake if only the people would leave! At this point some analysis became possible and we discovered behind the impatience and anxiety a bitter hatred against her 'friends'. As a result of this piece of analysis the anxiety subsided; the friends eventually departed, but the hatred against them remained practically unaltered.

Now, this pattern was already well known to both of us. Anybody approaching her in friendship is equipped willy-nilly with 'angel wings' which (subjectively) means a blissful

[1] Paper read at the Seventeenth International Psycho-analytical Congress, Amsterdam, 1951.

expectation that now she will *really* be loved, and she will be able to love *safely*. In this incident we discovered once again that it is impossible for anyone to live up to her expectations, that everybody must fall short of them because everybody has *also* his own life, needs, interests which are of necessity independent of, and so practically always different from, hers.

Her whole life has been an endless repetition of this same pattern. She has always been terribly in need of love and affection; several times it has happened that she has thrown herself away at the first signs of some slight attention. The person in question was then equipped with the 'angel wings', and for a short while she lived in blissful expectation. Then because of the other person not being identical with her, certain privations were automatically and unavoidably imposed upon her which she interpreted as heartlessness and cruel neglect; the result has always been a painful disappointment. This soon turned into hatred; the partner was discarded as bad, heartless, rotten, cruel, etc. Quite often, as in the incident reported here, the hate had to be repressed and severe anxiety appeared in its place.

Now let us consider what happened here. The sequence of events doubtless is: love—hate—anxiety. The change back from anxiety to hate can be fairly easily achieved with our psycho-analytic technique, whereas the next step, the change from hate to love, appears much more difficult. A number of problems arise here. The first question is, is the form of love described here love, or something quite different? Can one say that my patient 'loved' her friends before the fatal visit or not? At first this appears to be an unimportant, innocent and somewhat academic question, but as I hope to show, any answer to it involves us unavoidably in very serious theoretical commitments. My contention is that the patient *did love* her friends, but she did so in a queer, very primitive way. Other workers in psycho-analysis have other ideas about this primitive relationship. I propose to sum up these other ideas very briefly before discussing my own views.

Before doing this, however, I wish to stress a very important point. And that is that this kind of love is markedly different from what we call mature love. On the other hand, the hate and anxiety shown by my patient cannot be called either mature or infantile, or primitive. I am inclined to think that this difference is a fundamental one, i.e. there is both a mature and a primitive form of love, whereas anxiety (and to some extent hate) exist only in primitive forms.

The various attempts at explaining the nature of the difference between primitive and adult love are usually treated as rivals, and as mutually exclusive. I prefer to consider the several descriptions as complementing each other by throwing light on one aspect or another of this complicated structure or, in other words, as overdetermining factors.

One attempt stresses the *weakness of the ego* in the infantile form of love. Because of this weakness the individual is unable to bear any serious frustration and has to mobilise all sorts of defensive mechanisms against it, especially anxiety. But, if we accept this, should hate be considered also as a mechanism of defence? Closely associated with the idea of the weakness of the ego is the other, stressing the *undeveloped or faulty reality testing* which then allows the persistence of infantile hopes and expectations far beyond what is really possible.

A third attempt lays the emphasis on *strong innate sadistic tendencies* (according to one theory originating from the archaic death instinct), as the result of which either no safe fusion with libidinal tendencies develops, or, if one does develop, it is unstable and easily upset by any privation. Such people can only have ambivalent relations to their objects, their love being easily smothered by their destructive tendencies or their sadism. Another attempt also based on the idea of strong sadistic tendencies answers our question by stressing the importance of *splitting processes* both in the mind and (especially) in regard to objects. The love-objects of such people are easily split and/or changed from extremely good to extremely bad; these latter are then pictured as indifferent, heartless, hateful and cruel, or, in one word, persecutory, giving rise in the individual to feelings of hatred and anxiety in place of love.

Yet another attempt at explaining this difference between mature and primitive love is to relate the inability to maintain loving relations for any length of time to *strong narcissistic tendencies*, whether innate or acquired, i.e. scars of early frustrations. Closely linked to this idea is that which explains the inability to love by *depressive fears*, i.e. by an impaired ability to bear 'normal', inevitable depressions. Such an individual cannot accept as unavoidable even the slightest amount of frustration by reality, and must resort to hatred and anxiety, whereas a normal individual although aggrieved within reason, can bear it.

The last but one theory I wish to discuss uses the conception of strong oral tendencies, especially that of *oral greed*. Nowadays this theory is perhaps the most fashionable. Every desire or need, if difficult to satisfy, is thought to be a derivative of this oral greed; every desired object of such need represents milk; every person towards whom such desires are directed stands for the 'good' or 'bad' mother (or breast).

It has been said time and again that 'oral' describes only one of several aspects of such very primitive object-relation, although admittedly a very conspicuous one. Other aspects equally important are warmth, bodily contact, familiar smells and tastes, or in one word, proper care and nursing. We all know that physiologically most proper food given without adequate nursing and especially without adequate bodily contact usually brings bad results, whereas with less proper food but with understanding and devoted nursing children thrive and develop well. Thus, if 'oral' were not used literally but only metaphorically, on the basis of *pars pro toto* I could raise no objection to it.[1] Unfortunately this is not the case.

In the same way I have to object to the use of 'greed'. 'Greed' does not describe the true situation, it gives only a subjective impression of it in adultomorph language. To us adults a child (or my patient) appears greedy because (1) if frustrated or compelled to wait, very noisy, highly dramatic and vehement symptoms appear, and (2) if satisfied hardly anything can be observed by an outsider as the gratification brings only a state of quiet, tranquil well-being. Our theory then values what is noisy as highly important, what is silent as unimportant (it is even possible that silent signs remain unnoticed by the theory, moreover it is certain that they are hardly ever mentioned), and thus develops a distorted picture of a highly greedy infant.

[1] See postcript to this paper on p. 156.

In my view in this peculiar form of love, proper and timely satisfaction of *all* needs is crucially important, because of the infant's (or the patient's) almost *absolute dependence* on the object. Or changing our point of view, not the infant is greedy but the object and the gratification are all-important. Because of this overwhelming importance of object and gratification, hardly any allowance can be made in their respect. *The object is indeed only an object* and must be treated as such, i.e. no consideration or regard can be paid to its interests, sensitivities, or well-being; it must be, and in fact is, simply taken for granted.

We find a very instructive example of this kind of object-relation in the adult's attitude to the supply of air. I do not think anybody would consider breathing as an expression of oral greed, although if the need for air is gratified we can see hardly any signs of satisfaction; on the other hand, if it is not and suffocation threatens, very noisy, dramatic and vehement symptoms develop. Moreover, the supply of air is taken for granted by all of us and we do not stop to consider whether the air does or does not like to be used by us for our own ends. Our attitude is simply: we need it and therefore it must be there for us all the time.

Another aspect of this peculiar love-relation or two-person-relation is *omnipotence*. The idea of omnipotence was very much in vogue till the time when ego-psychology came to the fore (*circa* 1925), then somehow got crowded out of our theoretical considerations. Recently it returned for the description of certain aspects of the primitive two-person-relation we are discussing. I am afraid it is another example of our thinking in adultomorph language. In fact 'omnipotence' never means a real feeling of power; on the contrary, a desperate and very precarious attempt at overcoming a feeling of helplessness and impotence. We call such an attempt 'omnipotence' if the following conditions are present: (*a*) certain objects and satisfactions can be taken for granted; (*b*) no regard or consideration need be paid to the object, the object can be treated as a mere object, as a thing; (*c*) there is a feeling of extreme dependence, the object and the satisfaction by it are all-important.

This is rather a surprising fact. We have found exactly the same dynamic structure in the case of 'oral greed'. A further, in my opinion, very important circumstance is that 'oral greed' and 'omnipotence' are practically always associated; that is if we find one of them in any two-person-relation, the other is hardly ever missing. This very close association and the almost identical dynamic structure point convincingly to a common origin.

2

All 'pregenital' or 'primitive' object-relations contain—in varying proportions—these three ingredients: despondent dependence, denial of this dependence by 'omnipotence', and taking the object for granted, treating it as a mere object, as a thing. Or, in terms of two-person-psychology: 'primitive object-relation' means a relation in which *only one partner is entitled to make demands*, the other is treated as an object, albeit as an instinct or love-object. An impressive argument for this conception is the practically non-sexual (i.e. sexually not dimorphous) nature of all such 'pregenital' relations; e.g. in the mother-child relation, the basic relation of all our theories, it makes no difference whether the child is boy or girl; anybody—father, mother, brother, sister, maid, etc., etc.—can be bullied equally well by a boy or a girl, and the same is roughly true of scopophilic gratifications.

The basis of all such pregenital or primitive object-relations is faulty reality testing, either still undeveloped (in infants) or stunted (in adults like my patient). That is why this 'omnipotent' or 'greedy' love is unstable, doomed to meet with frustration and to lead on to hate. In order to change to a more mature relation we need much more reliable reality testing. We have to realise that our needs have become too varied, complicated and specialised, so that we can no longer expect automatic satisfaction by our objects; we must be able to bear the depression caused by this realisation; and we must accept the fact that we have to give something to our object, something that he expects from us, in order to change the object into a *co-operative partner*. The object can no longer be taken for granted, it must be induced to enjoy giving satisfaction to us, i.e. must come to have his or her satisfaction at the same time, in the same *mutual action*. To establish this mutuality, to change a reluctant and uninterested object into a co-operative partner, means both tolerating considerable strains and maintaining a steady and reliable reality testing. I have called this *the work of conquest*.[1]

In contrast to the pregenital relation, this genital or adult relation is always sexual (usually heterosexual but may be homosexual), whereas the pregenital object-relation is usually non-sexual (sexually not dimorphous). Closely linked with this change from non-sexuality to sexuality is that other development, which has already been pointed out, from taking the object as a mere object to treating it as an equal partner, as a sexual human being.

If the work of conquest has been successful and the subsequent work of preserving is adequate, love and harmony may develop on the basis of mutuality.

3

Where is the place of hatred in this development? Is hatred just as normal and natural as love? Or is it something different?

Our theory based on the assumption of the two archaic instincts of life, and death, would suggest an equal status for love and hate. Moreover, our clinical experience seems in a way to confirm this view. A really healthy man must be capable of both love and hate; if his faculty for either is weak, his health is somehow unstable. There is a further similarity: quite primitive hate is unconnected with any reality testing, being in this respect very much like pregenital love. On the contrary, mature hate means taking into full consideration what would most hurt the object of our hate. A child would hit back at the table leg which hurt him without consideration and without testing whether it will cause pain to the table leg or not. The adult form of hate is perhaps best illustrated by an anecdote of the time of the Nazi régime. A group of Jews,

---

[1] 'On Genital Love', 1948. This vol., pp. 135–6.

refugees from Germany, are sitting in a café, and discussing what should be done to Hitler after victory has been won. All sorts of cruel retaliations are proposed until one silences the discussion: 'We shall sit here in this café and you, Schwarz, will say to me: "Look, there, at the next table, there is Adolf Hitler!" And I shall say: "So what?" '

In our first approach we found a kind of equal status for love and hate, but we must ask how far this parallel holds true. In my opinion, closer examination reveals important differences. Love in a healthy man ought to be fairly constant, steady, unchanging, almost unshakable. Slight or even serious frustrations should alter it hardly or even not at all. Real love is understanding, forgiving and forbearing. Hate, on the other hand, in a healthy man is only potential or incidental. When a really serious reason for it is present, strong or even vehement emotion should arise and be maintained. But it should be more like acute anger; in contrast to love, hate should easily and speedily dissipate if the situation changes for the better. Somehow it seems as if hate and health could tolerate each other only for short intervals, while love and health appear almost as inseparable comrades over long periods.

How shall we explain this important difference? I wish to submit for discussion one explanation which I know is neither the last nor the deepest, but one that perhaps can account for a number of the characteristics of hate discussed here. In my opinion *hate is the last remnant, the denial of, and the defence against, the primitive object-love (or the dependent archaic love)*.

This means that we hate people who, though very important to us, do *not* love us and refuse to become our co-operative partners despite our best efforts to win their affection. This stirs up in us all the bitter pains, sufferings and anxieties of the past and we defend ourselves against their return by the *barrier of hatred*, by denying our need for those people and our dependence on them. In a way, we reassure ourselves that those people, though important, are bad, that we no longer depend on the love of *all* the important people, that we can do without the love of the bad ones of them.

This theory would explain the ease with which love can change into hate and the great difficulty of changing back hate into love. The change of love into hate is a subjective, intra-psychic process. The object itself need not take any part in it, may often remain completely unaware of this process. On the contrary, the change of hate into love can happen only if, in addition to the intra-psychic process, the object too can be changed into an affectionate partner, i.e. a considerable change in the external reality is also needed.

This theory enables us to understand why hate, especially persistent hate, makes us suspect a somewhat immature ego. In fact, persistent hate has never been left untouched by psycho-analytic treatment and under analysis it has always revealed itself as a derivative of frustrated love.

On the other hand, incidental, not persistent, hate appears in the light of my idea as on the whole a good institution. It is a not-too-expensive guardian of our maturity, preventing us from sliding back into the archaic object-world, into the infantile dependence on the affection of our environment.

The more mature an individual is, the less is his need for barriers against regression into primitive forms of object-love, and so the less is his need for hatred. But not all of us can reach this high standard, and so for most of us the need for some hate remains. Perhaps this ideal standard of complete maturity is the true meaning of the traditional ending of the fairy tales: 'They lived happily ever after'. People who have reached that stage of maturity can be thought to be able to solve all their problems of love without resorting in any way to hate.

If we accept my idea then love and hate have no equal status. Love is the more general notion, more people and things can be loved than hated, because hate has the additional condition of a denial of dependence. It is easy, for example, for a Londoner to find an elephant or a giraffe in the zoo 'lovely', but very difficult to hate it. Love has no bounds, everybody and everything can be loved that has ever satisfied our needs, or from whom or which we may expect any satisfaction in the future. Hate has the additional condition that only people and things on which we depend can be hated. Hate is a measure of inequality between object and subject; the smaller the inequality, the more mature the subject, the less is his need for hate.

4

It is high time to stop and examine where we have been led by this train of thought. We have come to have serious doubts whether hate can be given the same status as is given to love. Love—or at least a very primitive form of love—appears now, in the light of these considerations, as a more general and above all more primitive form of object-relation; on the other hand, hate becomes less general and secondary, its range of potential objects is considerably more restricted, its dynamic structure more complicated, and above all it cannot be so easily tolerated by a healthy ego, as can love.

This is dangerous ground indeed, as it involves us in the re-examination of the vexed problem of the two archaic instincts of life and death. If hate proves to be of secondary nature as compared with love, then very likely the status of the death instinct needs careful re-examination too, and with it the theoretically assumed primary aggressiveness, primary sadism, primary narcissism and possibly many more. It is certain that in this case our ideas about masochism must be reconsidered too. A really formidable task, so let us see whether there is a way to get round it.

One way would be to assume that the primary, archaic, object-relation is so primitive that it cannot be called either love, hate or narcissism, or anything; all these are contained in it in rudimentary form as yet indiscriminable from one another, and they appear and become discernible only during later development. This is certainly an attractive idea; to say the least, it would enable us to continue our endless discussions about the true nature of the infantile mind.

But, we ought to ask ourselves, what else would we gain by this idea? And, moreover, what is the price to be paid for it? Every theoretician will agree that conceptions having only negative characteristics are very reassuring and comfortable; one can go on talking about them without much effort as it is almost impossible to be caught out. If one's opponent argues from any positive finding, one can easily defeat him by pointing out that nothing positive can relate to the original conception. If the primitive object-relation is neither love, nor hate, nor narcissism, and in spite of this all these are contained in it *in nuce*, then everything in the world, and in addition the opposite of everything in the world, can be postulated as pertaining to this primitive object-relation.

A further difficulty will arise in connection with two of our fundamental clinical experiences: regression and fixation. One dynamic factor in every mental illness—whether neurotic or psychotic—is the establishment of some primitive form both of satisfaction and object-relation in place of the mature one. This is brought about either by a stunted development, i.e. fixation, or by being thrown back from a higher level, i.e. regression. I am certain there will be no difficulty in finding examples in any analyst's practice for the form of primitive love described in this and in several others of my papers. But, I do not think anybody could give instances of the theoretical primitive object-relation possessing only negative qualities, that is, a relation which is neither love, nor hate, nor narcissism, in my opinion, because no such state exists. Though I must admit that it is possible to argue that any observed and observable state has *not yet* regressed far enough to reach this theoretical state. I think I have proved the inherent fallacy of any argument using the words 'not yet' in my paper on 'Early Developmental States of the Ego'.[1]

And, thirdly, what shall be our ideas about the dynamic mechanisms that start and then maintain the processes that change this primitive form of relation into a mature one? Are these inherent in human biology, i.e. at least potentially innate, or are they mainly external, i.e. originating in the environment? Considered from this angle we must admit that our work as analysts consists above all in providing well-aimed and well-controlled external influences for the release and maintenance of such evolutionary processes. I think we may also agree that the chances of any considerably regressed individual for emerging on his own from regression are not very good; on the other hand, given 'proper' analytic help, his chances become considerably better. From this angle 'proper' analytic help means very favourable external conditions for changing a primitive object-relation into a mature one. I think we may

[1] This vol., pp. 103, 104, 108.

further agree that 'proper' analytic help—from the point of view of the analyst—means as little ambivalence as possible, i.e. very little hate, a very fine and never-relaxing control over the analyst's own satisfactions in the analytic situation, an ever-present alertness to respond in the 'right' way to any need or demand of the patient, a constant watch over any possible over- or under-stimulation of the patient by the analytic process, resulting especially in inhibitions and anxiety, and dissolving any such anxiety or inhibition pre-eminently by means of understanding interpretations. These are only a few outstanding characteristics of the complicated rôle that the analyst has to play, but I think this much will be enough to prove that the rôle is—in many ways—that of the object of the primitive love described in this paper; an object that can be taken for granted, to whose interests, feelings, sensitivities no regard need be paid, who is always there when needed—in fact, who can be used and treated as a mere object, as a thing.

To sum up: assuming a primary state which, though object-related, cannot be described either as love, or hatred, or narcissism, is profitable only in so far as it permits us not to commit ourselves in any way. I cannot see that it could be useful in any other way. States, met with in patients, however deeply fixated or regressed, do not correspond to such a theoretical assumption; on the other hand, they fit exactly into the picture of primary object-love. An equally weighty argument is that the other partner of this primitive two-person-relation, the analyst, agrees in every respect with the 'object' of the primary object-love, both in his actual behaviour in the analytic situation and in the rôles he has to play in the patient's phantasies.

5

This leads us to our last topic, the significance of my ideas for our technique. I think this is such an important question that I intend to examine it in a separate paper. Here I wish only to point out that what we call analytic situation is almost exactly the same as what I call 'primitive object-love'. The analyst is taken for granted and is treated as an object, as a thing. The patient, on the other hand, shows all the characteristics described in the introductory part of my paper. These are: considerable weakness of his ego, faulty reality testing, strong sadistic tendencies, splitting processes both within his own mind and with regard to his objects, resulting in a paranoid picture of the world, strong narcissistic features, marked fears of any depression and above all 'oral greed' and despondent 'omnipotence'. I wish to add to this description that all these affects, feelings, sentiments, develop only under the impact of the analytical situation but are practically independent of the analyst's age, sex, personality and—within surprisingly wide limits—even of his individual variant of technique.

For a long while the therapeutic process consists in studying and analysing this or that facet or component of this complicated and precarious object-relation, which—for want of a better word—is usually called transference. Sooner or later changes appear in the patient's emotions, associations and behaviour which we call *genital transference* in contradistinction to the former *pregenital transference*. (These two terms are shortened expressions for the correct 'transference of emotions, feelings and attitudes, etc., characteristic of genital—or pregenital—object-relations'.) On closer examination all these changes appear to point into one direction, which is accepting the analyst as a 'real' person. That means that the patient tries to find out his analyst's wishes and desires, interests, needs and sensitivities and then is at pains to adapt his behaviour and associations, even his use of phrases and forms of speech, to the image formed of his analyst, in order to find pleasure in the analyst's eyes. I wish to call attention to the almost exact correspondence between this 'genital transference' and what I called 'work of conquest'. The aim of both is to induce a recalcitrant object (the analyst in this case) to become a co-operative partner.

The third and last stage on this road leading towards health is what we call '*transference to real objects*'. The patient gradually realises, understands and accepts his analyst's shortcomings, especially in relation to himself (the patient). Parallel with this process he renounces bit by bit his wish to change the analyst into a co-operative partner, i.e. to establish a harmonious relation in which the two partners—patient and analyst—will desire the same satisfaction in the same *mutual* act, and turning towards the world of reality tries to find someone else there, better suited for such a purpose.

I am fully aware that my description of the complicated therapeutic process is scanty, meagre, highly condensed and simplified. My only aim is to provide a frame in order to put into proper perspective the consequences arising out of my ideas about the origin of hate.

The first phase, which may be called pregenital transference, or more correctly establishment in the analytic situation of an object-relation according to the pattern of the primary object-love, or briefly: *primary transference*, comprises all the factors which we found active in the formation of hatred. These are, once more: despondent dependence, denial of this dependence by 'omnipotence', and 'oral greed', or in other words: establishment of an oppressive inequality between subject and object. It would mean carrying coals to Newcastle to prove that in every analytical treatment a momentous amount of hatred is inevitably evoked,[1] and if not dealt with adequately may either wreck the therapeutic result or—despite a good result—may colour for a long time, even for good, the patient's feelings towards his former analyst. We say that in such cases the transference was not properly resolved. Although true, this statement is not specific enough. What in fact happened was that the patient remained dependent on his former analyst, the inequality between his object and himself did not cease to exist, and so one possible solution for the patient was the erection of a *barrier of hatred* against his object, the analyst.

We know also of another solution, and this is the *perpetuation of the dependence* in the form of an interminable analysis. In such a relation any suggestion of a possible termination of the analysis mobilises anxiety and hatred, which have to be dealt with by further analysis, and so on for ever. I know of cases in which this vicious circle could be broken only by some heroic procedure. It is easy to say that in a 'properly' conducted

---

[1] In addition to hatred, in every analysis there occur periodically blissful expectations and serious attacks of anxiety. In my opinion this triad is a characteristic diagnostic sign of primary object-love in an adult.

analysis such an outcome should not occur; practical experience, however, shows that even analysts of the highest repute have occasionally had such a case. In other cases the dependence can be greatly diminished, the treatment eventually terminates, but the patients remain in the peripheral orbit of the analyst as his 'faithful children'.

This leads to the third, perhaps still less pathological, solution which might be called *idealised*, or more correctly: *dependent identification*. Here too the dependence is perpetuated, albeit in a sublimated form. *Identification with the aggressor* would describe another aspect of this outcome. If one cannot conquer the object, the opponent—and the analyst is but very seldom conquered—in order to avoid hating him, one must accept him wholesale. Then there is no hate on the surface, but to a large extent the patient himself disappeared with his hate—and love. Uppermost is his unconquerable and inexorable analyst with all his terms, happy phrases, theories, his ways of experiencing emotions and his ways of expressing such experiences, even with his petty habits.

In some cases, perhaps, this dependent identification may be a not-too-bad solution. After all, some people with weak muscles and flabby joints need supports; without their supports they are cripples, with their supports they may live a useful and fairly contented life. Although this is not a goal to aim at without some compelling reason, I do not see any justification to reject it altogether, even as a second or third best solution. Furthermore, some traces or even considerably more than traces of 'dependent, idealised, identification' can be detected easily in most successfully terminated analyses. It seems that if any human being has been exposed to the primary object-relation, either in the original form as in infancy, or in a transferred form as in the analytical situation, for ever his mind will bear some marks reminiscent of it. Moreover, it may be that it is only possible to alter an already established mental structure by subjecting the individual to the impact of this primary object-relation.

To sum up: in some cases the result of treatment will be health behind barriers of hatred, a costly but not-too-bad protection against the wish to regress. In other cases the result will be a perpetual dependent identification, defending by idealisation the object against our hatred. And lastly, in favourable cases, the lasting marks of this fateful primary object-relation, of the primary transference, may amount only to unforgettable memories, sweet and painful at the same time. When describing such fortunate people, may I quote again the traditional ending of the fairy tales: 'And they lived happily ever after!'

POSTSCRIPT TO PAGE 144

I WISH to call attention here to the distressing and pathetic one-sidedness of our theory. Practically all our technical terms describing this early period of mental life have been derived from objective phenomena and/or subjective experiences of the 'oral' sphere; as for instance: greed, incorporation, introjection, internalisation, part-objects, destruction by sucking, chewing and biting, projection according to the pattern of spitting and vomiting, etc. Sadly enough, we have almost completely neglected to enrich our understanding of these very early, very primitive, phenomena by creating theoretical notions and coining technical terms using the experiences, imagery and implications of other spheres. Such spheres are, among others, feeling of warmth, rhythmic noises and movements, subdued nondescript humming, the irresistible and overwhelming effects of tastes and smells, of close bodily contact, of tactile and muscle sensations especially in the hands, and the undeniable power of any and all of these for provoking and allaying anxieties and suspicions, blissful contentment and dire and desperate loneliness. It is highly probable that because of this omission, the time will come when our present theories will be considered as badly deficient and hopelessly lop-sided.

Part Two
PROBLEMS OF TECHNIQUE

IX

CHARACTER ANALYSIS AND NEW BEGINNING [1]

(1932)

I

I T is generally accepted that today quite different demands are made of a 'terminated analysis' from those made a decade ago or even earlier. Today, for instance, Breuer's Frl. Anna would certainly not be released from analysis as cured; yet all her symptoms had disappeared, and she declared herself to be fit for work. Surprisingly perhaps, patients who, like her, have for long been free from symptoms, today continue their treatment. What do we want of them and, still more important, what do they require of us? The removal of infantile amnesia, a recovered memory of the primal scene . . .? I believe our patients would not remain with us for many months because of such reasons. What keeps them at their analytic work is their wish, often unconscious, to be able to love free from anxiety, to lose their fear of complete surrender.

Any of us could cite several cases in which the marked neurotic symptoms disappeared through the treatment in a relatively short time, but there still remained a complete incapacity or only a very qualified capacity for love. This state of affairs became particularly clear to me in working with so-called 'organic' patients.

Moreover, we are quite often sought out by people who at the very first consultation present just this picture. It is difficult to place them under any diagnostic heading. Their chief complaint is that they cannot find their place in life. Nothing is actually wrong with them or, at most, they have some quite insignificant neurotic symptoms; but they take no pleasure in anything. Naturally the picture of their sexual life is the same.

[1] Paper read at the Twelfth International Psycho-analytical Congress, Wiesbaden, 1932. Published in German in *Int. J. of PsA*. (1939), **20**, 54.

They perform the act, if they are men, with a fairly reliable erection, are not really frigid if they are women, nor is the terminal pleasure quite lacking, but in spite of all this the whole process brings them no relieving joy.

In analytical work with such people it can be proved, without exception, that they suffer from a special anxiety. This anxiety surpasses every other symptom, and it indicates a fairly strong theoretical prejudice that this has not been rightly appraised by psycho-analysis till now. These people are afraid, dreadfully afraid, of excitation, even of the gratifying pleasure itself. They cannot enjoy because they do not dare to. This fear compels them to evolve all kinds of stratagems to rouse themselves out of a surrender to enjoyment, to bring themselves as quickly as possible out of the state of self-forgetfulness back to their senses. They think fixedly of a certain subject, say the multiplication table to themselves, recite endless poems, etc. They also make innumerable stipulations as to the behaviour of their partner and the duration of the act, and if only one of these should not be exactly fulfilled then they have again a reason to escape enjoyment. In the analytic working through of these generally known phenomena I always came to the same result: these patients simply cannot bear it, or only with great difficulty, if their sexual excitation is raised somewhat higher; and if they are brought—by whatever means—to expose themselves to this increase, great anxiety breaks out.

In tracing back this anxiety, the psycho-analytical work always led back to childhood, to a similar situation. Usually it was grown-ups who had, by their actions, evoked sexual excitation, thereby producing in the defenceless child amounts of pleasure it was not yet able to bear. These actions may have been, much more frequently than one would imagine, directly sexual, even in the genital sense, but need not be so necessarily. Even so-called 'innocent caresses', such as kisses, embraces, stroking, rocking, all kinds of sliding games, etc., may have the same unfortunate results. Naturally this does not mean that one should abstain from all tenderness towards children; on the contrary. Yet we analysts should know that there are neither innocent nor guilty caresses—both are in essence sexual actions and inevitably evoke sexual excitation. We know also that parents live out a great deal of their own repressed sexuality in the bringing up of their children. *How much* is lived out here, and *which component instincts* play the chief rôle in it, are determined almost without exception by the *unconscious of the parents* and only in a very small degree by the needs of the child. And here lies the danger. There is surely much truth in the statement that a child consists almost entirely of sexuality, but sexuality of its own kind, with its own laws, its own needs. Infantile sexuality is distinguished from that of grown-ups not only in that it is still unorganised, or more correctly not so strictly organised, but also, as Freud pointed out long ago, that it does not yet know end-pleasure. The capacity to bear such great amounts of sexual excitation as are necessary to bring about end-pleasure seems to be lacking in the child. Whether this is conditioned biologically or psychologically is still un-decided. It is however very probable that this incapacity for end-pleasure discharge represents one of the most important primal causes of the notably great anxiety-proneness in children.

There is another economic trouble in the childish libido balance which though of a different kind produces the same result. Many parents purposely treat their children with cold-ness or even with spartan severity. It is noteworthy that many adults who were brought up in this way also react to every increase of sexual excitation with anxiety. Here there can certainly be no question of a traumatic over-excitation in childhood. But we must consider that with these children the normal need for tenderness, warmth, etc., far exceeds the given possibilities of libido discharge and can therefore evoke anxiety. Consequently there is also a relative over-excitation which in principle goes back to the same error in upbringing, that of not paying attention to the specifically infantile needs.

To these biological dangers is added a psychological one. If the children have been sexually excited, whether by them-selves or by the actions of grown-ups, and openly show this excitement and would like to live it out in their own sexual mode of expression, they meet, almost without exception, not only with an energetic rejection, but over and above this with severe reproof arising from moral indignation over their dreadful depravity. And usually the more clearly the signs of sexual excitement, partly conscious, partly unconscious, appear in the grown-up, the sharper is the reproof. Since Ferenczi [1] drew our attention to it situations like this have been found in nearly every analysis. In this way the children's capacity for discharging excitement, which in any case is somewhat precarious, is still further restricted; the children are forced to hide their excitement, even to deny it. Quite naturally a dread of every increase of sexual excitation arises from this situation, or at best such excitation will be allowed only when they are quite sure of being undisturbed, i.e. the children are directly driven to secret self-gratification. *To be excited in the presence of other people is synonymous with danger and hence is charged with anxiety.*

Now let us return to the patients described above. Our therapeutic aim is quite clear. These *mistrustful* people must learn in the course of treatment to be able again to give themselves up to love, to pleasure, to enjoyment, as fearlessly and innocently as they were able to do in their earliest childhood. In other words, they must be brought to the point of exercising anew certain instinctual functions which till now could not be performed at all, or only with anxiety, or if without anxiety, then without pleasure.

How can we be of assistance to our patients in this task? Freud describes this situation, as far as I know, only on a single occasion, in his often quoted paper: *Recollection, Repetition and Working Through.* According to him the aim of our work is to let the patient remember. To some extent this cannot be wholly realised; one has to allow the patient some acting out. This should, however, be kept as far as possible within strict limits. What does the patient really repeat, or act out? 'He reproduces everything in the reservoirs of repressed material that has already permeated his general character—his inhibitions and disadvantageous attitudes of mind, his pathological traits of character'.[2] Today this must be somewhat amplified. The patient naturally acts out not only the pathological, but *all* his traits of character, he behaves as he really is, he cannot do

---

[1] 'Confusion of Tongues between the Adults and the Child', *Int. J. of PsA.* (1949), **30**, 225. First published in German in 1933.

[2] *Collected Papers*, II, p. 371. First published in German in 1914.

otherwise. To prevent this is impossible. What we need to do is to control our counter-transference. That is, we must induce him to develop the analytical relation, even in its subtlest details, as far as possible from his own side only. And only then, when we have succeeded in maintaining the transference undisturbed, can we show him where, when and by what means he is protecting himself against a full surrender to love and against its counterpart, a full surrender to hate. In this period of work, therefore, repetition necessarily comes first and recollection later.

At the same time it also becomes clear that the patient has always behaved in the same way; only with other people the picture was distorted through the disturbing effect of the partners' counter-transference. Now the partner, the analyst, is passive, the relation is being developed as the patient unconsciously wants it. This interpretation almost regularly evokes violent affects, such as anger, pain, hurt feelings, shame. The analyst should, however, not be led astray; all these affects are only interposed to keep back the development of anxiety. This anxiety is directed against the full surrender, against the unbearable excitation; as this becomes conscious the situation in childhood usually also comes to light where the child's trust was betrayed. One would expect that now a change would set in, but this very rarely happens; even though the patient understands now these connections. We know what must now take place. The analyst has to point out that what was once actually rational behaviour is, today, irrational; the patient has grown up since then, today he can bear much more than he could at that time. The real situation, too, is different; then powerful grown-ups stood over against him, who had to live out their unconscious instincts in relation to him; whereas today he has to do with the analyst, who strives not to live out anything on his patient. In short, today he can himself determine the amount of excitation which he is capable of bearing.

That is the crucial point: *That the amount of excitation, the degree of the tension, is actually determined by the patient himself*. This explains why in many cases the otherwise useful active interventions (such as those recommended by Ferenczi) remain ineffectual. At first they were called commands and prohibitions;

they were in fact given rather emphatically, sometimes even—as in the fixing of a time limit—apparently irrevocably. Ferenczi himself was the first to see the uselessness of this form and inaugurated a new, much milder form, that of 'advice'. Accordingly one tried to trust to the patient to determine himself the amount of tension or excitement he could bear. In many cases what Ferenczi intended with active intervention can be reached in this way, i.e. to free the patient from his spastic toleration of tension forced upon him through anxiety, and instead to set up a new régime based on spontaneous insight and practical adjustment. In many other cases, however, we cannot reach this aim by 'advice'. This shows that even the milder form of advice sometimes corresponds only to our unconscious wishes, i.e. that it means for the patient a still disproportionate increase of tension.

Where advice has shown itself to be useless there is nothing left but to revise it, and again and again to consider how much tension can be put on the patient at any moment without evoking too great and deterring a development of anxiety. This revision must in some cases be extended over the whole analytic situation. Doubtless patient waiting and interpreting is the surest and, in most cases, the most efficacious method. But not in all cases; consequently this method, which we may admit is the easiest for ourselves, sometimes needs revision.

I cannot today go into the question of what this revision means; without clinical examples, any discussion of technique is useless. I should only like to mention that it is always a question of assigning to the patient a certain amount of tension, naturally with his agreement. In principle, therefore, nothing new, in fact only a continuation of some ideas, inspired principally by Ferenczi, especially in his papers: 'Child Analysis in the Analysis of Adults' [1] and 'Confusion of Tongues'.[2]

If the form and the degree of this consciously evoked tension, and also its moment, were rightly chosen, a great outburst of affect generally occurred and there regularly appeared fragments of memory not previously accessible; on one occasion it even led to an intensive hallucination, which was only subse-

[1] *Int. J. of PsA.* (1931), **12**, 468.
[2] *Int. J. of PsA.* (1949), **30**, 225. The German original appeared in 1933.

quently recognised as originating in the past. But this is only part of the result. Equally important are the reactions, which lie in the direction of what I would like to call the *'new beginning'*. By this I mean a change in the behaviour, more exactly in the libido structure, of the patient. Freud in his technical writings mentioned that it was really a great disappointment to him that no improvement followed when he had disclosed to his patient what had previously been repressed. We have long known that the result of such a disclosure is often only an increase in the resistance. Later we have all experienced with him the second disappointment. After much work we brought our patient to the point where he could himself remember that he had repressed this and that at one time. Sometimes his symptoms thereupon disappear, sometimes not—but anyhow he will not feel himself cured. What is still lacking is that he should finally drop the many conditions which he always had to impose in order to be able to love without anxiety. It is therefore not enough for the patient to know that in fact the object of these conditions was to protect him from the surrender, from the excitation which was too much for him; even if he also knows the trauma from which these conditions arose, he still has to learn anew to be able to love *innocently, unconditionally*, as only children can love. This dropping of condition I call the *new beginning*. This must naturally always be infantile. The development must be taken up again at the point where, at the time, it was diverted from its original course by the trauma. One patient, for instance, wished me to reach her a finger which she clasped with her whole hand like a baby. Another in this period brought day by day a dream, in which she herself appeared as a child; this child was somewhat older in every dream and did nothing but love; the different ways of loving in the dream series repeated her whole development.

This enables us to understand why the tracing back of the libido development, either through remembering or through repetition, is absolutely necessary. To be able to begin something anew, one must go back to the point of interruption. The return itself, that is, the remembering, the disclosure of the repression, means no change as yet; it is however an absolutely necessary prelude to the change—to the new beginning.

What happens now? Sometimes only after some new timid attempts, at other times without them, there appears like an eruption an almost insatiable longing to repeat again and again such newly begun infantile manifestations of love. After this dies down, which only rarely takes any considerable time, the anxiety disappears and the patient is able to recognise and accept his newly begun wishes, and either to realise them in reality or eventually to renounce them. It is very seldom that the analytical work is finished with one single phase of this new beginning. Usually it is only step by step that patients allow themselves to drop the many conditions and formulas on which they made their surrender, their preparedness to love, conditional.

This period is certainly one of the most interesting in the analytical work. I believe it is the same as that which Freud called 'working through'. But in spite of the fact, stated by himself, that 'it is the part of the work that effects the greatest changes in the patient',[1] he deals with it only very briefly in the essay previously quoted; only the two last paragraphs are devoted to this problem. He also gives no further advice to the analyst for this phase of the treatment, apart from the usual ones: patience and adherence to the fundamental psycho-analytic rule. As long as I worked exclusively with this classical technique I did, in fact, observe reactions that looked like a new beginning, but could not recognise the regularity and significance of these phenomena. This situation may perhaps suggest one reason why Freud dealt with this important question so disproportionately briefly.

This last stage in the analytic treatment, the working through of the resistances, or as I should like to call it: *the search after a new beginning free from anxiety*, always brings with it an extension of the capacity for love and enjoyment. From now on also such functions are exercised, and exercised with pleasure, which up till now were impossible because of the obstructing anxiety.

2

Certainly this extension also implies a change of character. And so we reach the vexed question of character analysis. Can

[1] Freud, op. cit., p. 376.

our work alter a character, and if so, how far? Is it right to do so? Since the introduction of training analysis which really brought up this subject, the question has continually hovered in the air, and it has by no means been finally answered.[1] On the contrary, very experienced analysts are rather sceptical about this question; others, equally experienced, answer it definitely in the affirmative. The assertion that by changing the capacity for love the character is also changed, speaks for the one solution, but the disquieting problem remains unanswered as to why experienced analysts have maintained the contrary. Now, it is an old experience that if in a science such contrary opinions are to be heard among serious research workers, the question referred to has never been formulated exactly enough.

Let us begin with colloquial usage. Character derives from χαράσσω which means something like to scratch on or to chisel on. χαρακτήρ means in the old Greek a kind of chiselling tool, the mark caused by it, and only in the figurative sense the character. We Hungarians have for it a word 'jellem', that has as root the word 'jel' = mark. In German also 'charakteristisch' and 'bezeichnend' mean the same. In this sense, character is a mark that makes its bearer recognisable.

One certainly speaks also of characteristic body-marks, but in general the word is used for the behaviour of a person. Thus in everyday language we call a person a strong character, who in the most varying circumstances, under the hardest temptations, acts, thinks and even feels according to recognisable rules and laws; Horace described him in his famous ode: 'Justum ac tenacem propositi virum . . .'; on the other hand, we call someone a weak character whose actions and ways of thinking do not obey any similar rules and laws. We say of him also that he may be capable of any and every abominable action. First of all we must consider the term independently of the social prejudice which came to light in the above phrase, i.e. only as a psychological diagnosis. According to this, character is a set, fixed, rigid form of reaction and action respectively.

To be sure, this rigidity varies in different people. From

[1] Written in 1932. The question has been settled since in the sense suggested in this paper (Postscript in 1951).

almost automaton-like forms of reaction it shades off into quite incalculable forms. Besides, the relation of a man to his own character can also differ widely. In fortunate cases a person recognises his character as an important part, even as the core, of his self. In other cases, however, he feels it as a strange force which is more powerful than himself. The greater part of mankind falls somewhere between these two extremes.

With all these variations it is always a question of one thing, whether it is permissible or not to do, think and feel in a certain way. This I call the form-problem of characterology. I would like to emphasise at once that with this form-problem characterology is by no means exhausted. To name only the most important of the further problems, men differ from one another also in the intensity, not only in the form of their actions. Here I can only call attention to this question of intensity, but not contribute anything worth mentioning to its solution.

Let us then examine the problem of form. For the study of set character reactions the simplest psychological stimuli are useless. The determination of the vision, of the reaction time, for instance, yields much valuable material as to the individuality, the constitution and the present disposition of the subject concerned, but nothing to the study of the subject's character. Character is certainly individually different, but it does not make up the whole individuality. We must therefore turn to more complicated stimuli.

It is easy to give examples. We must examine whether a man can forgive a person he loves and to what extent; whether he can persevere in a matter important to him, or whether he abandons it easily; how he helps his friends in need, and how he stands up against his enemies; whether he is impatient when something turns out to be different from what he would like to have; what he does when something goes according to his wishes and what if it goes against them, etc. All these and similar observations supply important features to the make-up of his character. But have all these apparently heterogeneous stimuli something in common? I believe I have found this common element. All the stimuli here enumerated, and all others that I have examined, lie without exception in the sphere of thinking, feeling, acting, which can be defined by the two verbs: to love and to hate. *Character therefore controls the relation of man to the objects of his love and hate.*

We must bear in mind, however, that character always means a quite distinct way of loving and hating, and indeed not only renders other ways of loving and hating difficult, but in many cases makes them simply impossible, so that we come to the simple statement: *character always means a more or less extensive limitation of love and hate possibilities.* And further, if through external circumstances other possibilities of love alien to his character are offered to a man, or even forced on him, he will neither be able to love, nor—and this still less—to enjoy. *Character therefore means a limitation of the capacity for love and enjoyment.* In other words, people with a strong character are generally at a disadvantage over people with a weak character; they must actually suffer considerably in certain situations which persons with a weak character experience with pleasure. The envy resulting from this may well furnish a weighty reason for the condemnation, indeed, contempt, of the weak characters by those having plenty of character.

I have called character a set, rigid form of reaction. This is to say that at an earlier time other reactions also were possible, the form was even still capable of transformation; it was only later that it became fixed and rigid. The moment when rigidity set in may be approximately assigned. It takes place in extra-uterine life, and certainly not quite in the beginning. The elaboration of such complicated stimuli is surely not the task of the first days. But I would like to emphasise that this only holds good for the character form; the intensity of the character seems to be determined much earlier.

In psycho-analytic literature one always finds fear of punishment as the primal cause of the formation of character. This punishment originally threatens the child from the parents and educators; later, when the super-ego has been established, from his own conscience also. The intention of punishment is always to force the child to identify himself with the punishing authority, therefore to transform his ego in order to enable him to avoid further punishment. Later this statement became generalised; by punishment is now understood not only corporal punishment, but also the threat of withdrawal of love. I wanted to point out that, besides this, the fear of disproportionate (i.e. too great) release of pleasure also plays an important rôle in character formation.[1]

Now we understand, also, why character controls the relation to the objects of hate and love. The danger, be it sexual excitation or punishment, threatens above all from one's nearest and dearest, the love-objects. Indifferent persons and objects are indifferent, one might say undangerous, because they can excite neither desire nor anxiety. And the greater the love, the attraction, the greater is the danger of disproportionate sexual excitation and anxiety. One could venture the statement that men suffer only because, and in so far as, they love.

One function of character certainly is to ensure man against disproportionately great sexual excitation, that is against love. This is attained by the person associating his love-preparedness, his share in the mutual excitement, in the gratification, with more or less rigid conditions. These are just his character traits. In psycho-analytic treatment he will not only become acquainted with the origins of these traits but also learn to regard them as defences. In this way he becomes able to abandon some of them which have now become useless and represent an obstacle, only historically justified, to harmless joy. That is the answer to the question of whether and how far analytic treatment is able to alter the character.

The two other questions, whether one should alter, or is

[1] These two kinds of anxiety—however different they may appear—have still much in common. Certainly punishment, even when mildly called withdrawal of love, is sometimes a considerable sexual gratification for sadistic parents, therefore for the masochism of the child also. The punishment (withdrawal of love) could be summarised as disproportionate sexual excitation, by which I do not at all want to deny that in *ultima analysi* this always means a real threat of death for the helpless child. Similarly, too great a sexual excitation means a real danger, therefore also a death menace for the child. It is then not at all impossible that both sources of anxiety: the real threat of death through the withdrawal of love or over-great excitation, and the disproportionate sexual excitation through the pleasure and punishment actions of the parents, are fundamentally related. It seems to me certain, however, that they are the most important causes of the character becoming rigid. The biological basis is again the defencelessness of the child, his being delivered up to the arbitrary will of the grown-ups.

allowed to alter, characters are not so easily answered. As we have seen, character is a compromise formation. Its two factors are the interests of the individual and the interests of society. A man with a strong character is a gain for society, a man with a weak character an everlasting worry, an everlasting danger. But for the individual, too, it is more comfortable to possess a character which makes reflection and choice unnecessary in many situations, and also decidedly lessens the subsequent responsibility.

But this is only one side of the question. On the other lie the many missed joys, the many spoiled pleasures, the many longings for complete surrender, which are never realised. And fortunately we are not much bothered by this question. The people who come to us, including the training candidates, long for freedom—freedom from the many oppressing demands of their character—and do not bother themselves about questions of principle.

But with that I do not wish to evade the question as to whether character analysis is justified in every case or not. As we have seen, our task is to free the person from his many compulsory rigid conditions of love and hate. In my opinion this is in many cases not only justified but also necessary. These conditions—in spite of the fact that they have been long ago built into the ego—are really the results of errors of upbringing. These once-committed errors we must render ineffectual. This can certainly be achieved. What we cannot achieve with an adult is to alter the make-up of his instincts and to undo the fact that he was brought up by a society. Our aim is therefore an elastic, practical adjustment to external reality, while—if possible—completely preserving the inner freedom. As a colleague of ours, Johann Scheffler, or by his self-chosen name, Angelus Silesius, described this so pregnantly some hundred years ago in his *Cherubinischer Wandersmann*:

> *Mensch werde wesentlich, denn wenn die Welt vergeht,*
> *So fällt der Zufall weg, das Wesen, das besteht.*

Now, the task of character analysis is just this: to teach our patient to distinguish in himself the essential from the accidental.

APPENDIX

According to the foregoing interpretation, regression is not a single event, not a definite shifting from one libido position to another, but rather a lifelong dynamic process, fluctuating to and fro, enforced by an anxiety-danger which blocks full genitality and causes incapacity for experiencing end-pleasure. Thus a young man during a certain period of his treatment regularly got violent diarrhoea if the proximity of the girl he was in love with excited him. Another protected himself against sexual excitation on such occasions by vomiting. A man of mature age, as soon as he felt himself attracted by his partner, became rough, harsh and quarrelsome. In all these cases it could be proved that these patients reacted with anxiety to an increase of genital excitation, that this anxiety grew with the excitation, and finally became so great that a further increase became unbearable, and another means of discharge, free of anxiety, had to be found. This process is regression, since apart from genitality every other sexual activity is by definition pregenital.

Similarly, repetition in individual life assumes a somewhat altered meaning. It forms the counterpart of regression. As soon as sexual excitation is adjusted through pregenital discharge (to keep to the above-mentioned examples—diarrhoea, vomiting, quarrelling, unpleasantness), the anxiety-danger is lessened and the libido moves again in the direction of genitality, i.e. the already traversed path of individual development is repeated again and again. If the excitation along this path again becomes unbearable, then the other swing of the pendulum, regression, sets in.

In the sexuality of every person these two points may be recognised. How far he can allow himself to approach full genitality without anxiety, this is the genital point; and how far anxiety drives him back, this is the fixation point. If we also add to this the amount of anxiety released, most known psychosexual situations can easily be represented schematically.

If anxiety can be released over a wide field, even by a small amount of sexual excitation, then the genital point approaches the fixation point and so originates an almost permanent condition of regression—the picture of a psychoneurosis. If the anxiety is only released by greater excitation, that is to say only over a narrow field, but its amount is still rather great, we have the description of the aforementioned sexual disturbances. If the person can finally bear a moderate quantum of excitation, and if the amount of anxiety released by the excitation is nil or small, we have a so-called healthy person with more or less rigid character traits.

According to this, character has also the function of protecting a person from a too intense pleasure. Genetically described, it means that there is no *successful repression*, i.e. a repression without a permanent change in the ego. In the worst case a neurotic symptom results, but in a case where formerly successful repression was supposed, a penetrating analysis discovers a series of more or less rigid character-traits, which are direct derivatives, one could say keloid scars, of past repressions.

X

ON TRANSFERENCE OF EMOTIONS [1]
(1933)

PSYCHO-ANALYSIS has been built up on two well-established facts of clinical experience. The one is *resistance*. During the flow of free associations the patient often feels an impulse not to tell the next idea (or a series of ideas) because it would be unpleasant, ridiculous, unessential, painful, etc. The analyst notices the resistance by the unequal flow of the associations, i.e. sudden deviations, accelerations, retardations or even complete interruption of speech. These experiences have been the source of the assumption of the unconscious mind, of repression, and in general of the dynamic conception of psychic processes. The facts, the basis of these ideas, are so obvious, so easily observable by everyone, so undeniable, that the above-mentioned ideas—though sometimes under different names—have already been accepted by the scientific world; nowadays a completely hostile criticism is scarcely ever heard.

The situation is entirely different with regard to the second, equally important observation: transference. This important fact of experience which led to a psycho-analytic theory of instincts, and recently to the beginnings of a psycho-analytic characterology, has been challenged, often disapproved of, even completely rejected. This attitude has two main causes. The one is that transference, though in the same way a general phenomenon, needs a trained, unprejudiced observer; the other is that it is intimately connected with the field of emotions. Let us begin therefore with some—not very dangerous—examples. In a hot dispute it may occur that one or the other disputant hits the table with his fist, as it were to give more weight to his arguments. Or it may happen that one hears things which make one angry; if one's excitement has not cooled down by the end of the talk one may bang the door

[1] Paper originally read in 1933 to the Hungarian Psychological Society. British examples substituted later. Published in Hungarian *Gyógyászat* (1933), **73.**

when going out of the room. Or, after taking leave from his best beloved a young man may notice that she has forgotten her gloves; again it may happen that the young man feels still happier in the possession of these valuable objects, even that he kisses them.

Let us study these rather uninteresting examples more closely. We see that in each of them a very intense emotion takes hold of the person. Obviously, this emotion is caused by, and directed towards, a certain person; yet it is lived out on something else. Our man is not at all angry with the table or with the door, not at all in love with the gloves, and still they have to suffer, or to rejoice as the case may be. Described in scientific language: our man has transferred his feelings, his emotions, from the original object to something else.

My next task is to show you with what an important, general phenomenon we are dealing, a phenomenon which permeates the whole of our social life. It is not at all an exaggeration to say that there is scarcely any sphere of social, religious, political life where transference is not a very important factor. First of all there is the realm of symbols: the National Ensign, the British Lion and Unicorn, the crest of a family, owe their great importance to transference of feelings. The same holds true for the Queen's uniform, or for the officer's epaulettes. It would mean carrying coals to Newcastle should I try to prove the significance of symbols for inciting or appeasing feelings to a British audience. 'British' itself is such a symbol, carefully chosen not to hurt the feelings of any nationality of the United Kingdom. Then each corner of a postage stamp bears a symbolic flower: the rose, the thistle, the daffodil and the shamrock. A criminal act is taken as having injured the sovereign, and all prosecutions are in his name, *Regina v.* N. Every official envelope bears the imprint 'On Her Majesty's Service', and it cannot be left unmentioned that the vast Commonwealth of British Nations is legally held together not by institutions, treaties or laws but mainly by a symbol, the Queen's person.

Less important symbols are the colours of the universities (e.g. dark blue and light blue) or those of clubs. Of much greater importance are the religious symbols: the cross, the genuflexion, the different ways of ringing the church bells. It is quite obvious that the symbol itself is almost valueless, its immense value is due to the transferred emotions.

Social and political life often tries to make good use of transference, frequently it is intentionally provoked for certain premeditated effects, e.g. inventing a new slogan or a new way of greeting.

Another field where transference plays an outstanding rôle is tradition. Very often the usage, the institution itself, is time-worn and decrepit, often even very boring and annoying, still we stick to it, as is often said, because of our honour and love for our fathers. That means that the usage, the institution, has inherited the feelings which, by rights, belonged to our fathers. As one of the innumerable examples let me quote the wigs worn by the Speaker, Judges, Barristers, etc.

A very similar phenomenon is reverence, the basis of which is always transference. A letter, a valueless object like a glove, a cane, a dried flower, a hideous piece of furniture, are kept with the same care, with the same love, which were due to their owners. A very instructive proof is a visit to a so-called Memorial Museum. In Weimar, for instance, Goethe's wash-basin and even his chamber-pot are reverently kept, and with the same reverence the Manchester Literary and Philosophical Society exhibited the top hat and the bedroom-slippers of Dalton in a glass case.

A further inexhaustible sphere for studying transference is *love*. It is impossible to imagine or even invent an object which could not be used, and occasionally has not been used, for transference. Beginning with punched tickets, used when together, and pieces of clothing worn by her or by him, everything in the world was, is and will be taken by lovers to represent him or her, to be kept in love, honour or adoration in his or her place. Quite recently I heard of a dental surgeon who kept a girl's tooth extracted by him in high esteem for two years and married the girl afterwards.

A very frequent technique of joking is based on transference. To quote only one famous story: the dilemma of a husband who surprised his wife with his partner. If he throws out the wife, he has to give the dowry back, if he throws out the partner, his business will go bankrupt, and thus, finally, after long hesitation, he throws out the couch.

In linguistics, too, transference plays an important rôle. To prove it I have only to remind you of such phrases as: the front of a house, the leg of a table, the brow of a hill; then: the pale moon, the blushing sky, a happy day, distressful years, etc.

This enumeration could be continued endlessly. I hope this much is enough to show that transference really is a general phenomenon. It is not difficult to detect both the causes and the aims of transference. The cause is always the circumstance that (at that moment) the emotion cannot be lived out on the original person or object or even cannot be lived out on it at all. This is clearly demonstrated by our story of the couch. The same is true of reverence where the original person is either dead or remote. Sometimes the original person is present, but some other feeling, e.g. fear, compassion, love, etc., prevents us from *doing* to him what we would like to do. As you see, transference has a great economical value for the mind; it enables us to live out emotions which otherwise must be carefully controlled, and so frees us from unnecessary strain —e.g. after having banged the door or hit the table we feel easier—and in the same way it is easier to endure the loss of a beloved person if we have something to keep him or her in our memory. This economical function is one of the aims of transference.

I am afraid that for the present you may see hardly any connection with psycho-analysis. This is my fault. I have deliberately omitted something. Up till now we have studied transference from the standpoint of the transferring subject only, and we have not even asked what the object, on to which —deservedly or undeservedly—the emotions had been transferred, will say to it. To wit, we have not yet asked what the triumphantly waved dark-blue piece of cloth, the reverently preserved glove, or the angrily banged door would like to say! I know this question sounds odd or even funny. But I can confess now that I have aimed at this effect, I have intentionally selected only such examples where the object, being inanimate, cannot say anything. Only this procedure made it possible for me to demonstrate to you such clear, obvious situations. The whole picture at once becomes different when emotions are transferred on to a human being, to whom it matters considerably whether he has been caressed or hit, honoured or despised. He certainly will not remain unimpressed and will react according to his aroused emotions, hopelessly disturbing the clear psychological situation. And more than that, transference being an absolutely general tendency, he too will strive to get rid of the strain existing in him, i.e. he will strive to transfer his non-abreacted emotions to everyone within his reach. A complete mess.

You remember I said that transference, though a trivial experience, cannot be as easily observed as resistance. Here we have the explanation. I want to add one more explanation only. We all know what is needed to bring about a clear situation again. One of the two persons concerned has to undertake the by no means easy task of behaving—in the first approach— as passively as the flag, the glove or the door. This person is the analyst, and the resulting situation has been called 'the psycho-analytic situation'. What will happen if the analyst abandons his passive rôle? A very trivial thing, namely the same which constantly happens among men: he will be glad if he has been treated gently, if he has heard nice words; and on the other hand, he will be angry if he has been hit, bitterly reproached, told off or railed at, i.e. he too will react and transfer his emotions on to his patient. Thus the psycho-analytic relation will change into a trivial human relation of friendliness or hostility, sympathy, love or hate, or even indifference.

On the other hand, if the analyst has been able to preserve his elastic passivity, by not bringing anything from his side into the developing relationship, then the patient alone has to form it. Only under such condition is it possible to show up the effects of the patient's transference and to follow them in detail. I cannot sufficiently emphasise how difficult this task can be. Generally it is thought that the real difficulty for the analyst is to remember the innumerable data, events, details, reported by each of his patients, or to keep apart the different material concerning the different patients, or to interpret it. All these tasks are not at all difficult compared with the preserving of this elastic passivity, with the benevolent conducting of the transference, with the absolute mastering of his own counter-transference; these are the touch-stones of the analyst. Analytic treatment requires something similar to surgical or bacteriological sterility; and as these cannot be learned from books, but only by practice, so there is only one way to learn this analytic sterility: the didactic or training analysis. As is well known, this means that the student has to undergo the same procedure which he intends to use with his future patients. I think a lot of polypragmasy could be prevented, should it be possible to introduce this requirement into the general medical and especially surgical curriculum.

I would like to illustrate with a few examples the difficulties waiting for the analyst. At the same time you will see how cunning the unconscious mind can be in inventing ingenious devices with the single aim of forcing the analyst to abandon his passivity. E.g. one day a man appears to consult me about his nervous complaints. He tells me his name, his family relations, really everything, a very complicated story. As usual, before asking anything, I tell him that he would do better to refuse to answer than to answer not quite sincerely; this makes a deep impression on him, and he readily answers all my questions. Nevertheless I cannot get a clear enough picture of his problems and I tell him so, when after more than an hour I have to end the interview. We agree that in a few days he will ring me up again. He does so, he comes again and continues his story. After a while I interrupt him with the confession that I am still unable to understand the situation: the more he tells me, the less clearly I see. My man takes a deep breath and says: 'At last—a sincere man'. Then he tells me that his name is different, the whole story—family relations, nervous symptoms, everything was invented; he wanted to test me first, because he wants a truthful man to whom to disclose his secrets. He has already tried several physicians in the same way, but each of them fell into the trap, giving him advice and prescriptions for his faked symptoms. Of course I agreed with him, really nobody ought to be trusted before being tested, but I added that it was rather an expensive and very tiresome method of testing; there are certainly ways of arriving at the same result with less cunning and at a smaller price. As you can see, this man came in a prepared attitude, entirely independent of my personality; this attitude, the transference, was—in this case—a severe obstacle to be overcome before he could establish a workable relation between his physician and himself. The attitude in this case was conscious, even well rationalised. It is true that the energy required was not in proportion with the result aimed at. With such a disproportion it is certain that the scheme of transference has—besides its conscious source—also a powerful unconscious one, but the discovery of this usually requires long and tiresome analytic work. In this case there was no time for it. Therefore it is advisable in such a situation simply to agree with the patient, but at the same time to show him how uneconomic his attitude is, and thereby to try to change his 'natural' attitude into a problematic one.

The end of the analytic session is another example of such a transference, again consciously well rationalised. Usually we work an hour a day with our patients, the end of the time being signalled in rather a stereotyped form. People react to it in various ways. There are some who get up at once, say good-bye and are already gone. Another cannot go away, he would like so much to tell just this one idea then certainly he will go, he knows that the next patient is already waiting; but just this one story is so nice, etc. . . . A third feels it as a grave offence that I am ending the session and not he; during a great part, often the greater part, of our working time, he has to prepare himself to endure this unjust blow. A fourth is very matter-of-fact, no emotions at all; the time is over, he has to go; but he has to tell me that something very important came into his mind just at this moment; certainly he has to wait with it till to-morrow—if he does not forget it, which undoubtedly would be a great pity, caused by the analyst's rigidity, indifference and impatience, etc., etc., in thousands of variations.

As you see, each of them feels his attitude to be logical and natural. But to us it must appear suspicious that each thinks that his is the only understandable attitude. To us, who see the whole picture, the particular attitude is not so much natural as characteristic for that certain person. With this we have arrived at characterology. You know that there are as many characterologies as authors investigating this problem. Each of them introduced a new classificatory system, supposed some new fundamental characters or temperaments different in many respects from any previously described. The main cause of this mess is the 'unsterile' way of investigation. The different authors brought their own likes and dislikes, their own character and temperament, into the material and observed and described the phenomena through the spectacles of their own transference. The result of such work is naturally a psychology or a characterology of the psychologist himself.

Psycho-analysis has gone a different way. Instead of beginning by supposing some basic types, it investigated the mature character-traits by studying their actual working in the analytical situation. Each man has his more or less automatic forms, even schemes of reactions, and some of these have been assimilated to such an extent that any other form is not only impossible, but literally does not exist for the person in question. We call these forms the character-traits. How are they to be treated in an analysis? First of all the analyst must not react to them. That means, taking the end of a session as an example, he does not find it natural that even after an agitated hour his patient should be able simply to go away without a moment's rest to collect himself; neither does he allow the conversation to slip into a pleasant chat; nor is he frightened that something very valuable could be irreparably lost, etc. Thus keeping the analytic situation free of his counter-transference, the analyst can demonstrate the automatisms working in the patient, often without his being conscious of them. It is a big step if not only the automatism itself but also the effect which is aimed at can be made conscious. So, keeping to the examples given above, the patient who habitually runs away at once was possibly a too-well-trained child, who has become unable to feel and still less to express a desire. The other, who cannot stop the new ideas coming into his mind, is skilfully hiding the fact that he cannot acquiesce in simply being sent away. The third, who suffers almost from the beginning of the session from the expectation of being sent away, is often a spoilt child, with a lot of aggressiveness behind his sensitivity. The fourth, though seemingly very submissive, really wants to throw the burden of responsibility on the analyst.

A still further step is to demonstrate that though this automatism can be economic under certain conditions, it is not always so; very often it leads to unmanageable situations. The next aim of the analysis is to look for the original situation, to which this form of reaction was well adapted, often the only possible adaptation. This found, we are able to follow up the whole process which led to the establishing of this particular automatism, or, by its other name, of this character-trait. As you see, this way is thoroughly different from that hitherto used in characterology. We have no idea how many and which are the basic types of character; we are simply collecting data in the hope that the material will arrange itself with our increasing knowledge.

I want to show what is meant when I stated that every character-trait has its individual history. We may get something unexpected too, namely that quite unimportant trifles may let loose a storm of transference. Therefore I have to begin with such unimportant details. For a time my consulting-room was so arranged that the couch was quite near my writing-desk. A rather big plant used to stand on the corner of the desk, throwing its shadow on the couch. One day the plant had been taken out of my room to be washed and had not been brought back. Neither I nor the first one or two patients noticed its absence. The next one—contrary to his habit—began the session by remaining silent. It was quite obvious by his whole behaviour that he was feeling uneasy, was almost suffering. Finally, after some encouragement, he burst out violently: 'Why do you do such things to me? And if it has to be done, why so brutally?' Only after further encouragement was he able to tell that until now he felt so comfortable in the shadow of the plant, it was so reassuring, so homely. But now that the plant had been taken away, he felt like one expelled, an outcast, a prey to the whole world, defencelessly handed over to every evil. You have to imagine that he was a physically absolutely healthy youth, an athlete, a champion weight-lifter and a member of his university eight. At that time I already knew that he had had to leave his home when nine years old for a very severe boarding school, run by Jesuits. The political situation at that time, i.e. the end of the war, three revolutions rapidly following one another and the Rumanian occupation of Hungary, made it impossible for his parents for about two years to take him home, or even to come to see him; so he had to stand on his own feet. Outwardly he was quite successful; a 'cheerful' child at school, he developed into a sincere and frank man who was always popular with everyone. Now we had to learn what was the price he had to pay for it. In his childhood he had to struggle against the same emotions of being thrown out without mercy, but as there was no hope of finding understanding, even a big risk of being laughed at, he had to appear as a strong, robust man, and to keep his real, tender feelings to himself. Even today nobody knows what he really feels; he has numerous good companions, not one intimate friend. If possible, he sits in a corner, shielded by the walls, speaks very little, is always on his guard and, curiously enough, he does not like to do anything by himself, e.g. when preparing for an examination he looks for somebody with whom to work together, when rowing he always tries to make someone accompany him in order not to be alone in the boat, even if he has to do the work of two. Of course his sexual life, his love affairs, show the same picture: a strong longing for human proximity with inability to maintain a real intimacy. The picture is in fact not simple, there are many ramifications, but two tendencies are obvious: the fear of disclosing his affectionate feelings and the striving not to become conspicuous. Needless to say, the unveiling of this part of his history was an important step in his analysis.

Let us take another case. The patient is a woman, of about thirty-five, single; a very difficult case. I am her second analyst; the first analysis was almost a failure. The main obstacle to the analytical work is her peculiar behaviour. Should there be anything in her mind which is disagreeable or only inconvenient for her to tell, she keeps silent or begins to chat about petty affairs of the day. At times I can show her that she tendentiously tries to avoid a specific subject in her associations, as often as not even then she tells lies in order to escape. Days later, when her emotions have gone, she admits her fears and insincere tricks. Of course, in this way we need an immense amount of time for the simplest matters. She knows very well that her whole life has been made a hopeless mess by just such behaviour.

In one of our last sessions she produced again the same 'comedy'—which is her own word. From the beginning it was quite obvious that she was keeping something back. It cost more than half an hour of hard work—for both of us—till she could tell me that she had received a letter of recommendation from her family doctor, and that in this letter she was described as a conscientious and reliable person. On this occasion it was possible to analyse some aspects of her behaviour. Here, naturally, I can report only the main tendencies brought to light. First of all, in her opinion it is a bad thing to be a grown-up; really everyone should be afraid of it. In fact, it means to be sentenced to hard labour for the rest of your life, and more-over to be fully responsible for everything that you do. On the other hand, a child is permitted to do what he likes, he has no responsibility—if anything should happen the parents are the persons responsible; then there is no compulsion to work; everybody finds it natural and even lovely when a child spends the time playing. And really no one can demand hard work of a little girl, not even a psycho-analyst.

Consequently her behaviour means: I am a little girl, you should love me as I am, and you should not try to make me work. This attitude could be traced back to her childhood. The mother was and still is a fanatic for work; life for her, I quote her own words, is 'work, sweat and duty'. She is the father's second wife, and he probably married her because he wanted somebody to work for him. The father, who died some years ago, was a happy-go-lucky fellow; he did not like my patient, his only daughter, but preferred his sons.

Her whole life is but a series of similar stories. She makes an excellent start; later, when she notices that people take her seriously, begin to expect something of her—i.e. expect her to work—she gets frightened of the responsibility, she begins to 'play the comedy', i.e. she demonstrates that she is a little girl, quite irresponsible. E.g. at school she was one of the best pupils, a candidate for a scholarship, was offered the position of prefect—the result was that in a couple of weeks she made herself quite impossible, and had to leave the school before her

H.S.C. In several jobs she did the same trick; once she worked as a nurse to two children, everybody was entirely satisfied with her, the parents offered her a rise in salary—then in an amazingly short time she turned everything upside down and left the post. Obviously she does not want to be a grown-up because it would mean leading a life similar to that of her mother. The following day she reported that she presented herself with the letter and took up a job. Very characteristically she became the secretary of a domestic agent, i.e., in her own words, she sits by the telephone and sends the others to work. Needless to say, that almost every day she comes with new reasons as to why it would be advisable for her to quit her job.

What can we see in all these examples? The behaviour of these people is not free, is not well adapted to the actual requirements. There is a pattern working in them, and this pattern determines their attitude towards important persons in their life. This attitude, this pattern, is more or less automatic, either constantly present, as with the last-mentioned patient, or a very small stimulus is sufficient to activate it, as was the case with our athlete. The main thing is that this pattern prescribes the emotions felt towards a certain type of person; the persons themselves have very little or even no part at all in evoking these emotions. All these patterns have an individual history, and if this history—I mean the original situation, in which this emotion was first felt as a reasonable response to the real situation, and all the subsequent changes of this response—if this whole history can be brought to consciousness the pattern becomes less imperative and the way to a new, more elastic adaptation is opened.

Does this mean that all character-traits are based on transference-patterns? Certainly not exclusively. But I would not like to embark upon this endless subject of characterology, with all its fine discriminations between style, character, personality, etc., and with all its complex involvements between psychology, physiology, endocrinology, genetics, sexual-biology, etc. My only purpose was to show that transference of emotions plays a very important part in shaping our character.

I should finally like to draw your attention to an important point of detail which we have not yet discussed. All the reported cases, without exception, show that the transferred emotions, though often very intense or even stormy, are in fact somewhat childish. This clinical fact, once a most surprising discovery, led to a much deeper understanding of the so-called Oedipus situation. You know that by that term psycho-analysis denotes all those complex, often contradictory but always very intense feelings and emotions which originate in every child during his first years of existence. A great part of these emotions must remain without any outlet or with an inappropriate outlet only, many desires without proper gratification. It is general knowledge that desires, especially love and hate, can live unnoticed for very long periods and return at a favourable occasion in their old strength. Psycho-analysis was able to show that these ungratified mental tendencies are not only persistent but that they cause a considerable strain in the mind, because they have to be kept in an inactive, so-called repressed, state. One means of alleviating this strain is transference.

Now we understand better why all of us always can, and actually do, transfer emotions on to everyone who is available, why the whole of our social, cultural, religious, political life is entirely permeated with transferred emotions. All these emotions originate from the immense reservoir of the Oedipus complex. This explains too why no attention was paid to these phenomena before Freud, and how he came to discover them. The psycho-analytic situation resembles in many respects the Oedipus situation. It is understandable that under such circumstances emotions are always transferred. It is not a paradox to state first that our whole cultural life is permeated with transference, that transference plays a paramount rôle in shaping our political, religious, social life, and then to assert that the same transference is childish. There is no contradiction, because we are speaking of the psychology of transference, and not of its cultural value—which are two entirely different aspects.

These two attributes of transference, (a) the seemingly loose connection between stimulus and reaction, and (b) the childishness, would lead us, if followed to their origins, to infantile sexuality.

Before ending I would like to enumerate some of the important problems which I have had to leave out: the qualitative study of the transferred feelings and emotions which leads to problems of the psychology of instincts. The cultural function of transference, which is no longer a purely psychological problem. Next the difference between conscious and unconscious transference, and the difference between individual and cultural (mass) transference, which would lead to the problem of repression, to very interesting problems of ego-psychology and the question of the interrelations between culture and the individual. Then transference as one of the main factors of psycho-analytic treatment, a purely technical problem; and last but not least transference as one form, may be the only true form, of manifestations of the unconscious mind.

With this enumeration I wanted to demonstrate that transference is a very intricate subject, not at all as simple as shown in this lecture.

Anyhow, I am at the end. We have seen that transference is a general feature of human life, everybody is always transferring his emotions to everybody within his reach. It is impossible to get a clear, understandable situation, if the object of transference is a second human being, because (a) the second person will react to the transferred feeling and (b) he too will try to transfer his un-abreacted emotions on to the first. The only way to see clearly is what I called the 'sterile' way of working, namely the elastic, tactful passivity, the complete mastering of the analyst's own transference.

XI

THE FINAL GOAL OF PSYCHO-ANALYTIC TREATMENT [1]

(1935)

ONE can confidently describe psycho-analytic treatment as a natural process of development in the patient. If, then, I inquire into the final goal of our therapy, I do not mean by this a prescribed final state, which, deduced from some philosophical, religious, moral, sociological, or even biological premise, requires that everyone should 'get well' according to its particular model. I ask rather: is our clinical experience sufficient to define the final goal, or at least the final direction of this natural development?

There are special cases particularly suitable for this inquiry. I am thinking of those people who—like Freud's famous Wolf-man—break off the analysis with only partial results, and then, after an interval of years, continue the treatment, possibly with another analyst. The resumed work offers a very favourable opportunity for a fresh investigation of the former non-adjusted obstacles, and a cure in such a case supplies the proof that it was precisely those obstacles that had previously blocked the way to recovery. [2]

[1] Read before the Thirteenth International Psycho-analytical Congress, Lucerne, 1934. First published in German in *Int. Z.f. Psa.* (1935), **21**, 36–45. In English: *Int. J. of PsA.* (1936), **17**, 206–16.

[2] I do not believe, in fact, that smoothly running cases, which terminate without complications, can offer much for our purpose. First of all, in these cases one can never be quite sure whether our therapeutic work did not merely set going some mechanism which remains hidden from us, and whether the patients did not recover with the help of this—to us—unknown process. Secondly, it often happens that one can only observe the result and not the process of recovery. We can learn far more from an analysis that does not run smoothly. Firstly, one is, of necessity, bound to reflect more upon it; in a difficult case one notices a problem much sooner than in those where results are easily obtained. Secondly, an obstinate, unchanging obstacle, on which the treatment comes to grief, is more easily perceived than the very subtle changes which finally bring about recovery.

A case of this kind first set before me the problem of how our patients become cured and what is really the final goal of psycho-analytic treatment. As the case offers nothing of special interest apart from this, I will mention here only what is of importance for the formulation of our problem. The man in question, who was well on in his forties and whose illness presented a picture in which phobic and obsessional neurotic features were originally to the fore, had already undergone some four years of thorough analysis. When, after an interval of two further years, he came to me since he was not able to return to his former analyst, his neurosis had taken the form of a fairly serious conversion-hysteria. We worked some further 500 hours together. The analysis came to an end two years ago, and the result is one of the best in my practice. Now this was attained without anything new that is worth mentioning being brought to light from the unconscious. Everything had already been partly remembered, partly reconstructed, in the previous analysis, and during this second period of work, which was certainly very intensive, and also successful, no change occurred in the picture, already familiar to the patient, of his infantile and subsequent course of development. In spite of this—and I can assert it without exaggeration—the man was cured during this time.

I would remark at once that this is not an exceptional case. Ever since this case taught me to pay attention to such processes I have been able regularly to observe that in all cases where the analysis was deep enough, the final phase turns out similarly. In the last months fresh material is only rarely made conscious, and infantile incidents which were not already known or had till then remained unconscious are hardly ever brought to light. Nevertheless, during this time something very important must have happened to our patients, for before it they were still ill, and during it they became well. I know that all this is already familiar; it was precisely such observation that supplied the material for the concept of 'working through'. But that concept, or, more correctly, the clinical factors on which that concept is based, were not adequately taken into consideration by the different investigators when they attempted to describe the goal of psycho-analytic treatment.

For this reason all the descriptions proposed have fallen short.

One group of these descriptions of the final goal deals only with the structural changes in the mind; this we may call the classical group. The other lays stress on the dynamic or the emotional factor; this could be called the romantic group. All descriptions of the first group derive from Freud. According to him the goal of the treatment was *the making conscious of the unconscious*, or, *the removal of infantile amnesia*, or, *the overcoming of the resistances*. The three descriptions are almost synonymous. In my opinion they go too far. As we have seen in the case described, after a certain point in the treatment no really new material came to light, nothing worth mentioning could be added to the picture of the development in early childhood, and in spite of this the neurosis was cured. On the other hand, it is generally known that even analysed people still dream, and that dream analysis encounters resistance with them also. Consequently, even after the end of an analysis, at least so much remains unconscious in the mind as is necessary for dream formation, and enough resistance unresolved to be able to disturb a dream-analysis considerably. Others, also, have surely had the experience that after a finished analysis, months or even years later, patients suddenly remember fragments of their infantile history. Often we had already been able to reconstruct these in the analysis, so that the suddenly emerging memories are only a confirmation of the analytic work; sometimes, however, these pieces bring to light material which was never even suspected and never used in the analysis, and though these pieces fit in well with the known picture they are none the less quite new. These three descriptions of the final goal of the treatment consist therefore of attributes which, to use mathematical terminology, are neither necessary nor sufficient.

Now let us turn to the second group of descriptions. They are all either paraphrases or more precise restatements of the old description which dates from the time of catharsis. According to this the final goal of our therapeutic efforts is '*the abreacting of the strangulated affects*'. This is doubtless correct but it is stated too generally. We have as yet no means of telling whether all the strangulated affects have in fact been dealt with, nor whether those already dealt with suffice for a cure. Since the theoretical clarifications of the repetition factor, not a few attempts have been made to arrive at some more precise criterion for judging this point. Ferenczi and Rank describe the goal as *'the complete reproduction of the Oedipus relation in analytic experience'*.[1] Since we know how complicated the early infantile Oedipus relation is, this description, though it doubtless signifies a notable advance, seems to say too much. Rank claims the final goal to be *'the abreacting of the birth trauma'*.[2] So much has already been written on the merits and defects of this theory, that further criticism is superfluous. V. Kovács's formulation, *'the unwinding of the repetition factor'*,[3] emphasises, in contrast to the two previous ones, the dynamics of the curative process, but is still too generally stated. W. Reich comes to almost the same conclusions as I.[4] But he gives as the final goal *'the attaining of full genitality, of orgastic potency'*. This is partly correct; nobody is healthy who lacks the capacity for a regular periodic orgasm. If I have understood him rightly, however, he seeks to explain by means of the vague concept of 'constitution' the cases in which, in spite of a deep analysis, orgastic potency cannot be reached. On the other hand, most of us have seen, and even observed analytically, more than one person who, in spite of perfect orgastic potency, is decidedly neurotic.

Since the descriptions already proposed do not entirely satisfy us, I shall venture to discuss this question on the basis of the views which I put forward at Wiesbaden.[5] I have been able regularly to observe that in the final phase of the treatment patients begin to give expression to long-forgotten, infantile, instinctual wishes, and to demand their gratification from their environment. These wishes are, at first, only faintly indicated, and their appearance often causes resistance, even extreme anxiety. It is only after many difficulties have been overcome

[1] *Entwicklungsziele der Psychoanalyse*, Int. PsA. Verlag, Wien, 1924, p. 54–5.

[2] *Das Trauma der Geburt*, Int. PsA. Verlag, Wien, 1924.

[3] 'Wiederholungstendenz und Charakterbildung,' *Int. Z. f. Psa.* (1931), **17**.

[4] *Charakteranalyse*, 1933.

[5] 'Charakteranalyse und Neubeginn', *Int. Z. f. Psa.* (1934), **20**. ('Character Analysis and New Beginning.') Reprinted this vol., p. 159.

and by very slow degrees that they are openly admitted, and it is not until even later that their gratification is experienced as pleasure. I have called this phenomenon the 'New Beginning', and I believe I have established the fact that it occurs just before the end, in all sufficiently profound analyses, and that it even constitutes an essential mechanism of the process of cure.

Let us now turn to some criticisms. First, as I remarked at Wiesbaden, a single New Beginning is hardly ever enough. On the other hand, the patient need not make a New Beginning with all of the early instinctual wishes that were important for him. Moreover, after the analysis has ended, instincts may remain whose gratification brings no pleasure and even causes pain.

At this point a host of technical questions arise. Assuming that with the New Beginning we have in our hands an important criterion for the termination of the treatment, then one would like to know how many such recurrent waves of New Beginning are necessary and sufficient. Further, for which component instincts is a New Beginning obligatory, for which accidental, and finally, for which superfluous? I cannot answer any of these questions, and therefore I propose to examine the New Beginning more closely; perhaps we shall come to the opinion that these questions, however important they may appear to us now, do not arise from the actual facts of the case, and are therefore unanswerable.

Since all these phenomena appear only in the last phase of the treatment, and since, unfortunately, not a few analyses have to be broken off on practical grounds before this phase is reached, it was naturally some time before I became aware of a significant characteristic of these newly begun pleasurable activities. *They are, without exception, directed towards objects.* This discovery rather surprised me. According to our generally accepted theory of today, the first and most primitive phase of the libido is auto-erotic. I tried to reconcile my findings with the theory by arguing that the earlier phases of the development of the libido (auto-erotism and narcissism) were dealt with in the middle period of the treatment. Naturally, then, the carrying-over of the libido to object-relations must remain as a task for the final phase.

But I remained dissatisfied. The activities realised in this New Beginning period, as well as its phantasies, were so childish, so natural, so absolutely unproblematical, that I simply could not regard them as the final links in a complicated chain of development. And, to go farther, we have long known that in analytic treatment it is precisely the most deeply hidden, the most primitive layers that come to light last. Then came another constantly repeated observation. As I pointed out at Wiesbaden, after a first, and usually very timid, performance of the activity in question, a passionate phase habitually follows. The patients are seized, as it were, with an addiction. For days on end they can simply do nothing else but continually repeat these newly begun pleasurable actions, or, at least make phantasies about them. This is a dangerous situation for the continuation of the treatment. The patients were mostly so happy that they were able to deceive themselves and to begin with, I must admit, myself also. They feel ultra-healthy, and some made use of this fact, with my consent, to break off the treatment. This state of passionate happiness, resembling that felt by a drug addict, unfortunately does not last. As I learnt from a psychologically perceptive patient who came back to me, it degenerates into ever more and more extensive demands which at last can no longer be satisfied by any real object. The end is an intensified narcissism with overweening pride, self-importance and outstanding selfishness, veiled by superficial politeness and insincere modesty. (Perhaps this provides an explanation for the very similar behaviour of real addicts.)

If, however, both patient and analyst hold out, this passionate phase passes and in its place a true object-relation, adjusted to reality, develops before our eyes. Thus, to put it shortly, there is first an unmistakably primitive-infantile object-relation, and this—if not rightly understood and treated—ends in unrealisable demands and a narcissistic state, very disagreeable for the whole environment (as is the case with a spoiled child); if rightly guided, however, it gives way to a relation without conflicts for the subject as well as for those around him. These observations do not harmonise at all with the usual doctrine of the analytical libido theory, according to which auto-erotism should be the primal state of sexuality. A solution of this discrepancy can only be offered by a theoretical picture which is able, at the same time, to explain both the former theory of libidinal development, founded on innumerable clinical data, as well as these latter observations. This solution I found not only suggested but already to a considerable extent built up by Ferenczi.

In his favourite work—*Thalassa*—he describes a process which he calls the development of the erotic sense of reality. He sets forth three stages whose goal always remains the same, and which are distinguished only in that they strive to reach this common goal by different ways, better and better adjusted to reality. This goal is the return to the mother's womb (according to Ferenczi the primal aim of all human sexuality) and the three stages are: passive object-love, the auto-plastic or masturbating phase and finally the alloplastic phase, or, as I should like to call it—active object-love.

What is important for our problem is that the child, as Ferenczi has often pointed out, lives in a libidinal object-relation from the very beginning, and without this libidinal object-relation simply cannot exist; this relation is, however, *passive*. The child does not love but *is loved*. For a time the fostering outer world can fulfil its requirements; but with advancing age these become ever greater, more numerous and more difficult of realisation, so that some time or other real frustration is bound to come. The child replies to this with well-founded hate and aggressiveness, and with a turning away from reality, i.e. with an introversion of his love. If upbringing does not work against this change of direction, i.e. does not attempt to bind the child to reality with enough love, there follows the period of auto-erotic distribution of the libido, the period of various self-gratifications, of defiant self-sufficiency. In my opinion the 'anal-sadistic' and 'phallic phases', i.e. the observed forms of object-relations, theoretically comprised under these concepts, are artefacts. They do not represent stages or even points in the normal development of psycho-sexual relations to the outer world; they are not in any respect normal phenomena, but where they can be observed they point to a considerably disturbed development. They are signs of a rather sharp deflection in the normal psychosexual relations to the outer world, occasioned by a consistently unsuitable influence on the part of the environment—above all, by a lack of understanding in upbringing.

I have already given further evidence in support of this seemingly bold assertion before the Budapest Psycho-Analytical Society, and I hope to be able to publish them shortly in a separate paper.[1] Here I will only quote two passages from Freud. He shows in his *Introductory Lectures* that many component instincts of sexuality (such as sadism, for instance) possess an object from the very beginning. He continues: 'Others, more plainly connected with particular erotogenic areas in the body, only have an object in the beginning, so long as they are still dependent upon the non-sexual functions and give it up when they become detached from these latter'. Oral erotism is here referred to. The other passage runs: '*The oral impulse becomes auto-erotic*, as the anal and other erotogenic impulses are from the beginning. Further development has, to put it as concisely as possible, two aims: first, to renounce auto-erotism, to give up again the object found in the child's own body in exchange *again* for an external one.' (What follows does not relate to our present theme.) [2] Here it is explicitly declared that the oral instinct, which has hitherto served in theoretical discussions as the perfect example, as it were, of auto-erotism, passes through a stage of object-relationship at its very outset. What was new in my Budapest paper was the attempt to build up a theory which should take into account this fact, which is generally known but has never been fully appreciated.

According to this theory, all instincts, including those originally described as auto-erotic, are primarily bound to objects.[3] This primitive object-relation is always passive. This passive primal aim of human sexuality—the desire to be gratified, or, the desire to be loved—is preserved throughout life. Reality,

[1] 'Critical Notes on the Theory of the Pregenital Organisations of the Libido', this vol., p. 49.

[2] *Introductory Lectures on Psycho-analysis*, G. Allen and Unwin, London, Fifth edn., 1936, pp. 276–7. (The italics are mine.)

[3] I may refer here to a paper on 'The Development of the Capacity for Love and the Sense of Reality', by Alice Balint (published in Hungarian at Budapest in 1933) in which the author anticipated me in arriving at almost the same results by a different path. A later version of the paper 'Love for the Mother and Mother Love', in this vol., p. 109.

unavoidable frustration from without, forces man into by-paths, and he has to be content with these. One by-path is auto-erotism, narcissism: if the world does not gratify me, does not love me enough, I must gratify and love myself. The other by-path is active object-love; this attains the original aim better, but at a sacrifice. We love and gratify our partner (this is the sacrifice) so that in the end we may be gratified and loved by him in return.

If all this is true, then it is easily intelligible that every New Beginning has to take place in an object-relation. One cause of neurosis is always real frustration. Usually the analyst under-estimates the importance of this cause, because its counterpart in the aetiological complemental series, the endogenic factor, is continually pushed into the foreground by the analytic work. What we work at for months, even years, are the structural defects of the soul, the torn connections, the psychical material that was rendered incapable of becoming conscious. But one thing we should never forget is that all these defects of de-velopment, which we group under the collective name of 'the repressed', were originally forced into that state by external influences. That is to say, there is no repression without reality, without an object-relation. It is to the lasting credit of Ferenczi that, in the years during which interest was centred upon what was called 'ego-psychology' and upon the investigation of mental structure, he never tired of continually stressing the importance of external factors.

How necessary this was, and still is, I will show by a single example, and for this purpose I have chosen from among many other works one that can well bear criticism, since its excellent qualities are very generally recognised. I refer to Melanie Klein's illuminating book.[1]

If we turn to the index of that work we shall look in vain for the following words: lack of understanding in upbringing, parental sadism, unkindness, harshness, spoiling, want of love, and the like. It is a remarkable fact that the word 'love' is itself

---

[1] *The Psycho-analysis of Children*. Int. PsA. Libr. London, 1932.

[2] Naturally all these subjects are discussed, but the fact that they are absent from the index is of symptomatic importance. (The remarks in the text apply, of course, to the index of the German edition.)

absent.[2] (This word is absent too in the index to Fenichel's *Hysterie und Zwangsneurose*.) This corresponds to another feature of the book: the prominence which it gives to the structural factor and the innate constitution. I will give one example. Everywhere in the book (as well as in her Lucern Congress paper) Mrs. Klein speaks of the split 'good' and 'bad' mother imagos which the child creates in order to have an object always at hand for his constitutionally intensified sadism. Naturally, then, he must always be afraid of the vengeance of these hated and maltreated 'bad' imagos. But could it not perhaps be put in this way—that in the eyes of the child his parents are capricious beings who, quite unaccountably, are sometimes bad to him and sometimes good? And the more neurotic the behaviour of the parents the harder is the task of adjustment for the child, who, in the end, has no choice but to treat his mother, for instance, as two fundamentally different beings. Sometimes the 'fairy' is there, and sometimes the 'witch'. The fear of vengeance would then be revealed as a fear *determined by reality*, and the 'constitutionally' intense sadism as the effect of lack of understanding in upbringing. That something in my assumption is true is shown precisely by the success of child analysis. With an understanding upbringing on the part of a mother imago who does not behave neurotically—I am thinking of Mrs. Klein—the way to adjustment is opened to the child. I am of the opinion that it is a pity to stop at the structural defects of the mind; our path can lead us still farther, namely to errors of upbringing—or, as Ferenczi expressed it in his Wiesbaden paper, to the 'confusion of tongues' between the adults and the child.

Now we can understand also why the question as to the necessary number and origin of the newly begun gratifications turned out to be unanswerable. The question arose from a way of thinking that had become schematic and not from the actual facts of the case. It is not particular component instincts that must be begun anew but object-love itself.

With the help of these reflections I believe I have been able to formulate the final goal of psycho-analytic treatment more exactly. A person becomes ill because, from his childhood, he has been treated with more or less lack of understanding by those around him. Gratifications were denied him which were necessary to him, whereas others were forced on him which were superfluous, unimportant or even harmful. His mind, moreover, had to submit to external force: it had to build up various structures and, above all, what we call a super-ego, in order to make him able automatically to avoid conflicts with his reality. He comes to us; we co-operate in a study of his biological and mental structure, and try to bring this into connection with his conscious and primal history. Finally he understands his own nature, and also the long and painful process through which he was formed into the man he now knows. Many people who were not too severely damaged in their object-relation are content with the relief which comes with consciousness, with the accompanying better control of their actions and the extended capacity for pleasure. As the work progresses they become slowly, almost imperceptibly healthy. With them the real end phase of the treatment is absent, or, at most, is merely indicated.

With the others, however, who were made to suffer severely from the 'confusion of tongues', whose capacity for love was artificially wholly stunted by lack of understanding in their upbringing, quite a peculiar situation finally arises. Everything turns on one decision. Shall one regard all past suffering as over and done with, settle accounts with the past for good, and, in the last resort, try to make the best use of what possibilities there are in the life still lying ahead? This decision to begin to love really anew is far from easy. Here the analyst can help considerably. Right interpretations are important; by them he shows that he understands his ward and will not treat him with lack of understanding as was once the case. The most important thing here, however, is that one should take notice of the timid attempts, often only extremely feebly indicated, towards the New Beginning of the object-relation and not frighten them off. One should never forget that the beginnings of object-libido pursue passive aims and can only be brought to development through the tactful and, in the literal sense of the word, 'lovable' behaviour of the object. And even later one must treat these newly begun relations indulgently so that they may find their way to reality and active love.

Unfortunately not everyone can achieve this decision for a New Beginning of love. There are people who cannot give up demanding ever fresh compensation from the whole world for all the wrong ever done them, who know, indeed, that such behaviour is obsessive, and at the present time quite unreal—simply a transference—but, nevertheless, cannot give it up, who want only to be loved and are not able to give love. On a few occasions, though not often, I have come to this point with patients, and have not been able to bring them farther. These isolated cases, which, incidentally, showed considerable improvement, but which I was not able to cure, forced me to recognise the limits of my therapeutic powers. With my present technique I can only cure such people as, in the course of the analytic work, can acquire the ability to attempt to begin to love anew. How those few others are to be helped I do not at present see. But I do not believe that we need let ourselves be defeated by the constitutional factors. Ferenczi always used to say that as long as a patient is willing to continue the treatment, a way must be found to help him. Those who knew his way of working know that with him this was no empty phrase. He made many experiments, and he also succeeded in helping many who had already been given up by others as hopeless. Unfortunately not all. The old proverb has proved true again: *ars longa, vita brevis*. It is the duty of the pupils to carry on the work which the master began.

I am at the end of my paper. I believe I have shown that it was one-sided to base our theories and our way of thinking principally on structural considerations and on the instinctual constitution. Without wishing to detract from the great achievement of the researches made in this direction, I have endeavoured to point out that the study of loving object-relations, which has been gravely neglected in recent years, can contribute much towards the understanding of the human mind and towards the improvement of our therapeutic powers. In my opinion there is today too much talk about constitutionally determined sadism and masochism in analytical theory. Thus the motto of my paper would run: less sadism and more love.

XII

STRENGTH OF THE EGO AND ITS
EDUCATION [1]

(1938)

Since the publication of Freud's *The Ego and the Id* in 1923, the conception of the 'weak ego' has been commonly accepted. It is curious that this has come about so rapidly and with so little opposition in spite of the established psycho-analytic theory tracing all neurotic symptoms to the conflict between the sexual instincts and the interests of the ego. If the ego is in fact weak, how can it be such an energetic advocate of its own interests that in this struggle it forces a continual compromise, thus producing a constant neurotic symptom? This and other similar questions, however, have not been asked. Instead, the theory explored another path, keeping close to the assumption of the weak ego and even exaggerating it. The interests of the ego disappeared almost entirely from our theoretical considerations, and their place is now taken by various demands, such as those of the id, the environment and the super-ego. The ego itself is regarded as having almost no interests of its own; and the theoretical discussion is occupied solely with its dependence and the tasks that it has to fulfill. The result of this view becomes evident in the subject indexes of books by psycho-analysts, where there is less conscious revision than in the text itself. Thus it will be seen that in all works that have appeared since 1930, the headings 'Interests of the Ego' and 'Strength of the Ego' are no longer to be found.[2] This is all the more remarkable because already in 1926 in 'Inhibition, Symptom

---

[1] Paper read at the Fifteenth International Psycho-analytical Congress, Paris, 1938. Published in German in *Int. Z.f. Psa.* (1939), **27**,417; in English: *The PsA. Quart.* (1942), **11**, 87.

[2] See: Fenichel: *Hysterien und Zwangsneurosen*, Vienna, 1931; Fenichel: *Perversionen, Psychosen usw*, Vienna, 1931; M. Klein: *Die Psychoanalyse des Kindes*, Vienna, 1932; Nunberg: *Allg. Neurosenlehre*, Bern, 1932; as also the annual indexes of *The Psycho-analytic Quarterly* and *Ztschr. f. psa. Pädagogik*.

and Anxiety,'[1] three years after the publication of *The Ego and the Id*, Freud warned us not to forget that the ego can also be strong. It is true he only cited a few cases in which this strength was clearly noticeable, but that is because he was then merely concerned with proving the occasional strength of the ego. Our theory has not paid much attention to this point and the organisers of the Congress [2] are to be congratulated for putting this much-neglected theme up for discussion.

What do we today understand by the 'strength of the ego'? The concept, as has so often happened with new ideas—as though by purpose—in the history of psycho-analysis, has never been clearly defined. In clinical work with patients, however, what is meant when we speak of the strength of the ego is roughly understood. It quite often happens that we hesitate as to whether to give a particular interpretation to the patient or to wait. In such cases we are uncertain whether there is not a danger of the patient reacting so violently against the interpretation that his peaceful collaboration may be greatly endangered, the id being aroused and the ego incited to defend itself. What, then, does the analyst hope for when he allows some days, weeks or even months to elapse? Certainly not a revolutionary change in the id; it is in any case open to question whether the id in adults can be changed at all by our technical means. Rather, he hopes for a strengthening of the ego, that is to say, that it may gradually become capable of a calm acceptance of what would have excited it earlier. This is an extremely important technical problem. The analyst, whether consciously or not, gauges at each of his technical measures the actual strength of the ego, and bases his behaviour towards the patient, above all his interpretation, upon this. The words in which he puts it, and also the time when he gives it, are so chosen that the ego, even though with considerable strain, can bear it.[3]

---

[1] *Gesammelte Schriften*, XI, p. 34.   [2] Paris, 1938.

[3] Both conditions are equally important: The bearing of the interpretation (the technical measures in general) must, where possible, impose a strain on the ego; not, however, one so acute as to incite a still greater defence. On the one hand there is the danger that the interpretation may not provoke any reaction at all, on the other that it may provoke a useless defence, which considerably increases the difficulty of the analytic work.

Let us consider the case of a correct interpretation, e.g. one that reveals a hitherto automatic form of defence, with the result that this particular defence mechanism can now only be consciously made use of. Should the patient attempt to resort to it again automatically, this will be pointed and followed by a repetition of the interpretation. Freud calls this more or less persistent struggle 'working through'. This form of defence is, when all goes well, finally abandoned, and the ego becomes capable of bearing this specific kind of tension. Thus 'strengthening of the ego' and 'working through' are conceptions which describe very similar, if not identical, clinical experiences. We are now faced with the task of describing the very important concept of 'working through' in terms of the psychology of the ego.

By 'working through' is to be understood a gradual change of the ego. Its progress is measured by the varying ability of ego to endure a specific kind of instinctual tension (the one that is being 'worked through') to an increasing degree. Perhaps we can also speak of a growing capacity of the ego in relation to this type of tension, and are thereby reminded of an electric condenser, say a Leyden jar, which has the remarkable characteristic of collecting electricity, or energy, without any considerable increase in tension. The charge of energy can be very high and still, given a correct structure, there is no danger of a sudden undesirable and useless discharge.[1]

The capacity of a condenser is determined by two factors: (a) its dimensions; (b) the efficiency of the insulation, i.e. by the degree to which faulty places occur in the dielectricum used. Now it is worthy of note that just these, and only these, two variables are used in theoretic descriptions of changes in the ego. It is commonly said that the ego grows, or, as the case may be, shrinks. So, for example, Freud defines the task of analytic therapy as aiming at the result: where id was, ego

---

[1] Actually I am putting it the wrong way round. The tool 'condenser' was unconsciously made from the image of the human ego, and is thus, like most tools, a projection of one of the human organs. Cf. S. Ferenczi: 'Zur Psychogenese der Mechanik', *Imago*, **5**, 1917–19 (reprinted in *Populäre Vorträge*, Vienna, 1922). English translation in: *Further Contributions*.

shall be.[1] All topographical descriptions of 'making conscious' use the idea of growth of the ego. Federn [2] speaks of the broadening and narrowing of the ego boundaries. Widening of the ego is a term often used as synonymous with introjection, just as shrinking of the ego is with projection. In other attempts at describing the process, the stress is laid not on the dimensions but on the degree of insulation. Freud often pointed out that in an analysis it is especially the faulty points in the structure of the ego that must be repaired. These originate from a disturbance in the development of the ego, and are the *loci minoris resistentiae* which can either facilitate an undesired short-circuit or breakdown, or, on the other hand, have to be carefully guarded against by reaction-formations. In the same way a condenser will be most likely to break down at any faulty point in the dielectricum or, alternatively, its capacity will be considerably diminished if we make the insulation unnecessarily thick.

Considered thus, our image of the ego as condenser, and of the strength of the ego as capacity, is perhaps something more than a metaphor, especially when we take the Lamarckian conception into account, according to which the attributes of living beings can be altered by desire and practice. Whether or not Lamarck's theory in this general form is true remains undecided, but it is undoubtedly completely valid for certain functions of the ego.[3] Let us consider, for example, piano playing or ski-ing; these aptitudes can certainly be altered by practice and desire. One has only to recall the history of world records: performances which thirty years ago were looked upon in astonishment are often not sufficient today to ensure the athlete a modest placing in a provincial competition. What can so simply and incontestably be proved with regard to the physical performances of the ego can hardly be denied to its

[1] *Gesammelte Schriften*, XII, p. 234.
[2] cf. *Imago* (1936), **22**.
[3] Much very sound ego psychology is contained in the theories of exact natural science. It is quite impossible for us to do our thinking except on anthropomorphic lines. While our experiences cannot be anthropomorphic, the explanation and understanding of them can only come about by projection or introjection, and has, therefore, unavoidably an anthropomorphic foundation.

mental ones. Furthermore, the far-reaching human capacity for discipline, as seen in the practice of Yogi, in religious orders, as well as in military service, and in education in general, supplies sufficient convincing examples of the markedly alterable character of certain mental activities of the ego.

For the sake of simplicity I should like, at first, to leave out of account the influence of the super-ego. This, incidentally, does not play a decisive part in certain activities (ski-ing, for example). The above-cited alterations doubtless take place in the ego. The result, in every successful case, is a strengthening of the ego. It can now perform, at will, what it was not previously capable of. The process by which this new ability has been acquired is that of *learning*. This word has two meanings. One is the reception and proper registration of sensory impressions and intellectual correlations; that is probably its newer meaning, and in English 'to learn' has almost solely this significance. The second, and probably the older meaning, is best demonstrated by the German compounds such as: *'ertragenlernen'*, *'aushaltenlernen'*, which imply the sense of bringing a faculty to full development.[1]

These two meanings of the verb 'to learn' correspond to the two factors which determine the capacity of the condenser. Intellectual learning, the reception of new elements, corresponds to the enlarging of the dimensions, while learning to endure corresponds to an improved insulation. We have already seen the close relationship between 'strengthening of the ego' and 'working through', and now we may ask should 'learning'

---

[1] This meaning is somewhat nearer to that of the English verb 'to train', though this I feel lays much too much emphasis on the goal. The accepted root of the word 'lernen' is 'leis', 'ich habe erfahren, erwandert', out of which the active 'lêrjan' = 'lehren' = 'erfahren, wissend machen' is derived; and from its participle then originated 'liznan' = 'lernen' = 'erfahren, wissend werden'. The related word 'list' was used in Old German and Middle High German in a praiseworthy sense as 'experience' or 'experienced'. (See: Kluge-Götz: *Etymologisches Wörterbuch der deutschen Sprache*, 1934. I am indebted to Dr. E. Lüders for drawing my attention to this work.)

In Hungarian the corresponding word has a root 'tanu' = 'a witness'. 'lehren' = 'tanitani' actually means 'to make a witness of someone', 'to turn (someone) into a witness'; 'lernen' = 'tanulni' thus means 'to become a witness', 'to be changed into a witness'.

be included in the same category? The question then arises, however, that if 'strengthening of the ego' is synonymous with, or even only related to 'learning', it follows that psycho-analysis and education are also closely related, from which there arises the seeming danger of the analytic treatment degenerating into pedagogy.

One may, however, recall that Anna Freud has described how children must often first be made capable of analysis, 'educated to analysis'. In spite of initial resistance, this method has established itself and an ever-increasing number of analysts describe it as an unavoidable phase of the treatment. Ferenczi has written of a *Child Analysis in the Analysis of Adults* ('Kinderanalyse an Erwachsenen'[1]) in which similar facts were observed. As the analytic method has approached, ever more boldly, the great problem of the treatment of psychotics, it has had to recognise—however reluctantly—that such patients in the early period of their treatment must, in fact, be 'educated to analysis'.

Finally, it should not be forgotten that the entire analytic situation is an artificial one to which patients—many of them only after overcoming considerable difficulties—must consistently be educated. There are cases in which they have to learn to appear punctually at the beginning of the session and —what is far more difficult—to leave punctually at the end. Further to be considered are the free associations, as well as sincerity and frankness, to which our patients must also be educated. The interpretations are certainly of considerable help in this development, but the entire procedure is, especially through its rigidly determined goal, far more akin to education than, for example, to the eradication of a neurotic symptom.

From the standpoint of the analyst all patients, whether children, neurotics or psychotics, have to be educated; that is to say, they must learn. Their ego has not the strength to meet the demands made by an analytic treatment, and so its primary task is to strengthen the ego. We have now four closely related concepts, each with a solid clinical basis: 'strengthening of the ego', 'working through', 'learning or training', 'education to

[1] *Int. J. of PsA.* (1931), **12**, 468.

analysis'.[1] It is clear that education for analysis and learning are descriptions of the same process; it only remains to show that 'strengthening of the ego' and 'working through' also describe the one and same process. Let us turn back for a moment to our condenser and see where and how it is used in practice. It will be employed wherever a spark formation, that is, wherever a useless loss of energy is to be avoided or lessened. The condenser prevents any sudden rise of tension and gathers the surplus energy into itself, without considerable increase of tension, so that it can later release it again with hardly any loss. Freud's idea that the free floating energy of the primary process is tonically bound by the secondary process until it can be discharged in a manner adapted to the demands of reality, seems like a paraphrase of this process.

Freud developed these ideas in the first edition of his *Interpretation of Dreams*; they have, however, scarcely ever been tested, and never actually been used as a working hypothesis. Since the introduction of the concept of the super-ego these ideas have become specially difficult to integrate into the rest of our theory. We are used to ascribe all forms of endurance summarily to obedience to the commands of the super-ego; only the dependence of the ego has been studied, its structure and proper functions hardly at all. I do not deny that in very many cases the ego is obedient to the super-ego in enduring the inflowing stream of stimulation from the id, but this is not always so. There are many occasions where it is demonstrable, beyond doubt, that the ego endures considerable strains for its own purpose, one might say out of pure joy, and even against the commands of the super-ego. The best examples of this are to be found in the field of sports from simple hiking to acrobatic rock climbing, from easy keep-fit exercises to the keenest competition. Here we find the individual acting against the

[1] Thomas M. French in 'A Clinical Study of Learning in the Course of a Psycho-analytic Treatment', *PsA. Quarterly*, **5**, 1936, develops similar ideas on learning and working through, without, however, stressing the connection between these two concepts and that of the strengthening of the ego. He goes on to give a very clear description of the way analysis constantly sets the patient various tasks, but does not draw the conclusion that there obviously exists a certain relationship between analysis and education.

pleasure principle and, without any external compulsion, subjecting himself to the greatest strain and stimulation for the pure joy of it. Similar observations can be made in the case of those who learn for the love of it.

I think Rank [1] was the first to call attention to the fact that 'we seek to increase pleasure by creating 'internal resistances'. It is unnecessary to document this thesis with a mass of proofs. For present considerations it is unimportant whether all these resistances arise from an introjection of external commands; whether, that is, they come from the super-ego. It is only important that they and the condenser functions of the ego are reciprocally involved. Without these resistances the attainable pleasure remains slight because only too small amounts of stimulation can be accumulated; without a sufficiently strong ego, a slight intensifying of excitement will lead to a short-circuiting discharge.

These relations can be most instructively studied in the sphere of the orgastic function.[2] The pleasure in orgasm depends on the intensity of sexual stimulation arrived at during the act of intercourse. *Artes amandi* in all literatures are simply instructions on how to deliberately increase the stimulation before and during orgasm. This intensification is both pleasant and unpleasant at the same time—Freud called attention to this already in the 'Three Contributions'—but the bearing of this strain is a test of the power of endurance, from which only persons with healthy egos will emerge successfully. To return once more to the condenser, small amounts of energy can be easily accumulated without danger of a haphazard discharge. But should a spark really be wanted, it will be a much more powerful one than any that the same source of energy could produce without a condenser.

Can the endurance, and still more the deliberate increase of sexual excitement during coitus, be explained as obedience to the commands of the super-ego? Surely it is obviously more of a conscious infringement of such commands often amounting to an offence against shame, disgust, pity, etc.; and therefore a

[1] Rank, Otto: *Der Künstler*. Heller, Vienna. First edn., 1907.

[2] Balint, Michael: 'Eros and Aphrodite'. (1938). Reprinted in this vol., p. 73.

triumph of the ego over the super-ego? A further proof is given by the analytical cure of *ejaculatio praecox*. Sexual excitement can be better endured after the analysis, certainly not because the super-ego, but because the ego has been strengthened. I think this much is enough to show that the endurance of strain does not only take place at the command of the super-ego, but that it can also run counter to any such command and constitute an autonomous function of the ego.[1]

All this we have long known and have even acted accordingly. The aim of every analytical treatment has always been to modify the severity of the automatically functioning super-ego, and in its place to develop in the patient an ego capable of bearing heavy strains. Thus, in practice, it has always been taken for granted that perseverance and endurance can also be proper functions of the ego. Theoretically, though, this fact, firmly based on clinical experience, has been left out of account; and this is undoubtedly because it has always brought us up against the theoretically unsolved problem as to what the significance and the function of pedagogy within the analytical treatment actually is.

Two very telling experiences can be brought to bear against the combining of psycho-analysis and pedagogy. Every analytical session brings us new proof of how disastrously education can influence the capacity for pleasure, the sense of the joy of life, or mental health in general. We know only too well that in the highly emotional atmosphere of transference the analyst's every word carries a very great authority, and can have very marked and unforeseen effects. Analysis has naturally been very careful to avoid this responsibility. On the other hand, we tried to apply the results arrived at by psycho-analysis to pedagogy. Thus there arose a valuable criticism of educational methods, though at first a merely negative one. The later positive advice, given tentatively, had at first to be modified, then considerably qualified and finally withdrawn, as Anna Freud most convincingly did in her address given on the occasion of the Second Four Countries' Conference in Budapest in 1937. This address culminated in the statement

---

[1] It is certainly not necessary to show that this endurance cannot be a function of the id.

that, after years of intensive work by some of the best psycho-analytical research workers, we are certain only that there still exists no practicable psycho-analytical pedagogy.

Psycho-analysis, both in its negative criticism and in its positive advice, has hitherto largely, if not exclusively, concerned itself with only one branch of pedagogy. This branch includes all the restrictions imposed by society on the individual, such as those in regard to cleanliness, feelings of shame and disgust, pity, aesthetics, morals, reverence, etc. These are the feelings which draw their strength from the super-ego. Psycho-analytic pedagogy has been chiefly a pedagogy of the super-ego, and its main problem was to find out what type of educational method, and applied in what degree of intensity, was best fitted to achieve an optimal formation of the super-ego.

That the general problem of education appeared to us in this particular form was due directly to the fact that psycho-analytical theory had been largely developed on the basis of the study of obsessional neurosis and depression. The problem of hysteria, although this was the sphere in which Freud began his investigations, has been more and more neglected in later theoretical discussions. To mention only a single but very telling example of this: Anna Freud in *The Ego and the Mechanisms of Defence* [1] does not even mention among the ten forms of defence the two which are characteristic of hysteria: displacement and conversion. This omission well characterises the now dominant attitude of psycho-analytical theory.

The obsessional neurotic has in general a rather well-developed ego with a considerable capacity for enduring tension. It is not rare, for instance, that persons suffering from severe obsessions can practise their callings in such a way that often no one is aware of their illness. Theoretically this is quite understandable; one of the main conditions for the formation of an obsession is that the stimulation, though divided into small quantities, remains within the ego and is neither repressed nor converted. The analysis of an obsessional neurotic will, correspondingly, far less often have to trouble, after making the repressions conscious, about strengthening the ego —a task which very often, indeed almost regularly, has to be

[1] Int. PsA. Library, The Hogarth Press, London, 1937.

faced in cases of hypochondria, hysteria or similar diseases. It is interesting to recall in this connection the well-known case of Anna O., who, having consciously remembered all the pathogenic events, intentionally exposed herself to a reproduction of the former pathogenic situation, although in a modified form, and thereby inaugurated the intermingling of pedagogic and analytical methods.[1] Her disease became known as a classic example of hysteria.

Psycho-analytical ego psychology has also largely been founded upon the study of obsessions and depressions. When more closely considered, it reveals itself as a psychology of dependences, or, to put it differently, to a small extent as a psychology of the id, but in the main as a psychology of the super-ego. In it the ego itself becomes merely a battle-ground. As psycho-analytical ego-psychology and psycho-analytical pedagogy are almost of the same age, they have had a far-reaching influence on each other's development. From the beginning both have been dominated by an emphasis on the rôle of the super-ego.

We know, however, that there is to be a true psychology of the ego and a genuine ego pedagogy, but also that they will have to be much more complex than that of the super-ego. Everything connected with the super-ego remains within the realms of psychology. But the ego is, above all, a body ego and the problems that arise here make manifold encroachments on to the field of biology, taking 'the mysterious leap into the organic'. One of the reasons why psycho-analysis has occupied itself less with this sphere has undoubtedly been this complexity, although it is here that answers to such problems as auto- and alloplasticity, sublimation and, above all, the discharge of fore- as well as end-pleasure may be found. What we know about these processes and their laws is very little when compared, for instance, to our knowledge of the primary process. Only so much is certain, that these four phenomena are functions of the ego. It is true that they are built up on inherent abilities but must all the same be laboriously learned.[2]

---

[1] Breuer-Freud: *Studien über Hysterie*, 1916, Vienna, Third edn., p. 32.

[2] As Byron so well said in his remark about his poetry being one-quarter inspiration and three-quarters perspiration.

Moreover, one of their conditions is reality testing, which is also something that has to be learnt.

'To learn' then, as we have seen, does not only denote the introjection of commands which, as super-ego, are further developed and strengthened. On the contrary, 'to learn' signifies in its original sense 'to become experienced', to enrich and develop the ego; just what, in fact, has for long been the aim of psycho-analytical treatment. *Making the unconscious conscious is only one aspect of this, the other is the strengthening of the ego.* The unconscious material brought to light varies in individual cases and is determined by the previous history of the patient. The strengthening of the ego, the teaching it to endure what hitherto had to be repressed, the strict maintenance of the analytical situation, the continual pressing forward towards full sincerity, the education to analysis, the 'learning' or 'experiencing' of new correlations, etc., are the ever-constant elements of every analytical treatment that are independent of the patient's individual history or form of disease. The problems to be solved are not here determined by the patients but by us. All this also is education but it is an education of the ego, contrasted here intentionally to the education of the super-ego.

To avoid possible misunderstanding, I would like once more to stress that the education of the ego is not a technical measure specially to be employed during the treatment; *it is rather an immanent component of the analysis.* Analysis has not been recognised as an education of the ego because to us pedagogy has simply meant education of the super-ego, that is to say: exhortations, moralising and especially the laying down of values. Naturally, within the analytical treatment, all this, in fact the whole education of the super-ego, must, for obvious reasons, now as ever, be strictly rejected.[1]

Psycho-analytical treatment certainly does not work in favour of but rather against the super-ego, because it aims at making what has become rigid elastic again, and at turning the automatic 'categoric imperative' of the super-ego into

[1] The difference between strengthening the ego (training the instincts) and super-ego formation has been described by Alice Balint: 'Versagen und Gewähren in der Erziehung'. *Z. f. psa. Päd.* (1936), **10.**

decisions and actions of the ego freely made and adapted to the demands of reality. For this, however, an efficient ego with a suitable capacity is necessary, an ego which has also 'learnt' to endure a high degree of instinctual tension. In my opinion much too much attention has lately been devoted to the earliest states in the development of the ego and the never observable origins of its formation. It is time for us to study more closely the clinically observable changes in the ego, which we can do daily.

Both these factors—the again and again demonstrable disastrous and often severely pathogenic effects of education on the one hand, and the impossibility of evolving a practicable psycho-analytical pedagogy on the other—have led psycho-analysis to abandon without examination everything that shows any resemblance to pedagogy. Thus a kind of phobia has developed which was certainly justified as long as pedagogy was simply identified with education of the super-ego. If, however, we make the strict differentiation proposed here, between education of the ego and that of the super-ego, we need no longer be afraid of analysis degenerating into pedagogy. Instead, we can have grounds for hoping that in the more minute study of the processes within the ego during working through, during the education to analysis and, in general, during the strengthening of the ego, a psychological basis will be laid on which a sound pedagogy can and must be built. This can best be realised by concentrating our attention and investigations much more intensively on the problems of hysteria and related pathological forms, which is only to say that just as more than forty years ago we are once more in need of 'Studies in Hysteria'.

XIII

ON TRANSFERENCE AND COUNTER-TRANSFERENCE [1]

(1939)

Written in collaboration with ALICE BALINT

A QUESTION which frequently arises in psycho-analytical discussions on technical themes is whether transference is brought about by the patient alone, or whether the behaviour of the analyst may have a part in it too. On such occasions one opinion is always put forward emphatically by certain analysts. It runs roughly as follows: 'If and when the analyst has influenced the transference situation by any means other than his interpretations, he has made a grave mistake.' The purpose of this paper is to investigate whether and how far this opinion corresponds to the facts.

The phenomenon of transference can best be demonstrated if its object is an inanimate, lifeless thing, e.g. the door which was banged because the cause of our anger was behind it. With a living being, the whole situation becomes infinitely more complex, because (a) the second person is also striving to get rid of his unvented emotions by transferring them on to the first, and (b) he will react to the emotions transferred on to him by the first person. The situation is hopelessly inextricable, unless one of the persons involved will voluntarily undertake the task of not transferring any of his feelings on to the other for a definite period, i.e. to behave as nearly as possible like an inanimate thing. This conception is the basis of Freud's often quoted simile: the analyst must behave like the surface of a well-polished mirror—a lifeless thing. Analysis has also often been compared with a surgical operation, and the behaviour of the analyst with the sterility of the surgeon. Again, we have the condition of lifelessness, for the word 'sterile' originally meant 'not producing a crop or fruit'.

[1] First published in *Int. J. of PsA.* (1939), **20**, 223–30.

The fact that there can be transference on to inanimate objects as well as on to living beings settles one part of our problem; for it shows that transference may be a one-sided process, i.e. that it may develop without any assistance from another person. The opinion which demands that the analyst shall not in any way assist in the formation of the transference is undoubtedly strengthened by this fact. Let us inquire how far the demand for perfect sterility is satisfied by the actual analytic technique. That is, let us see whether the 'passivity' (which means in this connection the same thing as sterility) of the analyst is in fact quite free from any traces of his own transference.

Some of the elements which unavoidably trouble the ideal of perfect sterility were fully discussed by Freud,[1] and thus we need not consider them in detail. Freud has emphasised the fact that analysis does not take place in a vacuum: the analyst has a name, is male or female, is of a particular age, has a home, etc.; in a very broad sense, we transfer these elements of our personality on to our patients. To deal with the reactions caused by these elements requires, in fact, a certain amount of technical skill, and these problems are often discussed in control analyses as well as in our technical seminars.

There are, however, many more such personal elements, which, though often discussed by analysts in private circles and even with a very keen interest, have scarcely if ever been mentioned publicly.

A very typical detail of this kind is 'the problem of the cushion'. There are several solutions to this problem: (a) the cushion remains the same for every patient, but a piece of tissue paper is spread over it, which is thrown away at the end of the hour; (b) the cushion remains, but every patient is given a special cover, distinguishable from the others by its shade or design, and for each hour the cushion is put into the appropriate cover; (c) each patient has his own cushion and must use only his; (d) there is only one cushion or only two or three of them for all the patients and it is left to them to use them as they like, etc. Moreover these possibilities have to be multiplied by at least three, because the situation differs according to

---

[1] In his papers on technique, *Collected Papers*, II.

whether the analyst, the patient or a servant manipulates the cushion.

A bagatelle, it may be thought, which it is almost ridiculous to treat at such length. And yet such trifles seem to have a certain importance in the formation of the transference situation. For instance, one patient, who for external reasons had had to change his analyst, dreamt of his first analyst as working in a highly modern, white-tiled W.C., well fitted with every hygienic refinement, and of the second as working in an old-fashioned, dirty, stinking place. It is not difficult to guess which solution of the 'problem of the cushion' was favoured by the first analyst and which by the second. The dream analysis showed clearly that the patient drew certain conclusions as regards his two analysts' different attitudes towards cleanliness from the way in which they treated the cushion problem. No one is likely to dispute that an analysis conducted in an atmosphere corresponding to the first part of the dream will take a different course from what it would in an atmosphere corresponding to the second part. For the present we are not concerned with the problem of whether or not one condition is more favourable to the progress of an analysis than the other. We only wish to assert that there do exist differences in the analytical atmosphere which are brought about by the analyst himself. (One must however bear in mind that each of the two analysts maintained the same attitude concerning the cushion towards every one of his patients, that is to say, his personal contribution to the analytical atmosphere was the same in all cases. This is a point to which we shall have to return later.)

The same is true of a whole number of such details. Another important point, for instance, is the way in which the end of the session is announced. Some analysts get up from their chairs, thus giving the signal. Others simply announce it in stereotyped words; others again try to invent new formulas for each session; some begin to move to and fro in their chairs and the patient has to infer from the sound that the time is over; others again use alarm clocks, or keep a clock in front of the patient so that he may himself see the time passing. Then there is the couch itself, which may be low, broad, comfortable, or quite the contrary; the chair of the analyst; the arrangement of the consulting-room—shall it be furnished as a study or as a drawing-room? or shall it be left totally unfurnished apart from the couch and the chair?—the method of lighting the room, etc.

The items that have just been enumerated are—so to say—tangible features of the analyst's behaviour. Certainly it is not a bold inference to conclude that many more such 'personal' elements influence our intangible analytical attitude as well. For instance, some analysts are parsimonious with their interpretations, and give one only when its correctness is practically certain; others are rather lavish, even at the risk of giving a number of incorrect ones. Some analysts do not encourage a silent patient to speak, others frequently do so, and so on.

Then there is the very delicate and very intricate problem of what should be interpreted to the patient and when and how. It is remarkable that the advocates of the different methods of interpretation, as well as their critics, are inclined to think that only their own technique is correct, and consider all other methods bad or even harmful. This arouses a suspicion that some personal element may be playing a part in the evaluation of the various ways of solving the problem, since differences in effectiveness do not always correspond to the stress laid upon them, as was pointed out by Edward Glover at the Paris Congress in 1938.

In the last fifteen years several procedures have been suggested. Let us quote them, followed in each case by the appropriate criticism: (1) The characteristic behaviour of the patient should at once be interpreted, at the very beginning of the treatment, even in the first analytical session, and subsequently again and again; another opinion maintains that such procedure is likely to produce unnecessary resistance in the patient. (2) Above all and first of all the actual meaning, the one relating to the analytical situation, to the transference, should be interpreted; the contrary opinion declares that the threads leading to the infantile situations should first be followed up. (3) A deep interpretation should be given as soon as possible: the deeper the early interpretations the more effective they are; others advise one to be very cautious in this respect, to give deep interpretations only if the material is strong enough to convince a resistant patient unconditionally.

(4) The defensive mechanisms have first to be interpreted irrespectively of the infantile material, even though it may present itself quite clearly; others maintain that both the infantile material and the defensive mechanisms may be interpreted at the same time, etc.[1]

But besides these major differences, the very fine shades present in the formulation of an interpretation or even of a seemingly indifferent communication, the choice of one or the other of the many synonymous possibilities, the accentuation or non-accentuation of certain words, even their cadence or intonation, naturally vary from analyst to analyst. The best argument for the existence of a personal element in all this is the fact that in control analyses words are very often used by the controlling analyst to the following effect: 'What you said to your patient was quite correct; only I should have said it in rather different words, and certainly with a different stress.'

In addition to these variations in technique which characterise the general attitude of one analyst towards all his patients, there are others arising from our conscious adaptation to the requirements of particular cases. With a child, for instance, we shall have to behave differently from the way in which we do with a grown-up; it is a fairly common practice to call a child patient by his Christian name and also to allow him to call us by ours; he is permitted and even encouraged by us to play during the analytical hour; he may touch us, sometimes gently but sometimes aggressively, etc., etc. The situation is almost the same with psychotics. This similarity between child-analysis and the analysis of a psychosis has been described and emphasised so often as to be already a commonplace.

Of course, every patient has to be, and is actually, treated individually, i.e. differently, and thus every analysis carried out by the same analyst is different from every other one; nevertheless it is undeniable that there are several individually different ways of analysing, different analytical atmospheres, so to say, created and maintained by the individual analyst's technique and personality. Naturally certain psychological

[1] For literature see Ferenczi and Rank, *Entwicklungsziele der Psychoanalyse*, 1924; Strachey: 'The Nature of the Therapeutic Action of Psycho-Analysis', *Int. J. of PsA.*, **5**, 1934; Anna Freud: *The Ego and the Mechanisms of Defence*, 1937. Int. PsA. Library. The Hogarth Press, London.

features usually go together with certain of the more physical, tangible, details described above.

Remembering the metaphor of the mirror, is it not remarkable that there are so many individual ways of analysing? And is it not still more remarkable that if the analyst happens to be a training analyst, almost all of his pupils when they begin to work 'independently' are likely to use his methods, from the form of interpretation to the—let us say—way of furnishing their consulting-rooms and of announcing the end of the analytical hour, thus giving a convincing proof that the real source of all these recurring features is transference, which in the case of an analyst in the analytical situation is euphemistically described as 'counter-transference'. The danger of being stuck fast in such a transference is one of the arguments in favour of the demand that at least one part of each control analysis shall be conducted by some analyst (or better by some analysts) other than the training analyst.

Looked at from this point of view the analytical situation is the result of an interplay between the patient's transference and the analyst's counter-transference, complicated by the reactions released in each by the other's transference on to him. If this is so—and it really is so—are we to conclude that there is no such thing as the 'sterile' method of analysing? That the opinion quoted at the beginning of this paper is based on an ideal never attained in practice? Formerly belief in the absolute validity of the mirror-like attitude was so firm that contesting it was liable to be regarded as a sign of desertion. And now—not only in the present paper—the very possibility of such an attitude is challenged. The circumstance that two such opinions could be formed, and both on the basis of ample clinical experience, explains the frequent discussions upon this subject and justifies our writing this paper.

The solution of the controversy can be arrived at by clinical experience only. The second opinion would lead one to expect that the different analytical atmospheres created by the analyst's personality would exercise a decisive influence upon the actual transference situation and consequently upon the therapeutic results as well. Curiously enough, this does not seem to be so. Our patients, with very few exceptions, are able to adapt themselves to most of these individual atmospheres and to proceed with their own transference, almost undisturbed by the analyst's counter-transference. This implies that all of these techniques are good enough to enable patients with average disturbances in the development of their emotional life to build up a transference which is favourable to analytical work. Though the advocates of one or the other techniques, especially those of certain particular methods of interpretation, maintain that all methods except their own are less effective, actual analytical results do not seem to substantiate this claim. The statistics of the different local psycho-analytical institutes show, upon the whole, almost the same percentages of successful and unsuccessful treatments,[1] and, further, however different the individual variants of psycho-analytical technique may be, they do not seem able to influence the average duration of treatments.

One must reluctantly admit that for the average neurotic patient these individual variants of technique do not greatly matter. Why then the heated discussions and the comparative intolerance in matters of technique? The ardour with which the individual methods are defended is an interesting instance of the well-known social phenomenon known as 'the narcissistic overvaluation of small differences'. As we have seen, one main source of the analyst's individual technique is the transference of emotions; i.e. our technique, our analytical behaviour, has an important economical value too, being a well-adapted, well-rationalised, sublimated way of alleviating strains, especially those arising within us while we are dealing with our patients.

We have not forgotten, of course, that our technique has first to comply with the objective demands of our work and naturally cannot be only an outlet for the emotions of the analyst. Viewed from the standpoint of the mental economy of the analyst, each technique has to cope with these two different tasks. The objective task demands that a patient analysed in any of the many individual ways shall learn to know his own

[1] *Zehn Jahre Berliner Psychoanalytisches Institut*, 1930; The London Clinic of Psycho-Analysis: *Decennial Report*, 1936; Institute of Psycho-Analysis, Chicago: *Five-Year Report*, 1937.

unconscious mind and not that of his analyst. The subjective task demands that analysing shall not be too heavy an emotional burden, that the individual variety of technique shall procure sufficient emotional outlet for the analyst. A sound and adequate technique must therefore be doubly individual.

This means that we have highly personal motives for fervently defending our individual methods of analysing. But, in doing so, we do not fight for our mental comfort alone, but for what is, objectively as well as subjectively, the best method. Returning to Freud's metaphor, we see that the analyst must really become like a well-polished mirror—not, however, by behaving passively like an inanimate thing, but by reflecting without distortion the whole of his patient. The more clearly the patient can see himself in the reflection, the better our technique; and if this has been achieved, it does not matter greatly how much of the analyst's personality has been revealed by his activity or passivity, his severity or lenience, his methods of interpretation, etc.

There is only one method of psycho-analysis, that laid down by Freud; but there are different ways of achieving that aim. There is no such thing as an absolutely good technique, to be followed by every analyst in the world. But, on the other hand, the analyst must be required to make himself conscious of every emotional gratification brought about by his individual technique, in order that he may obtain a better control over his behaviour—and over his theoretical convictions. Every advance in psycho-analysis has had to be paid for by an ever-increasing conscious control over the investigator's emotional life. We believe that our technique can be still further improved, if we are able to bear still further conscious control over our everyday analytical behaviour.

XIV

CHANGING THERAPEUTICAL AIMS AND TECHNIQUES IN PSYCHO-ANALYSIS [1]

(1949)

I

I THINK it may be taken for granted that every analyst is at pains to learn from his own technical errors and mistakes. Conversely, this means that our individual technique is continually changing through gradually accumulating individual experience—let us hope, for the better. Are we justified in assuming that this is also true of psycho-analytical technique in general? Is the therapeutic work of the rank and file analyst of today different from that of his colleague of say thirty, twenty or even ten years ago? and if so, what is the difference and what has brought it about? As the title of my paper suggests, my contention is that psycho-analytic technique has changed, in fact has been changing continuously, ever since its first description by Freud in the technical chapter of the *Studies in Hysteria*.[2]

To put this process into true perspective, the survey ought to start with the techniques (in the plural) described by Breuer and Freud in their book. For the sake of brevity, however, I shall restrict myself to that part of the history of the technique which is contemporary with my analytical lifetime.

When I started to practise psycho-analysis (in 1922), the whole of our thinking was under the influence of two momentous works of Freud's: *From the History of an Infantile Neurosis* [3] and *Beyond the Pleasure Principle*.[4] Theoretically the aim of all

---

[1] Parts of this paper were read at the Sixteenth International Psycho-Analytical Congress, Zürich, August, 1949. First published in the *Int. J. of PsA.* (1950), **31**, 117–24.

[2] Breuer-Freud: *Studies in Hysteria*. Nervous and Mental Disease Monogr. Series No. 61. In German, 1895.

[3] Freud, S.: *Collected Papers*, III. In German, 1918.

[4] Freud, S.: London, 1920.

psycho-analytical therapy was defined by Freud—for all time to come, as we thought then—in his three famous synonymous formulae: 'overcoming the patient's resistance', 'removal of infantile amnesia', and 'making the unconscious conscious'. It is important to bear in mind that at that time 'unconscious' was equivalent to what we now call the 'repressed', and 'infantile amnesia' meant hardly more than the Oedipus situation, the 'nuclear complex' of all mental development. Accordingly, the practical task of an analysis was: (1) to reconstruct the patient's instinctual development, in particular to find out which of his sexual component instincts remained repressed and could not be integrated under the genital primacy; (2) to reconstruct the historical Oedipus situation; and (3) to relieve the castration anxiety, originating—as we then thought—from the Oedipus situation, mainly from the father, both for boys and girls.

Soon after (1922–26) we learnt from Freud his final ideas about the structure of the mind.[1] Since then it has been an established custom to view any neurotic symptom, in fact any mental phenomenon, as a compromise between the three factors: the id, the ego and the super-ego. The aim of therapy was, as reformulated by Freud: 'Where id was, ego shall be.' In practice this meant a new, an additional task: to help the patient to repair the faulty places in his ego structure, and in particular to aid him to abandon some of his costly defensive mechanisms and to develop less costly ones.

It is obvious that the three older formulations and the new one are not identical. In my opinion they are the psycho-analytic expression of the centuries-old dilemma of all the biological sciences: does function determine structure—*the functional or dynamic approach*—or does structure determine function—*the structural or topic approach*? [2]

[1] Freud, S.: *The Ego and the Id*, Int. PsA. Library. Hogarth Press. London, 1923; *Group Psychology and the Analysis of the Ego*, London, 1922; *Inhibitions, Symptoms and Anxiety*, Int. PsA. Library, Hogarth Press, London, 1936 (in German, 1926).

[2] It is an interesting problem, which certainly deserves proper examination, why in psycho-analysis—contrary to the general trend in medicine—the structural approach came so late after the functional, and why in spite of its late appearance it was able so quickly and so easily to attain such great importance in theory.

The relative importance of these two approaches dominated all theoretical discussions on therapy and technique in the following years. The dynamic approach laid more emphasis on 'content', was more concerned with the 'repressed' and the 'unconscious', which meant roughly the inhibited, repressed sexual gratifications, and was aiming at achieving a break-through of such repressed instincts,[1] at liberating them from repression, and establishing a free enjoyment of their gratifica-tion. To put it briefly, the main concern of the dynamic approach was the id. The topic approach, on the other hand, laid more emphasis on the study of the habitual defensive mechanisms, which roughly meant the developmental faults in the mental structure, especially the relative strengths of the ego and the super-ego.

It is perhaps interesting to note that all Freud's case histories —all dating, it is true, from before 1914—contain practically nothing but 'dynamic' or 'content' interpretations. And secondly that in *Studies in Hysteria*[2] Freud explicitly stated that his method of catharsis (or was it even then psycho-analysis?) could cure only hysterical symptoms and not a hysterical constitution; as far as I know, the statement has been neither revoked nor qualified.

A very important feature is that all the formulations of therapeutic aims put forward by Freud, i.e. both the earlier three synonymous ones expressing the dynamic approach and the newer one expressing the topic approach, are concerned only with the individual. I shall call this limitation the *physio-logical or biological bias*. This fact has been repeatedly quoted as a severe criticism of psycho-analysis, in particular by certain sociologists and anthropologists, from both the extreme left and the extreme right. This criticism, though not entirely unfounded, is in fact unfair and unjust, since it deliberately neglects certain important developments in our technique. It is true, however, that the fault is partly our own, for we have omitted to change our theoretical notions so as to include the results of our changed technique.

[1] e.g. Kaiser, H.: 'Probleme der Technik', *Int. Z. f. Psa.* (1934), **20**, 490–522.

[2] Freud, S.: loc. cit., pp. 228–9 (Third German edition).

2

This new orientation in our technique started almost imperceptibly by paying proper attention—in addition to the 'contents' of the free associations and to the detection of the patient's habitual defence mechanisms—to the *formal elements* of the patient's behaviour in the psycho-analytical situation. ('Formal' in English has two meanings: (1) perfunctory, or according to the rules of propriety; and (2) concerned with the form, not verbal. In this paper I shall use the word mainly in its second sense, but have no objection if the reader understands it to include both.) These formal elements include, among others, the changing expressions of the patient's face,[1] his way of lying on the couch, of using his voice, of starting and finishing the session, his intercurrent illnesses, even a passing malaise, and especially his way of associating.[2] At first such attention to, and subsequent interpretation of, these formal elements was thought to be a subtle trick or a lucky hit, and only gradually did we become aware of the immense value for therapeutic purposes of the consequent noting and interpreting of as many of these formal elements as possible. Nowadays this is fully recognised, and has become part and parcel of our everyday work, especially of our teaching activity in supervising our candidates.

The main results of this extensive study may be summed up under two heads. Firstly, these formal elements of the patient's behaviour in the psycho-analytical situation are very closely linked with the patient's *character*; it is extremely difficult to change them, even to make the patient become aware of their peculiar nature, since they appear absolutely 'natural' to him; obviously the force activating them must be very strong; as is well known, Freud classified it under the repetition compulsion. Secondly, these formal elements of behaviour are part and parcel of the patient's *transference*, expressing both his

---

[1] First observed and described by Freud in *Studies in Hysteria*, but I have not been able to find any reference to his interpreting it to the patient.

[2] All these first mentioned by Ferenczi. Cf. his papers Nos. 8, 14–15, 22–24, 27, 29, 45, 77 in *Further Contributions*, London, Inst. PsA. Lbr. Hogarth Press. 1926. (In German:1913, 1914, 1915 and 1919.)

general—lasting—sentiments towards the world, and his present—passing—attitudes towards a particular object—his analyst; consequently they have to be regarded as phenomena of some kind of *object-relation* —often of a primitive type—which has been revived in (or perhaps by) the psycho-analytical situation. The consequent study of these formal elements of the patient's behaviour in the psycho-analytical situation was, in my opinion, the main factor that brought about a fundamental change, indeed a very great improvement, in our technical skill; though I readily admit that other contributory factors were also at work.

This new orientation in our technique aims, first and foremost, at understanding and interpreting every detail of the patient's transference *in terms of object-relations*. In fact, Strachey[1] in an often-quoted paper maintained that transference interpretations alone have any curative (mutative) value. Whether we accept this statement or not, it is certainly true that nowadays hardly anybody tries to analyse neurotic symptoms or character-traits directly; they are dealt with *en passant*, so to speak, while analysing the 'transference'. And we may proudly say that our present-day technique is a very fine, safe and reliable instrument indeed for understanding, and dealing with, transference phenomena, i.e. object-relations.

At present we are in the queer situation that technically we can deal fairly well even with complicated problems of object-related attitudes or emotions which on the other hand are rather difficult to describe with our present theoretical concepts. (Later, when discussing Mrs. Klein's contributions, I shall have to qualify this statement.) To show how far our technique is ahead of our theory, let me quote one example. It is well known that we have no proper systematised classification of mental illnesses, not even properly defined pathological entities—only a fairly large collection of well-sounding labels. Today, to diagnose a case is always a difficult task; the result is usually an uncertain, rather haphazard, and not even very important label; and as soon as any particular label has been attached to a particular patient, a heated controversy breaks .

[1] Strachey, James: 'The Nature of the Therapeutic Action of Psychoanalysis', *Int. J. of PsA.* (1934), **15**, 127–59.

out challenging its correctness. To quote a few frequently recurring vexed questions: what is the difference between a mild epilepsy and a hysteria? or between a severe hysteria and an incipient schizophrenia? or between criminality and certain pathological characters? and so on. Our theory is very weak indeed on these points. Technically, however, we can deal fairly well with all these cases, despite their uncertain labelling.

3

The difference is striking. On the theoretical side we have excellent, concise, pregnant terms which, however, help us little; on the technical side we have well-founded, sharply delineated clinical pictures for the description of which we must use lengthy and clumsy formulae, often whole sentences, for lack of proper terms. I think that the cause of this queer and embarrassing situation is the same limitation that compelled Freud not to go beyond the individual when formulating the aims of psycho-analytic therapy. I called it the *physiological or biological bias*. It is a highly interesting fact that this bias is a self-imposed restriction; in his characteristic way, with matter-of-fact frankness, Freud conscientiously recorded his reasons for imposing the restriction upon himself.

In *Inhibitions, Symptoms and Anxiety* [1] he stated explicitly that he had deliberately chosen as the basis of his psychological theories *the clinical experiences with obsessional neurotics* because in this neurosis all conflicts and mental processes are internalised (in German: *verinnerlicht*).[2] For the future development of Freud's theories, as we all know, the study of *melancholia* was the paramount source. In recent years we have been able to watch Mrs. Klein, who—faithfully following Freud—has also used melancholia (depression) and still more recently schizoid and paranoid states as the main sources for the development of her ideas.[3] All these pathological forms have a common quality

[1] Freud, loc. cit., pp. 60–61.
[2] Freud, loc. cit., Chapters V and VII.
[3] e.g. Klein, M.: 'A Contribution to the Psychogenesis of Manic-Depressive States', *Int. J. of PsA.* (1935), **16**, 145–74; 'Mourning and its Relation to the Manic-Depressive State', *Int. J. of PsA.* (1940), **21**, 125–53; 'Notes of Some Schizoid Mechanisms', *Int. J. of PsA.* (1946), **27**, 99–109.

which may be called a bias; that is, the more or less complete *withdrawal from their objects*.

This bias becomes still more striking if we contrast these pathological forms with those which helped and compelled us to learn the new technique; which in fact initiated all analytical techniques. Firstly, there is hysteria, where everything happens with one eye on the objects; a very instructive history is that of Fr. Anna O.'s case, with the many changes of her object-relations to Breuer, which in turn compelled Breuer to ever new adaptations, i.e. changes in his technique.[1] Then the two types that make up a good half, if not two-thirds, of all our patients: the many forms of sexual disturbances and the acting-out type of character neuroses. In all these forms *objects are of paramount importance*. Whereas in obsessional neurosis or melancholia psycho-analytic theory was able to describe the clinical observations in concise dynamic terms, revealing the typical mental constellation that led to this particular kind of symptoms—in hysteria, in sexual disorders, and still more so in character neurosis our theoretical descriptions are rather primitive. We have not been able to isolate any well-defined, easily identifiable clinical types comparable to those in obsessional neurosis or in melancholia, and still less to describe them in concise dynamic terms. In fact, one is justified in saying that a clinical system of these latter illnesses does not as yet exist.

Here we meet the same queer situation, but from a different angle. Our theory has been mainly based on the study of pathological forms which use internalisation extensively and have only weakly cathected object-relations; our technique was invented and has been mainly developed when working with pathological forms such as hysteria, sexual disorders, character neurosis, all of which have strongly cathected object-relations. This, however, is only natural, as our true field of study is the *psycho-analytical situation*, a situation where relations to an object—admittedly a very peculiar object—are of overwhelming importance. A good deal of internal contradiction and of conflicting tendencies in psycho-analysis becomes

---

[1] Breuer-Freud: *Studies in Hysteria*.

understandable if we always bear in mind this double origin of our technique and theory.

Instead of speaking of a 'double origin' we might say that our theory and technique are differently biased. The bias influencing our theory led Freud to formulate the aims of therapy in a way that limited the description to the individual. I called it the *physiological or biological bias*.[1] It is much more difficult to find a suitable name for the bias influencing our technique. Suitable names or technical terms are usually the fruits of good theories—a good degree of skill is not sufficient for that—and, as I said, a good theory of our present technique does not yet exist. For want of a better term I propose to call this bias the *object* or perhaps *object-relation bias*.

The reason why it is so difficult to find a suitable name is that all our concepts and technical terms—except two—have been coined under the physiological bias and are, in consequence, highly individualistic; they do not go beyond the confines of the individual mind. The two exceptions are 'object' and 'object-relation', which have had a very interesting career indeed. Together with 'source' and 'aim', the 'object' of an instinct was made a technical term by Freud in his *Three Contributions*.[2] And it led a very modest existence in the shadow of its two much more important siblings. The 'source of an instinct' became the basis of classification in our theory of instincts; almost all the human instincts that we know of are called by names denoting their sources; which means that we think in terms borrowed from biology—or more correctly, *anatomy*—which knows only the individual and no object-relations. The development of the mind in its early stages, we thought, was determined by the instinctual aims, i.e. gratifications (and frustrations); the most gratifying instinct of the time, the prevalent instinct, organising the libido under its own rule, and prescribing what object was to be chosen and the individual's relation to it. Thus developed the theory of the pre-

---

[1] If I understood E. Kris (Zürich Congress paper) correctly, Freud, in his early letters and drafts which are shortly to be published, stated in so many words that he deliberately decided to develop his psychological ideas on physiological lines.

[2] Freud, S.: *Three Contributions to the Theory of Sexuality* (in German, 1905).

genital organisations of libido, in its most elaborate form, in Abraham's famous 'Short Study of the Development of the Libido' (1924).[1] The crucial factors in this development were thought to be the changing instincts, emerging during onto-genesis as the consequence of some unknown physiological process. The objects in this development were of secondary importance, a kind of chance substrata to be cathected by this or that instinct. Perhaps the recent views describing the very early object-relations which might be summed up as the theory of the 'exchangeable physiological objects' are only a logical consequence of this physiological train of thought.

As early as 1935 I pointed out several inconsistencies in this part of our theory and urged for a review which should pay more attention to the development of object-relations, especi-ally to the influences of the environment.[2] My proposition found hardly any response. Recently, however, there have been several unmistakable signs that our way of thinking about the development of the mind is changing. Here are a few such signs, none of them very important in itself, though rather impressive if seen together. Firstly: the term 'source of an instinct' is hardly ever heard or seen in print nowadays; equally the term 'instinctual aim' is definitely receding from our theoretical considerations; even the once very frequently used term 'aim-inhibited' is heard but rarely; in the foreground are, and in fact have been for some time, objects and object-relations; a further characteristic point which is important for my argument: they are hardly ever used in connection with their original adjective, 'instinctual object'; and I have never seen or heard 'relation to an instinctual object'. Secondly, the well-known terms anal, oral, genital, etc., are less and less used to denote the source or aim of instincts, but more and more to denote specific object-relations, e.g. 'oral greed', 'anal domina-

---

[1] Published in English in Abraham, K.: *Selected Papers*, Int. PsA. Library, Hogarth Press, London, 1942.

[2] Balint, M.: 'Zur Kritik der Lehre von den prägenitalen Libido-organisationen' ('Critical Notes on the Theory of the Pregenital Organisations of the Libido'), *Int. Z. f. PsA.* (1935), **21**, 525–34. Reprinted in this vol., p. 73; 'Frühe Entwickelungsstadien des Ichs. Primäre Objektliebe' (1937) ('Early Developmental Stages of the Ego. Primary Object-love'). Reprinted in this vol., p. 90.

tion', 'genital love', etc. Thirdly, the term 'sadistic' has been gradually going out of fashion, in my opinion because its implications are much too libidinous, and relate rather closely to instinctual aims, gratifications; in its stead terms like 'hostile' 'aggressive', 'destructive', are used, which have an unmistakable affinity to object-relations.

4

My contention is, that if we describe the events only from the point of view of the individual, using our well-developed technical terms and concepts such as repression, regression, split, establishment of a severe super-ego, introjection and projection, displacement, fusion or defusion, ambivalence, etc. —our description, though correct, will be incomplete, for every neurotic symptom means also a distorted object-relation, and the change in the individual is only one aspect of the whole process. Regarded from this angle the classical sources of psycho-analytic theory, obsessional neurosis and melancholia, because of the far-reaching withdrawal from their objects, are only borderline cases. They offer, it is true, simpler conditions for investigation, but their simplicity has perhaps been a mixed blessing because our theory, developed under their influence, has become incomplete and lopsided. What we need now is a theory that would give us a good description of the development of object-relations comparable to, but independent of, our present, biologising, theory of the development of instincts. And for that purpose we need a field of investigation where the conclusions drawn from the theory can be checked and validated, modified or refuted.

Here is the place to discuss Mrs. Klein's contributions.[1] Her theoretical ideas go a long way to meet the demands I have mentioned. In several papers she has described in more and more detail a theory of the development of object-relations, using only rarely the terms coined under the influence of the physiological bias, but creating new ones, such as part objects, which may be good or bad, can be split off or reintegrated,

[1] Klein, M.: *The Psychoanalysis of Children*, Int. PsA. Library, Hogarth Press, London, 1932, and the papers quoted above.

destroyed or repaired, introjected or projected, and so on. If we accept that introjection and projection, splitting, etc., mean some structural changes in the mind, then Mrs. Klein's theories can be regarded as an attempt at relating changes in the object-relations to structural changes in the mind. Obviously this is a very important step, and most likely is the transition between the old theories and the new ones demanded by me. And certainly any new theory will have to take account of the relevant results achieved by Mrs. Klein and her school.

The most important field of investigation for this coming theory must be the *analyst's behaviour in the psycho-analytic situation*, or, as I prefer to phrase it, the analyst's contribution to the creating and maintaining of the psycho-analytic situation. A very dangerous and awkward topic indeed, which I intend to deal with in a separate paper. Here I want to discuss only so much of it as is necessary for our topic. It is obvious that every human relation is *libidinous*. So is *the patient's relation to his analyst*, which we have called transference ever since Freud showed us its nature and dynamism in the famous Dora case-history,[1] but the *analyst's relation to his patient is libidinous in exactly the same way*; even if we call it 'counter-transference', or 'correct analytical behaviour', or 'proper handling of the transference situation', or 'detached friendly understanding and well-timed interpreting'; this relation, too, *is* libidinous.

It is as true for the patient as for his analyst that no human being can in the long run tolerate any relation which brings only frustration, i.e. an ever-increasing tension between him and his object. Sooner or later the tension must be relieved either by conscious or by unconscious means. The question is, therefore, *not* friendly objectiveness plus correct interpretation versus hugging and kissing the patient and using four-letter Anglo-Saxon words *à la* John Rosen,[2] *but* how much and what kind of satisfaction is needed by the patient on the one hand, and by the analyst on the other, to keep the tension in the psycho-analytical situation at or near the optimal level.

Observational data as to how this very queer object-relation,

[1] Freud, S.: *Collected Papers*, III. (German original, 1905.)
[2] Discussion on the 'direct' psycho-analysis of J. Rosen in the British Psycho-Analytic Society, Autumn, 1949.

which we call the psycho-analytical situation, develops and changes, is influenced by frustrations and satisfactions, and in turn influences the wishes, demands, conscious and unconscious gratifications, and frustrations of each of its two participants, will be perhaps the most important source of material for any developmental theory of object-relations. All the so-called technical innovations, starting with Frl. Anna O. through Freud, Ferenczi, Rank, Reich, etc., till the recent ones of Alexander and French, of Rosen and others, should be examined from this angle. A very important item of this examination will be the *language* used by the analyst for conveying his interpretations to his patient. By language I mean the set of technical terms, of concepts, the 'frame of reference' habitually used by the individual analyst. How much unconscious gratification lies hidden behind the undisturbed use of accustomed ways of thinking and of expressing one's ideas, is best shown by the often quite irrational resistance that almost every analyst puts up at the suggestion that he might learn to use or even only to understand a frame of reference considerably different from his own. I think it may therefore be accepted that the 'language' is always highly cathected by libido; the use of his own language is an important gratification to the analyst; acceptance or even tolerance of any other language is consequently a somewhat telling strain. This, however, does not mean that every 'language' is equally useful or correct, but that every 'language' must be examined in order to discover how much conscious or unconscious gratification it affords the analyst, and how much it contributes to the building up and shaping of the psycho-analytic situation.

A second important source of data for a developmental theory of object-relation will be the direct observation of children. One would have expected that the impetus for the revision of our theoretical concepts would have come from the direct study of children, especially now that we have so many excellently trained child analysts. But it seems that history will again repeat itself. It is a puzzling fact that apart from a few exceptions almost all important new discoveries in psycho-analysis were made in the psycho-analytical situation with adult patients.

The third source in my opinion will be experiences in group therapy. As I am a novice in this field I cannot claim any authority. My only purpose here is to call attention to this extremely important field where both object and subject can be observed together simultaneously; some transference of emotions invariably takes place from member to member, i.e. object-relations develop before our eyes. Transference, counter-transference, all sorts of object-relations, happen in our presence, and as it is not *our* counter-transference, its objective observation is considerably easier. It is possible that 'natural' groups will be still more important for the study than the 'artificial' groups of patients brought together by us. By 'natural' groups I mean neighbours' communities, works' groups, etc., where real object-relations, i.e. such as have always existed spontaneously, can be studied.

5

In lieu of summing up I shall describe what analysts did or may do even today with a silent patient. I hope this description will illustrate the various stages in the development of our therapeutic techniques and aims. So let us suppose that a patient remains silent for some time. His analyst might adopt the very early technique used by Freud in the *Studies in Hysteria*, i.e. urging and pressing the patient, demanding that in spite of his resistances he should say what has come into his mind. Freud even used to put his hand on the patient's forehead, and in the early case-histories phrases frequently occur such as 'under the pressure of my hand' or 'in concentration', etc., the patient was able to speak. Nowadays I think this method is seldom used, and, if at all, only in the case of minor obstacles.

Then the analyst may try to find out what the patient has been withholding and to say it in his stead, in some such way as this: 'It is obvious from this or that sign that you are occupied, say, with phantasies about my private life or with some of your own sexual activities, etc.' This is what is called 'content interpretation'.

Thirdly, the analyst may endeavour to link up all the instances when the patient remained silent instead of associating and to show the identical features in all such instances, e.g. 'Whenever this or that difficulty emerges, you escape from it by withdrawing into silence, by becoming numb, dead, by ceasing to feel anything', etc. As the second step he will try to show that at one time when this particular defence mechanism started there was some point in resorting to it. In the third step then the analyst will try to make conscious the fear or anxiety now arising in the patient and to link the present situation with some similar feature in the original situation; and in addition to point out the inherent differences between the two situations. This is what we may call the interpretation of the defence mechanism or even transference interpretation.

There is still another approach, and I think this latter will yield important material to a theory of object-relations. I propose to call it *creating a proper atmosphere* for the patient by the analyst, in order that the patient may be able to open up. If it is thought that this is too much to ask, I shall put it in a negative form: *avoiding* the creation of an atmosphere that shuts the patient up. Putting it in this way, it is obvious that silence is not due to the patient's transference, or to the analyst's counter-transference, but to an interplay of transference *and* counter-transference, i.e. to an object-relation.

With our terminology of today it is very difficult indeed to describe the development and the subtle changes of this object-relation. Without noticing it we slide into describing it in our accustomed individualising terms of instinctual tension, displacement, acting out, repetition-compulsion, transference of verbal or pre-verbal emotions, etc., with regard to the patient. On the other hand, with regard to the analyst we speak of friendly understanding, correct interpretation, alleviating anxiety, reassurance, strengthening of the ego, etc. All these descriptions are correct as far as they go. But as they do not go beyond the individual, they remain incomplete through the neglect of an essential feature, namely that all these phenomena happen in an interrelation between two individuals, in a constantly changing and developing object-relation.

I wish to quote here an idea of John Rickman's, of which unfortunately I heard only in April 1950, i.e. only after finishing this paper. If I had been able to use his ideas, several passages might have been formulated more exactly and more convincingly. As I had not time enough to re-write this paper, I took the second-best course of calling attention to this important train of thought which admirably explains the discrepancies between our theory and technique. According to Rickman: 'The whole region of psychology may be divided into areas of research according to the number of persons concerned. Thus we may speak of One-Body Psychology, Two-Body, Three-Body, Four-Body and Multi-Body Psychology.' [1]

Each of these psychologies has its own field of studies and ought to develop its own 'language' of technical terms, sets of concepts, etc., for the proper description of its findings. Until now this has been done only in the One-Body Psychology. Psycho-analytical theory—as I have tried to show—is no exception; almost all our terms and concepts were derived from studying pathological forms hardly going beyond the domain of the One-Body Psychology (obsessional neurosis, melancholia, schizophrenia). That is why they can give only a clumsy, approximate description of what happens in the psycho-analytical situation which is essentially a Two-Body Situation. Mathematicians have developed a special discipline—projective geometry—for the study of the laws (and of the many pitfalls) concerning the representation of an $n + 1$-dimensional body in an n-dimensional space (the best-studied case is that of the representation of a three-dimensional body on a two-dimensional plane). No such discipline as yet exists in psychology, and we have only some vague ideas but no exact knowledge about what distortions happen and how much we miss while describing Two-Body experiences (analytical technique) in a language belonging to One-Body situations.

[1] Rickman, J.: 'Methodology and Research in Psychiatry' (Contribution to a symposium at a meeting of the Med. Sec. of the Brit. Psychol. Soc.), April 26th, 1950. I understand that similar ideas were already expressed by Rickman in June 1948.

XV

ON THE TERMINATION OF ANALYSIS [1]

(1949)

I

THE criteria for termination can be classified under many possible headings. From among these I have chosen three, not only because they appear to me important, but mainly because I have studied them more closely than the others. The first heading is that of *instinctual aims*. That means a firmly established genital primacy, the capacity to enjoy full genital satisfaction, i.e. mature genitality. I wish to point out that I mean more than a simple sum-total of all the component sexual instincts; mature genitality is in my opinion a new function emerging about puberty, possibly as the result of a 'natural process' such as I tried to describe in 'Eros and Aphrodite'.[2]

The second group of criteria can be summed up under the heading: *relation to instinctual objects*. I dealt with this topic in a recent paper: 'On Genital Love'.[3] The gist of my thesis is that genital love is definitely not a natural spontaneous process but an artefact—the result of civilisation (or of education)—a complex fusion of genital satisfaction and pregenital tenderness; its psychological expression is genital identification with the object based on an exacting reality testing, and its aim the changing of an indifferent or even reluctant object into a loving and co-operating genital partner.

The third group of criteria can be summed up under the heading: *structure of the ego*. The ego must be strong enough to cope with tensions caused—*inter alia*—by: (*a*) the use of alloplastic instead of autoplastic methods for dealing with reality; (*b*) the acceptance of unpleasant ideas; (*c*) the sudden increase

[1] Contribution to a symposium on the Termination of Psycho-Analytical Treatment at the meeting of British Psycho-Analytical Society, on March 2nd, 1949. First published in the *Int. J. of PsA.* (1950), **31**, 196–99.

[2] *Int. J. of PsA.* (1938), **19**, 199–213. This vol. p. 73.

[3] *Int. J. of PsA.* (1948), **29**, 34–40. Reprinted in this vol., p. 128.

of excitement before and during an orgasm; (*d*) maintaining the genital identification with the partner even in phases of temporary dissatisfaction; etc. Obviously the common basis of all these functions is reliable reality testing which enables the individual to maintain an uninterrupted contact with reality even under strain.

I am aware that all this is well known. In the same way we know that these are rather perfectionist standards, which nobody can fulfil completely. A sceptical critic would be more than justified in asking at this point: Granted all these criteria, how much deviation from these high standards should be allowed before finishing an analysis? As this question cannot easily be answered, I propose to try another approach.

2

As the attempt to establish theoretical standards did not prove promising, we shall drop the search for external criteria and try to describe clinically what actually happens when an analysis terminates. In two of my papers [1] I have tried to describe this process which I called *new beginning*. Briefly what happens is: the patient gradually gives up his suspicious attitude towards the world of objects, especially his analyst; parallel with this a particular kind of object-relation emerges which could be called archaic, primitive or passive object-love; its main features are the unconditional expectation of being loved without being under the obligation to give anything in return, and of obtaining safely and without fail the desired gratification, irrespective of the interests of the object; an important point is that these vehemently demanded gratifications never go above the level of fore-pleasure. Naturally these wishes can never be fully met in the framework of the analytical situation, but—according to my experience— they must be fully understood and also met to a considerable degree. For only if the analyst has succeeded in leading this

[1] 'Charakteranalyse und Neubeginn', *Int. Z. f. Psa.* (1934), **20**, 54, 65; in English 'Character Analysis and New Beginning'. This vol., p. 159. 'The Final Goal of Psycho-Analytical Treatment', *Int. J. of PsA.* (1936), **17**, 206–16. This vol., p. 188.

patient through all these Scyllas and Charybdises can the patient develop from this newly begun primitive passive object-love to mature genital love. This development goes parallel to, and depends largely on, the patient's gradual allowing more and more rights to his objects, i.e. by developing his capacity for testing the reality with regard to his objects, and in this way endeavouring to arrive at an acceptable compromise between his and his object's demands.

If this process can develop in an undisturbed way a surprisingly uniform experience dominates the very last period of the treatment. The patient feels that he is going through a kind of re-birth into a new life, that he has arrived at the end of a dark tunnel, that he sees light again after a long journey, that he has been given a new life, he experiences a sense of great freedom as if a heavy burden had dropped from him, etc. It is a deeply moving experience; the general atmosphere is of taking leave for ever of something very dear, very precious—with all the corresponding grief and mourning—but this sincere and deeply felt grief is mitigated by the feeling of security, originating from the newly won possibilities for real happiness. Usually the patient leaves after the last session happy but with tears in his eyes and—I think I may admit—the analyst is in a very similar mood.

It is very important that we should not be led astray by the obvious symbolism of this description, although naturally we must remain fully aware of all the implications. But I think the real problem is much deeper than the symbolic expression, and the symbolism is only a clumsy language in which this deeper problem is expressed haltingly and rather incompletely.

This deeper problem, which I regard as the crux of our discussion, can be formulated in several ways, all of which try to convey the same content. I shall discuss only two such formulations.

The first asks the question: Is the analytical cure a 'natural' or an 'artificial' process? i.e. does the analyst's task consist only in removing the obstacles created by the individual and social traumata—after which the 'natural' processes will take charge of the cure?

(*a*) If the answer is Yes, we may expect rather uniform happenings in the end-phase; moreover, these events will probably be expressed in some general symbolic form, such as that of giving up an intra-uterine existence which retrospectively will be described as both good and bad; or (*b*) If the answer is No, we must expect widely varying experiences in the end-phase, dependent on—among other factors—the degree of the overall maturity reached, on the problems that happen to be the last ones to be dealt with, on the personality of the analyst, etc.

Another formulation—using more general concepts—may ask: (1) Is *health* a natural state of equilibrium? i.e. do processes exist in the mind which—if unhampered and undisturbed—would lead the development towards that equilibrium? or (2) Is *health* the result of a lucky chance, a rare or even an improbable event, the reason being that its conditions are so stringent and so numerous that the chances are very heavily weighted against it?

The two dilemmas are essentially identical. There are a few other possible formulations, but we need not trouble ourselves about them on this occasion. Analysts have not as yet been able to give a satisfactory answer to these questions. Roughly there are two camps. It is interesting to note that those who think that mature genitality is not simply a chance sum-total of a motley mixture of component sexual instincts but a function *per se*, also think that health is a 'natural' equilibrium and the termination of a psycho-analytic cure is a 'natural' process. And there is the other camp which maintains fairly unanimously that health, the termination of an analysis and mature genitality are similarly the result of the interplay of so many forces, tendencies and influences that one is not justified in assuming governing 'natural' processes.

3

Obviously the answer to this important dilemma lies with the clinical experiences, i.e. with the study of truly terminated analyses. Unfortunately the available material is very meagre and unconvincing. Still, it is worth while to examine it. The first source is my own experience. This cannot be really decisive because (a) it is subjectively coloured and (b) my numbers are too small. Taking all those of my cases which went beyond the trial period, I could observe the end-phase as described in this paper roughly in two cases out of ten. A very poor proportion indeed. Still, I remain convinced that in the main my description is correct. My principal reason is that in every case in which we failed to achieve a proper termination, I think I know what went wrong, although I must admit that once the mistake was made and the phase of new beginning was spoilt, it was hardly possible to remedy the situation. In such cases the analysis usually ended in a state of partial success, seldom of dissatisfaction or even of resentment, in spite of sincere goodwill and honest efforts from both sides. The reassuring point is that very often the processes started by the cure developed farther after the so-called termination, and in this way the final results have often become quite commendable—still a feeling of having missed something seems to persist for long periods with the patient as well as with his analyst. Obviously this is not very convincing material.

Control analyses should provide a second source of material. Unfortunately control work as a rule finishes before the analyses can be carried to their termination: a very unsatisfactory state of affairs both for the candidate and the supervisor—and not least for the patient. Apart from the real difficulties, an additional reason for our tolerating this grave fault in our training system is the unconscious and unformulated doubt mentioned above as to the possibility of any 'natural' termination of analysis.

The last source of material should be found in other analysts' cases. Unfortunately we know so little about our colleagues' techniques and we are so secretive about our own that only a very small fraction of all cases is available to an outsider. The small fraction about which an outsider may know something is the training analyses.

For several reasons one would expect fewer complications here than with neurotics; unfortunately the very opposite is the case. It is generally known —though not officially recognised—that quite a number of candidates continue their analyses without any break after qualification. This entails not only a short period for some tidying up, but honest all-out treatments. I think this fact, which I believe occurs in every Training Institution, is of crucial importance to our topic.

Our present training system is based on the empirical fundamental rule that no one shall analyse who has not been analysed himself. Obviously this must mean more than just having started analysis or having had, say, a few dozen sessions. Although the rule does not say it in so many words, one is led to assume that it implies that the candidate should finish his own analysis before being allowed to treat patients without any further compulsory supervision.

Apparently this is not the case, and we are working with two standards instead of one. Standard A, less stringent but publicly controlled and strictly enforced by our Societies and their officers, says that the candidate is healthy (i.e. trained) enough for starting to analyse patients on his own, for being qualified as a fully fledged analyst, but as yet not necessarily healthy enough to deal with his own neurotic unconscious problems. Standard B, more stringent but uncontrolled by our Societies and their officers, a matter of private agreement between the patient (a fully qualified analyst) and his training analyst, determines the criteria of the real termination. We know a good deal about Standard A, but unfortunately hardly anything about Standard B.

I wish to add that this dual-standard system is a comparatively new development away from what may have been too perfectionist an idea, a kind of coming-down-to-sober-reality policy. Some of the factors of this development which started, as far as I know, in the thirties, are known; they include, among others, incompletely finished analyses of several of our colleagues, which later necessitated a resumption of their analyses as a private venture; inefficient selection of the candidates at the start, the ever-lengthening duration of the normal training analyses, which in turn always leads to heavy external pressure, especially of a financial nature, etc. It would be a very important piece of research to find out more about the conscious *and* unconscious motives of this latest development in our training system.

As things are at present this source of clinical material does not yield a reliable answer to our problems either. Obviously standard A is useless to us; and of standard B we know as little as of any other terminated analysis.

4

To sum up: we have excellent theoretical criteria to decide whether an analysis has been properly terminated or not. Unfortunately we must admit that they are rather perfectionist standards, and we are not able to define what would constitute an admissible deviation from our criteria. I am well aware of the fact that other analysts prefer to use criteria partly or wholly different from mine. The above criticism, however, remains true for any set of criteria.

On the practical side, when examining the end-phases of my truly terminated analyses, we landed in the dilemma: is health a 'natural' state or is it only the result of extremely good luck, a very rare event? And we had to admit our inability to solve it.

And lastly, when looking for reliable clinical material the study of which might enable us to formulate an empirical, or at least a statistical, answer to our problem, we found that such material—even if it exists—is inaccessible to any other analyst, i.e. is available only to the analyst who actually conducted the analysis to its end. As for the time being there is no possibility of control or verification, all statements about truly terminated analyses are, of necessity, subjectively coloured and therefore not absolutely reliable.

This is, of course, as true of my own statements as it is of those of anyone else taking part in this discussion, until such time as reliable material is made accessible to all of us for proper criticism. As long as things remain as they are now, any contribution to this problem must run the risk of bringing but little to the solution of this problem while disclosing a good deal about the personality of the contributor, albeit in a highly sublimated form. I hasten to say that this holds good for this contribution too.

Still, in spite of this uncertainty, every year several analyses are terminated. Even if we take the cautious view that each member of our International Association who is a practising analyst finishes only one or two of his cases per year, the sum-total will be 1,000–2,000 per annum. Using my figures quoted in this paper, according to which at least two out of ten finished cases are truly terminated, we arrive at the figure of 200–400 per annum. This is a vast material indeed. I write these notes in the hope that they will stimulate some colleague to collect this material critically and to use it as a means of finding a real answer to our problems.

NEW BEGINNING AND THE PARANOID AND THE DEPRESSIVE SYNDROMES [1]
(1952)

I

I FELT greatly honoured when I was asked to contribute a paper to this number, as I cannot consider myself Mrs. Klein's pupil in the ordinary sense of the word. My justification for inclusion is a long-standing interest in her work, and—if I may call it so—a friendship dating back to our bygone Berlin days, when both of us were still under analysis, and by good luck for me we lived for some time only a few doors away from each other. In every other respect our positions were wholly different. I was a real beginner, fresh from the University, while Mrs. Klein was already an analyst of repute who was listened to attentively, even though at times ironically. She still had an uphill fight to face, being the only non-academic and the only child analyst in the midst of a very academic and very 'learned' German society. Time and again she caused embarrassment, incredulity or even sardonic laughter, by using in her case-histories the naïve nursery expressions of her child patients. Yet, despite this ambivalent reception she remained steadfast in her primary aim of showing that neurotic symptoms and defensive mechanisms found in adults can be observed also in young children, and very often, in quite relevant respects, can be studied better in children than in adults. Both Mrs. Klein and the analytic world have travelled a long way since those days. Many—though certainly not all—of her then hotly disputed ideas have since become an integral part of the body of accepted analytic knowledge.

As my tribute to her birthday I wish to show how her ideas helped me to understand an impasse in my work, and gave me hope that in the future this impasse might be avoided by better

---

[1] First published in *Int. J. of PsA.* (1952), **33**, 214.

knowledge and skill. In 1932 I described [1] a peculiar phase in the analytic treatment of patients. Since then on several occasions I have returned to the same theme, trying to describe it more and more exactly.

My clinical experience was briefly this: At times when the analytic work has already progressed a long way, i.e. towards the end of a cure, my patients began—very timidly at first—to desire, to expect, even to demand certain simple gratifications, mainly, though not exclusively, from their analyst. On the surface these wishes appeared unimportant: to give a present to the analyst or—more frequently—to receive one from him; to be allowed to touch or stroke him or to be touched or stroked by him, etc.; and most frequently of all to be able to hold his hand or just one of his fingers. Two highly important characteristics of these wishes are easily seen. First: they can be satisfied only by another human being; any auto-erotic satisfaction is simply impossible. Second: the level of gratification never goes beyond that of mild fore-pleasure. Correspondingly[2] a really full satisfaction followed by an anticlimax can hardly ever be observed, only a more or less complete saturation. Thus, if satisfaction arrives at the right moment and with the right intensity, it leads to reactions which can be observed and recognised only with difficulty, as the level of pleasure amounts only to a *tranquil quiet sense of well-being*.

This leads me to a very difficult technical problem: what the analyst should do about these wishes. The first task is obvious: both he and his patient must recognise them and understand their essentially primitive nature. This is a difficult task, because these wishes—like all other material produced by the patient— are overdetermined, and all the overlying determinants must first be resolved by the analytic work before their primitiveness can clearly emerge. In most cases this much is sufficient. There are, however, some patients whose analysis—in my experience —demands more. They belong to a class which can be

[1] In 'Charakteranalyse und Neubeginn', read at the Twelfth Congress of the International Psycho-analytical Association, published: *Int. Z. f. Psa.* (1934). Reprinted in this vol., p. 159.

[2] M. Balint: 'Eros and Aphrodite', *Int. Z. f. Psa.* (1936). *Int. J. of PsA.* (1938). Reprinted in this vol., p. 73.

described either as deeply disturbed or as people whose ego development was distorted by early traumas. These patients have the ability—or compulsion, or symptom—of regressing to a state of infantile helplessness in which they do not seem to be able to comprehend intellectual considerations, i.e. interpretations couched in words. These states are, of course, over-determined; they are a sign of strong resistance, an expression of intense fear, a bitter reproach, a way of demonstrating the disastrous effects of the trauma, a means of getting masochistic pleasure by repeating the surrender to the trauma and by inviting through helplessness another traumatic attack, etc. etc. In some cases—encouraged by Ferenczi's experiments [1] my patient and I agreed that some of the primitive wishes belonging to such a state should be satisfied in so far as they were compatible with the analytic situation. The terms of such 'agreement' are naturally very elastic, but in the mutually trusting atmosphere of this period they have proved quite workable.

To maintain this mutually trusting atmosphere between patient and analyst requires very great tact and careful skill. On one side lies the precipice of addiction-like states. If the analyst is incautiously indulgent, the patients develop an almost insatiable greediness, they can never have enough. On the other side are the horrors of the state of frustration. Perhaps the most striking feature of this state is the overwhelming flood of sadistic tendencies. Session after session may be completely taken up with the most cruel phantasies of how the analyst should be treated, as a retaliation for his indifferent and thus frustrating behaviour, and/or by equally cruel phantasies about what the patient must expect as the well-merited punishment of his aggressiveness. Similarly intense but well-disguised aggressiveness can also be demonstrated in the addiction-like states; the form of the disguise is usually inhibited masochistic pleasure in one's own sufferings. In both states—of frustration and of addiction alike—in contrast to the silent signs of well-

---

[1] S. Ferenczi: 'The Principle of Relaxation and Neocatharsis', *Int. J. of PsA.* (1930), **11**, 428; 'Child Analysis in the Analysis of Adults', *ibid.* (1931), **12**, 468; 'Confusion of Tongues between the Adults and the Child' (originally in 1933), *ibid.* (1949), **30**, 225.

timed and spaced satisfactions, one encounters vehement and noisy reactions, caused by very painful, almost unbearable tensions in the patients. It is anything but easy to steer an even course through all these difficulties and pitfalls. However, if one succeeds, this period proves to be very fruitful; rigid ego structures, character-traits and defensive mechanisms, ossified behaviour patterns and ever-repeated forms of object-relations, become analysable, understandable to both patient and analyst, and finally adaptable to reality which then usually leads to a true termination of the analysis.

I had two reasons for calling these phenomena *new beginning*. The main reason was psychological. The whole, very dramatic process struck one as if the patient—though only very cautiously—gave up, bit by bit, his accustomed automatic forms of object-relation, or in other words, his hitherto unchangeable, fateful ways of loving and hating. Simultaneously, he made timid attempts at trying out new ways which, however, could easily be proved to be really old ones which, in their time, had been spoilt for him by his frustrating, unresponsive or merely indifferent early environment. His ever-recurring bad experiences, amounting in some cases to real traumas, forced him at the time to start his neurotic ways of loving and hating. Now, in the safety of the analytical transference, he seemed to give up tentatively his defences, to regress to an—as yet— undefended, naïve, i.e. pre-traumatic state, and to *begin anew* to love and to hate in a primitive way, which was then speedily followed by the development of a mature, well-adapted, non-neurotic (as far as such a state is thinkable) way of loving and hating.

A piece of theory is the corollary of this train of thought. I consider this period of *primitive, or archaic, object-love* (at first— under the influence of S. Ferenczi—I used the term *passive object-love*) to be the *fons et origo* of human libido-development. The original and everlasting aim of all object-relations is the primitive wish: *I must be loved* without any obligation on me and without any expectation of return from me. All 'adult' ways of object-relation, i.e. of loving and hating, are compromise formations between this original wish and the acceptance of an unkind, unpleasant, indifferent reality. If a neurotic compromise (i.e. one economically much too expensive) is resolved by analysis, the original primitive form of love emerges again. This has to be realised and the patient must be allowed to go back, to 'regress', to this archaic, pre-traumatic state. The more the patient is able to divest himself of his acquired forms of object-relation, the more he is able to begin anew to love, the greater is the probability of his developing a non-neurotic 'adult' way of loving.

My additional reason for calling these phenomena new beginning came from biology.[1] In highly unfavourable external circumstances only those living beings can survive who are able to give up their well-differentiated organisation, and regress to primitive stages in their development, in order to begin the process of adaptation anew. Highly developed forms are more efficient but also more dependent on a special set of environmental factors. Primitive, undifferentiated states are elastic, capable of new adaptation in various directions. The similarity is striking. Highly differentiated forms, both in biology and in psychology, are rigid unadaptable; if a radically new adaptation becomes necessary, the highly differentiated organisation must be reduced to its primitive, undifferentiated form from which a new beginning may then issue.

2

Looking through my case-material, i.e. all the patients who continued their analyses beyond the trial period, I find that a proper period of new beginning, leading to a true termination of the analysis, could be achieved only in about 20 per cent. of my cases.[2] Another 20 per cent. could be described as

[1] M. Balint: 'Psychosexuelle Parallelen zum biogenetischen Grundgsetz', *Imago* (1932). English translation in this vol., p. 11.

[2] Being abstract, i.e. lifeless, figures are a dangerous matter. Quoted by themselves, without relation to experience, on which they are based, i.e. life, they can be very misleading. That is why I wish to add that my case-material includes all sorts of patients from a short-lived monosymptomatic psychosomatic illness to very severe paranoias, schizophrenias and depressions; cases with good prognoses and so-called 'hopeless' cases. The ages range from 16 to over 60, and there are a number of training analyses amongst them. In short: the very mixed bag of a general psycho-analytic practice.

practically cured and another 30–40 per cent. as considerably improved (the uncertainty is due to the interpretation of the adverb 'considerably'), while 20–30 per cent. must be considered as uninfluenced or not materially improved.

All these figures deserve thorough discussion. On this occasion I propose to examine what happened to the patients who achieved only a practical (not a theoretical) cure, and to those who could be improved but not cured. If my idea about the importance of the new beginning is correct, the first question in this examination must be: what happened to the patients during this period? I mentioned this problem already in my first paper on this subject,[1] but in spite of constant attention and endeavour ever since, I have not been able to arrive at a satisfactory theoretical clarification. Using some of Mrs. Klein's ideas, I think I can now take an important step towards a solution.

My clinical experience has been that patients proceed very cautiously towards what I call 'new beginning'. This cautiousness I interpreted—to myself, but also to my patients—as a precipitate of all the frustrations suffered during their development, on the lines of 'a burnt child dreads the fire'. Often we discovered that the patient's early environment was anything but loving, in fact quite often deliberately and maliciously frustrating. In other cases the environment apparently was not malicious, only careless or indifferent, which, however, was interpreted by the patient's phantasies as malicious or hostile—sometimes probably correctly. All this, naturally, was worked through both in the recollection and in the repetition, i.e. in the transference to the analytical situation.

Even so, in some cases the mutually trusting atmosphere of the new beginning would not develop. The patients remained suspicious and mistrustful towards their analyst, in spite of honest endeavours on both sides. And although they could speak as a possibility about their awakening primitive wishes—so characteristic of the period of new beginning—they could never relax, i.e. abandon their suspicious adult selves to the extent of feeling these wishes as an actual reality. They remained even in their most relaxed states split adults who 'took

[1] op. cit. (1934), see this vol., p. 159.

care of themselves'; they could not reach the state when they were 'one with themselves'.[1]

This state is, I think, reminiscent of that described by Mrs. Klein as the 'paranoid position' [2]: The patients, in their innermost selves, are convinced that everybody else is bad, hostile, malicious, an evil-wisher who grudges any happiness to anybody—and they readily admit that they too are hostile, bad and grudging. According to them the only true, the only possible relation between them and their environment, in fact between any two human beings, is that of guarded suspicion and never-relaxing watchfulness. People do *not* love each other, and if anybody says he does, or merely tries to show sincere interest (e.g. the analyst), it is the easiest thing for these patients to prove that all this is only hypocritical pretence, a make-believe, a clumsy attempt at misleading a fool in order to take advantage of him after lulling him into relaxing his guard. It is amazing how often these people succeed in creating a world around themselves in which all this is *really* true. And still more amazing that sometimes they can trap their analyst as well. In spite of keeping constant watch on counter-transference, I must admit I have not always been able to keep completely clear of this world of general suspicion.

Is one justified in calling this world of suspicion which the patient creates around himself out of his transference and the systematically provoked and nursed counter-transferences of practically all of his objects a world of persecutory anxieties? Mrs. Klein uses these two terms—paranoid and persecutory—as synonyms, perhaps even preferring the latter as a more general notion. As far as my experience goes, in the phase described above, which precedes the relaxation and abandonment of the period of new beginning, the attitude of the patients can be best described in terms of *delusions of reference* (Beziehungswahn). Everything, the most everyday happening, will inevitably be referred to the patient's own person; everything has some hidden meaning, and almost always this deep,

[1] Ferenczi: 'Notes and Fragments. Integration and Splitting', *Int. J. of PsA.* (1949), **30**, 241. (Originally written in 1932.)

[2] e.g. in 'Notes on Some Schizoid Mechanisms', *Int. J. of PsA.* (1946), **27**, 99.

'true' meaning is inconsiderateness and lovelessness. The question, therefore, is: Can persecution on the one hand and loveless, careless indifference on the other be considered as meaning the same thing? Or is this meticulous distinction only a later development, without any meaning for the primitive unconscious mind?

Even if I am inclined to accept this latter possibility for the patient's (and the child's) unconscious, I cannot do so for our terminology. Words have their inevitable associations, not only for the patient but also for the analyst; using one word instead of another of necessity summons up a whole cluster of associations, creates a very definite atmosphere in our minds—and in our discussions. That is why I wish, when describing this kind of environment, to stick to careless, loveless indifference, creating in turn fear and suspicion in the patient. This state of affairs is adequately described by 'paranoid' attitude or position, and I propose to use 'persecutory' and 'persecution' only in their proper sense, not as general notions.

Some people seem to be unable to overcome completely this barrier of suspicion. With my present technique, at least, I have not been able to resolve this world of suspicion in all my patients. With the patients who finished their analyses in the stage when they could admit—as a possibility—that they were feeling those primitive wishes but could not abandon themselves to break down the barrier between themselves and these wishes, the analytic cure usually achieved quite commendable results. After analysis these people could as a rule maintain a good social adaptation, achieve social and financial success, and show hardly any neurotic symptoms. They have no serious difficulty with their sexual life, usually no impotence or frigidity. But somehow their love-life is cool and colourless. They can never accept their partners as true equals; the partners, though quite attractive and pleasant people, do not mean much. The patients themselves remain all their lives independent, unattached, lonely people, somewhat suspicious, hypercritical and overbearing. Characteristically their criticisms, though never unjustified or incorrect, are always exaggerated, somehow out of proportion. Another interesting feature is that they do not feel ill and in fact they cannot be called ill.

If I was able to help my patients out of this paranoid position, another state developed; and here too Mrs. Klein's work has helped me a great deal towards a proper evaluation. Before describing this state I wish to add that the change from the suspicious state to this new one is a very gradual process fraught with several real relapses, and with still more that threaten but do not materialise. This new state is best described as depression. As a rule the patients say in so many words: I am worthless, unlovable; I know I ought to be different; I see it would be better for me and for everyone if I were different; I would be a much better man in every way, more pleasant, more lovable, perhaps even happy—but I cannot change, it is totally impossible. Sometimes they can even admit that they do not want to change or dare not.

Behind all that façade, however, there is the feeling of a deep, painful, narcissistic wound which, as a rule, can be made conscious without serious difficulty—somehow in this way: 'It is terrifying and dreadfully painful that *I am not loved for what I am*; time and again I cannot avoid seeing that people are critical of me; it is an irrefutable fact that no one loves me as I want to be loved.' From here it is an easy step for the patient to get back into the paranoid state by projecting the real cause of this ever-present experience on the general loveless indifference between man and man. If this can be prevented by correct and timely interpretations, the patient cannot but admit that he—or at least parts of himself—are not really lovable, or using Mrs. Klein's word, not really good. In this way a long-standing but carefully covered-up split becomes apparent and a very painful process starts in which one part of the patient's mind—the healthy part of his ego—has to struggle with the rest of his ego and his old super-ego—with some help, it is true, from the analyst.

This is a very hard and painful fight, giving up consciously parts of ourselves as unlovable and unacceptable to our fellow men—or using again Mrs. Klein's word—as bad. By now the patient knows the history of these parts, that they have been developed mainly as defences against an environment felt to be cruel, indifferent, etc.; but at the same time he knows also that those parts represent, albeit in a distorted way, the people most important and dearest to him; and—last but not least— these parts have been for many, many years and still are important parts of himself which he valued highly. An additional reason for the high emotional value of these parts to the patient is that they are, so to speak, the last survivors of his archaic object-relation; they are the remnants of the eternal wish that he may live without the strain of constantly testing the reality and without any obligation of regard or consideration for the wishes and sensitivities of people around him. All these wishes have become incorporated in the introjected archaic objects or, using another metaphor, the introjection of the archaic objects has enabled these wishes to survive in great force. The stronger these wishes, the greater the task of renouncing them consciously. During this very bitter struggle the patients show all the features described so poignantly by Freud: [1] 'A profoundly painful dejection, abrogation of interest in the outside world, loss of capacity to love, inhibition of all activity, and a lowering of the self-regarding feelings . . . culminating in expectations of punishment.'

Is one to call this syndrome melancholia or depression? Here I am fully on the side of Mrs. Klein, who hardly ever calls this state melancholia but speaks of depressive position and depressive anxieties.[2] In my opinion the clinical observations reported above have a significantly different mechanism from that studied and described by Abraham and Freud [3] for which I propose to reserve the term melancholia, while depression could be used in a wider sense which should include the classical melancholia, the early states described by Mrs. Klein, my clinical observations and very likely many more others.[4] I think it can be accepted that one condition, perhaps

[1] 'Mourning and Melancholia', *Collected Papers*, IV, p. 153.
[2] e.g. in 'A Contribution to the Psychogenesis of Manic-Depressive States', *Int. J. of PsA.* (1945), **16**, 145; 'Mourning and its Relation to Manic-Depressive States', *ibid.* (1940), **21**, 125; 'The Oedipus Complex in the Light of Early Anxieties', *ibid.* (1945), **26**, 11.
[3] Freud: op. cit.
Abraham: 'Development of the Libido', in *Selected Papers*, pp. 418 ff. Hogarth Press, London.
[4] cf. Balint, M.: 'On Punishing Offenders', in *Psycho-Analysis and Culture*, Int. Univ. Press, New York, 1951.

the distinguishing one of every depression, is a very painful split leading to one part of the personality rejecting the other part and trying to discard it altogether, even to annihilate it. (In paranoid states this fight seems to be successfully terminated: all the bad things have been projected outside, the ego feels whole, clever, superior and often overbearing—in fact like a true conqueror. Like every conqueror, however, the paranoiac, too, has to organise a police state around himself in which suspicion reigns supreme.) In classical melancholia—according to Fenichel [1] it is either the ego that fights against the super-ego and the introjects, or the super-ego that fights against the ego and the introjects. Neither of these two descriptions fits my case.

To show what I mean, I shall start with the everyday adaptation to reality. In every such process giving up part of our personality (certain of our wishes) for some time or even for good is unavoidably involved. As we know from Freud,[2] a very instructive example of this is mourning. Conversely every adaptation can be described as, and perhaps is, in fact, mourning. From here an interesting line of thought leads to the general problem of the acceptance of unpleasure; [3] certainly a most important facet of adaptation. All this—mourning, adaptation, the classical melancholia, in fact every form of depression—shows very strong *secondary narcissistic* features, usually taking the form of bitter resentment about an undeserved, unfair and unjust injury—a mixture of paranoid and depressive mechanisms. Mourning, again, is a good example. Under the pressure of the feeling of an unjust injury quite often markedly paranoid features develop, as can be often observed after the death of a beloved person: assuming hostile intentions in the doctors who did not treat our beloved with proper skill and care, or even accusing the dead partner of not taking enough care of himself, etc.—obvious projections of one's own unconscious tendencies.

---

[1] *The Psycho-Analytic Theory of Neuroses*, p. 398. Norton and Co. (New York, 1945.)

[2] Freud S.: *Collected Papers*, IV.

[3] Ferenczi: *Bausteine zur Psychoanalyse*, **1**, 84; *Further Contributions*, p. 366.

The depressive states, preceding the new beginning, in many points differ considerably from these forms. There is undoubtedly the fight of one part of the personality against the other (the pre-condition of every depression), but this time the aim is not to create or to widen a split but to remove it, to enable the patient to be 'one with himself'. The parts against which the patient's ego has to fight are not rejected, condemned or hated (although these feelings may be, and often are, present) but above all mourned for, and—*sit venia verbo*—buried with full honours. And lastly, the whole process happens all the time on two planes simultaneously: on a narcissistic plane in the patient's mind and on the plane of transference, i.e. in an object-relation. In my opinion, this last quality constitutes the crucial difference between all the other depressive states and the therapeutic depression, of which the phenomena in the new beginning period are but one example. In this benign form of depression the patient in his newly won courage allows himself to experience the actual revival of old, primitive object-relations; he admits them not only as mere possibilities but as actual wishes and feelings, although he is in no doubt that the analytical situation permits at best only very partial gratifications, and even these only for a very limited period; he does not shut himself off from the painful sweetness of these desires, i.e. does not repress them. In this way he may remain 'unsplit', the memory of these gratifications remains accessible, and even further gratifications of these infantile, primitive longings by a real object remain potentially possible, although admittedly somewhat comical because of their often very primitive nature.

I must add that my knowledge of these phenomena is still not so well founded as it is of the paranoid state, and consequently most of my mistakes used to happen here. Perhaps an added difficulty is the very high vulnerability of patients in the depressive period, which is far beyond that of the paranoid period; in fact it surpasses all expectation. Time and again I was surprised that in spite of every precaution and—as far as I know—the best of wills, one or the other of my patients felt deeply and unjustly hurt by an interpretation or even by a 'neutral' remark or an 'everyday' gesture of mine.

As in the paranoid state, it happens that some patients cannot be helped—by my present technique—through the depressive state, and so finish their analysis with a partial result. And similarly, although the therapeutic result is quite commendable, it is not as good as one would wish. These patients, too, usually show good social adaptation, a good measure of success in life, but somehow they remain discontented, they cannot enjoy their laurels. For them there is always some flaw in everything, fate is never as kind to them as to others. Despite this they are well liked, though often considered difficult and awkward; lots of people are willing to go out of their way to help them to a quite considerable degree which these patients accept and even demand as a matter of course. Their love-life runs on similar lines; they are usually fairly successful, people fall for them often quite unexpectedly, still their basic ambivalent attitude remains unchanged. They accept the love offered to them, even demand more and more of it, and then go on wondering about the true motives of the partner for choosing them, whether these motives are sound and trustworthy enough. The same applies to their physical sexuality; as a rule they are not impotent or frigid but never quite certain of it. Their whole sexuality seems to be rather precarious, but somehow it works. In contrast to the patients who left analysis during the paranoid period who do not feel ill and hardly ever complain, the patients leaving analysis before the depressive state could be resolved usually complain a lot, try to raise guilt feelings in their environment (and in their former analyst) by exhibiting and even flaunting their shortcomings, but they hardly ever want to make real efforts towards a basic change. Apparently they cannot renounce their right to expect miraculous help from their environment—a clear remnant of the archaic object-love.

3

To sum up my clinical experience (leaving out the technical difficulties): new beginning means the capacity for an unsuspicious, trusting, self-abandoned and relaxed object-relation. There are two clinically necessary conditions without which a proper phase of new beginning cannot develop. These are: (*a*) the relinquishing of the paranoid attitude, the realisation that the paranoid anxieties were unfounded or at least grossly exaggerated; (*b*) the acceptance, without undue anxiety, of a certain amount of depression as an inevitable condition of life, the confidence that it is possible—nay certain —to emerge from this kind of depression a better man.[1]

Is it justified to assume that the sequence: paranoid attitude —depression—archaic object-love, occurring regularly in the end-phases of my analyses, is significant, i.e. that it is determined by some principle of repetition? Or is this sequence accidental, caused merely by the peculiarity of my technique? In a paper recently published in English [2] I discussed in detail the reasons for preferring the first assumption with regard to the archaic object-love. But if we accept that the occurrence of primitive forms of object-love in the transference situation has the significance of repetition, the same must be assumed of its concomitant syndromes—the paranoid attitude and the depression.

The next objection will likely be: the sequence—paranoid attitude—depression—primary object-love—observed in adult patients, though perhaps of repetitive nature, is most likely so distorted that any inference to early states of development is unjustified without careful validation by direct observation of

[1] Professor Lagache who kindly read the MS. suggested that the idea of new beginning should not be restricted to the events occurring towards the end of a treatment, but to use it also in relation to all the occasions during an extended analysis when a patient gives up some complicated defensive mechanism for the first time. In his experience— which I can fully confirm—each time the patient first develops some form of the paranoid and depressive syndrome described in this paper, overcomes it and then starts some new attitude, usually of a primitive nature; further analysis proves in all such cases that the newly begun attitudes or activities are in fact repetitions of early forms. Such an extension is probably legitimate and I think it will prove to be fruitful, as it will almost certainly lead to a better understanding of the all-important problem of tolerating unpleasure, and through it to the general problem of adaptation to reality, especially to the reality of one's objects. I see, however, a number of complications and must therefore content myself with this short note.

[2] Balint, M.: 'Early Developmental States of the Ego. Primary Object-love', *Imago* (1937), *Int. J. of PsA.* (1949.) Reprinted in this vol., p. 90.

the child. This—on the surface—appears to be a legitimate argument which can be, and is, in fact, often used against any inference from adult to infant—except against the classical theory of primary narcissism. In the paper just quoted, I think I showed the fallacy of this argument.

But if we accept the view that the clinical observations described in this paper are at least partly determined by repetition of early states of human development, we have to face a very old and very vexed problem of psycho-analysis—that of chronology. The clinical sequence is doubtless paranoia—depression—new beginning. Moreover, till the full development of the last phase, the therapeutic situation remains precarious and the patient may relapse at any moment into either of the two previous states. Can one conclude that the above sequence describes the line of development of the human mind? It is a weighty argument that Mrs. Klein and her school think, in fact, that the first phase of the human mind is dominated by paranoid anxieties and mechanisms and that this is followed by the depressive position.

If I were to accept this chronology, I should have to give up the idea of the archaic object-love as the first phase; it is true, however, that even in this case the archaic object-love might be retained as a focal point of all later forms of object-love, but it would be preceded by the paranoid and the depressive phases. In other words, the sequence paranoid attitude—depression—archaic form of love, as observed in adult patients, corresponds to the sequence of early stages of the human mind. Mrs. Klein's theory of the persecutory phase followed by depression is correct; one has only to insert the archaic object-love between these two earlier phases and any later form of object-relation.

There are, however, several important clinical facts that speak against this conception. I have mentioned already that both the paranoid and the depressive states preceding the period of new beginning show many narcissistic features. According to my experience, narcissism is always secondary.[1] (If I am right, Mrs. Klein has recently come very near to this idea. In any case she has stressed time and again the presence

[1] Balint, M.: 'Early Development Stages of the Ego. Primary Object-love', This vol., p. 98.

of early object-relations, an inevitable corollary of which is that narcissism is secondary—unless it is assumed that object-relations and narcissistic attitude coexist right from the beginning of extra-erinute life, which, however, is contrary to my clinical observations discussed in the paper just mentioned.) If we accept the secondary nature of all narcissistic features, then it is very probable that syndromes incorporating many narcissistic traits are also secondary phenomena, forms of reaction and not primary phases.

A second, still weightier argument is the different fate of these three phases during analytic treatment under my technique. All three must be interpreted and worked through, none of them can be carried over unchanged into adult life. As I have mentioned, the paranoid phantasies must be worked through, recognised as originating from a greatly distorted picture of the reality, i.e. from faulty reality testing, and then be given up. The depression—caused by the realisation that the environment is largely indifferent towards us (or as someone said to me recently 'has not been cut to fit us') and that we must renounce certain of our wishes if we want any favour from our environment—must be accepted as inevitable, and the attempts at circumventing it largely given up. Or, in other words, removing the paranoid anxieties enables the patient to evaluate the everyday hardships of life in their proper proportion, while removing the depressive anxieties enables him to accept a certain amount of depression as caused by common frustrations and to arrange his life better by taking full account of them.

The fate of the archaic object-love is quite different. Although the difference is great, I find it difficult to express it in words. Both the paranoid and the depressive attitude preceding the period of new beginning appear to be markedly pathological, they must be overcome, put right; the archaic form of object-love is only undeveloped, and the healthy adult way of love may grow out of it in a straight line. The task of analytic therapy is only to assist this development. From another angle the same difference may be described in this way: both the paranoid and the depressive attitude are fraught with anxieties; analysis can reduce the intensity of these anxieties and then these attitudes lose their importance. There is no fear inherent in the archaic object-love—only naïve confidence and unsuspicious self-abandonment; the more paranoid and depressive anxieties and fears have been removed by analysis, the more clearly the phenomena of the archaic object-love—the new beginning in an adult patient—develop before our eyes.

I find it difficult to reconcile these clinical facts with the theory that the very first extra-uterine phase of the human mind is characterised by the paranoid attitude, out of which, then, the depressive position develops. The next argument, I expect, will be worded somehow in this way: there is no need to reconcile my observation with those of Mrs. Klein and her school; the two sets of observations are—because of the different techniques used—incommensurable. Although very plausible, I think this argument is unacceptable, as it is only a pusillanimous, and at the same time stealthily supercilious, attempt at avoiding the real issue, admittedly a very difficult one. The real issue is this: how far does the analyst's individual technique, i.e. his attitude in the analytical situation, his theoretical expectations, the set of technical terms used by him, etc., etc., influence among other things: (a) the patient's reactions and associations; (b) the analyst's observations; (c) the analyst's description of his observations. As may be expected, most analysts, including myself, superciliously admit the possibility, or rather the certainty, of such a 'distorting' influence by the technique of anyone not belonging to their own school, while pusillanimously stating that their own technique exerts no, or only a negligible, influence of this kind.

In my Zürich Congress paper [1] I dealt with some aspects of this cardinal problem, especially with the importance to the analyst of using his own accustomed ways of thinking and speaking, i.e. his familiar set of technical terms. I am fully aware that by this only the very fringe of the problem has been reached and that it will not be easy to penetrate farther. But what are we to do in the meanwhile, i.e. before we know with

[1] Balint, M.: 'Changing Therapeutical Aims and Techniques in Psycho-Analysis', *Int. J. of PsA.* (1950) **31**, 117–24. Reprinted in this vol., p. 221.

some certainty how far the analyst's honest account of his experience in the analytical situation is biased by his technique?

I wish to propose two interim working principles. First: for the time being we should accept every positive finding by any analyst as something that must be evaluated by, and then allotted some place in, any theoretical construction. A theory which cannot explain and place a clinical observation satisfactorily should be considered with due scepticism. On the other hand, negative findings need not necessarily be given such weight. The reason for this discrimination is that it is not impossible for one to miss this or that event in the long process of analysis, or not to attribute to it the weight it deserves, because of some emotional blind spot not yet dealt with by one's own training analysis or the subsequent self-analysis. On the other hand, it is not very likely that one could be misled to the extent of reporting something non-existent. Secondly: as long as we have hardly any well-founded knowledge of the dynamisms governing the relation of the various technical approaches to their respective theoretical findings, we have no choice but to accept most analytic techniques as peers. I wish I could add to this frighteningly sweeping statement: 'except a few obviously faulty ones'! The reason why I abstain from including this rider is that for the present I cannot see any criteria which would enable us to decide objectively what is an 'obviously faulty' technique and what is not, although, like every other analyst, subjectively I am convinced that doubtless there are some 'obviously faulty' techniques.

Honouring these two working principles, let us now return to the differing descriptions of our analytical experiences. Among the new terms introduced by Mrs. Klein we find a very important notion which must have been based on clinical experiences very similar to, if not identical with, those which lead me to the idea of the primitive object-relation. This notion is the phantasy of the 'idealised object'. Such an object is inviolate and inviolable, it has no needs and no demands, is eternal and never changing, and it can and does give bountifully everything that one can wish for. Obviously a very near description of what I would call an archaic or primitive object, though equally obviously it has a much richer content.

The first question we have to decide is, is this 'idealised object' a primary or a secondary phenomenon, or, in other words, does it have a history or not? I think it is correct to say that the general view is that the 'idealised object' is the result of a split, the other split-off part being the persecutory object.

But, if we accept this, we must ask ourselves, what was the original, the unsplit, the primary object? What was its history before the split and what will its fate be in later life?—e.g. does it disappear altogether in the turmoil of the archaic splitting? The present literature—if I am right—does not answer any of these questions, in fact has not even asked them.

Apparently we have reached a problem not yet solved, perhaps not even noticed. In my view there are two trains of thought which point to a possible solution; both of them are based on the fact that the concept of the 'idealised object' is much richer than that of the 'archaic object'. First, the 'idealised object' contains a very important element of denial, especially the denial of aggressive intentions against it. The true meaning of being inviolate and inviolable is, very likely, the bitter experience that the most violent aggressiveness has proved of no avail against it. This characteristic alone points irrefutably to its comparative lateness, to its secondary nature. In contradistinction there is no quality of aggressivity or its denial in the concept of archaic object-relation—only confidence and self-abandonment.

A second train of thought makes use of the interrelation between the development of libidinous object-relation, on the one hand, and that of reality testing on the other.[1] Primary, archaic, object-relation hardly demands any reality testing; there is no need to account for the object. A change is brought about by the experience of being frustrated or being compelled to wait for satisfaction by an indifferent, insufficiently considerate, or even hostile environment. This enforces upon the child a very primitive kind of reality testing, resulting in splitting the object into a frustrating bad, and into a gratifying good, part-object. Out of the former develop the phantasies

[1] cf. Alice Balint: 'Love for the Mother and Mother Love', in German, (1939). English: *Int. J. of PsA.* (1949), **30**, 251–9. Reprinted in this vol., p. 109.

about the hostile, persecutory or depressing objects, out of the latter—as a kind of reaction-formation or reparation—the phantasy of the 'idealised object'.

It is certain that there are many more phases in this complicated interrelation of two parallel developments (that of object-relations and that of testing the reality), the last rung of which is the mature form of object-relation with a fully developed sense of reality, enabling the individual to accept a certain measure of unpleasure as unavoidable, or in other words to accept reality as real and even to enjoy it as far as it is enjoyable. But behind every one of the many forms of object-relation there remains practically unchanged the eternal archaic wish: I shall be loved for every little bit that I am, by every one of my objects for whom I need not care, whose interests and sensitivity I need not consider, who shall be just there when I want them, and shall not bother me after my needs have been satisfied.[1]

Considering all this, I think that the unsuspicious, naïve, archaic object-love should be considered as the first post-natal phase in the development of the human mind; it is a centre or a nodal point from which all later developments radiate. One such development is narcissism: if I am not loved by the world (in the way I want it), I must love myself. Another direction of development is depression and paranoid attitude. These two are closely interlinked; each of them can be used as a defence against the other; quite often—even after the termination of an analysis—I remained in doubt whether to consider the change-over from one position to the other in that particular case as a progression or a regression. Several of these baffling clinical experiences have been mentioned in this paper, e.g. that patients who left the analysis without working through their paranoid attitudes usually appear healthier and feel better than those who went through their paranoid position but left the analysis before fully coping with their depressive attitude. All this prompts me to leave the chronology of these

[1] Attention was called to a very important new field for studying clinical phenomena closely linked with this idea by D. W. Winnicott in a paper 'Transitional Objects and Transitional Phenomena', read before the British Psycho-analytical Society on May 30th, 1951.

two phases undecided for the time being. Yet another direction of development, mainly due to certain educational influences, is what analysis describes as anal-sadistic object-relation. And last but not least there is that very complicated and rather precarious direction which we call adult sexuality and genital object-love.

Unfortunately the different lines of development are neither straight nor clearly separated one from the others. I have pointed out that both the paranoid and the depressive positions show many markedly narcissistic features; conversely, in the clinical picture of very narcissistic patients strong paranoid and depressive features are always present.

If we accept the view that a real adaptation—the acceptance of unpleasure—is only possible if one can face depression without undue anxiety, then the depressive position must be considered as a second focus through which every line of development associated with adaptation must pass. The relation between these two nodal points of development—archaic object-love and normal depression—is far from being clear; on the basis of my scanty knowledge I expect that they have a profound influence on each other. I could quote many more examples of such entanglement of directions of development or —using another metaphor—of overlapping.

I do not think, however, that a similar overall importance can be attributed to the paranoid position, which then perhaps means that the depressive position must be considered more fundamental, more primitive, than the paranoid.

I wish to mention one more complication. My experiences concern only adults and thus the conclusions reported here are inferences, based on the assumption that these processes, these positions or syndromes, have a fairly similar dynamism, stay in a fairly similar chronological and structural relation to each other, in adults and in children. Although, as far as we know, there is no proof against this assumption, it is only a plausibility, not a certainty. On the other hand, it must not be forgotten that practically all our knowledge about the infantile mind was acquired when analysing adults. The only exception of which I know are Mrs. Klein's ideas and theories which originated mostly—though not exclusively—in her work with children. Despite all these complications I think that a theory of human development, starting with the state of archaic object-love, is worth considering and worth examining again after more clinical material has been collected.

It is fair to say that the value of any new contribution to scientific theory or practice can best be assessed by the quality and number of problems that have emerged under its impact. Measured by this standard, the value of Mrs. Klein's contribution is high indeed. It is no exaggeration to say that her ideas are at present perhaps the most hotly discussed topics in our psycho-analysis. This is only the natural consequence of her dauntless courage in directing her research towards the very roots of human nature, in consequence of which her ideas cannot be but challenging.

In my tribute to her birthday I have tried to show how the challenge of her ideas has helped me to solve some of my old problems and led me to find many more new ones.

INDEX OF SUBJECTS

Abreaction
  of affects   190 [see also *Affects*]
  of birth trauma   191
Acting out   162
  [see also *Repetition, Transference*]
Active
  love, see *Love, active*
  technique, see *Psycho-analytic technique, active*
Adaptation [Adjustment, see also *Alloplastic, Autoplastic, Environment, Reality*]   40, *42–6*, 47, 57, 125, 171, 185, 197, 248, 254
  and acceptance of unpleasure   236, 254, 257, 263, 264
  erotisation as precondition for   43, 46
  genitality in the process of   134
  hysteria as model for   40
  mutual, in genital love   135–6
  to the object's wishes   122, 135
Addiction
  auto-erotism as   123
  – like states in the new beginning   97, 102, 193, 246
Adult   74, 170
  eternally a child   133
  fear of being one   184
  love, see *Aphrodite, Love*

and orgasm   74, 78
sexuality   147, 247, 263–4 [see also *Genital(ity)*, etc.]
'split'   249–50
Adultomorph language   144–5
Affect(s) [Emotions, see also *Abreaction, Emotional life*]
  outbreak of   84, 87, 181–2
  transference of   *174–87*
Aggression [Aggressiveness, Destructiveness, see also *Hate, Hostility, Sadism*]   5, 57, 60, 62, 93, 100, 230, 246
  against archaic object   262
  against 'idealised' object   262
  primary   150
  and true hate   111
  very early   94, 103
Aim-inhibition [see also *Erotism, Fore-pleasure, Playfulness, Tenderness*]   61, 68, 229
  love as   124–5, 131
Alloplastic
  methods   41, 200, 236 [see also *Adaptation, Autoplastic*]
  phase   194
Altruism   70, 110, 112, 120, 124–5
  in coitus   101
  in genital love   129

Ambivalence 57, 92, 94
    as derivative of oral erotism 51
    pseudo– 115
    secondary nature of 111
Ambivalent, object-relations, see
    Object-relations
Amnion 28, 29, 30
Anal (Anal sadistic)
    evacuation, sexual functions of
        the gametocyte 16, 25, 26
    evacuation, as model for the
        sexual function of plants 19,
        26
    gratification 71 [see also Grati-
        fication]
    instinct 49, 51, 229–30
    love (object-relations), see Love,
        anal
    masturbation 75
    organisation of the libido 12,
        25, 54, 55 [see also Libido]
    phase 50, 90
Analysis, see Psycho-analysis
Analyst, see Psycho-analyst
Analytic(al), see Psycho-analytic(al)
Anthropomorphism 28, 203
Anisogamous, see Gametes
Anxiety [Panic, see also Castration,
    Fear] 83, 86, 88, 93, 154,
    160, 162–4, 170, 172–3, 222
    acute state of 137, 141
    depressive, see Depressive
    during analysis 152
    form of 143, 170
    and hate 141–2
    love free from 159, 166
    and oral-sadistic impulses 92
    and orgasm 74, 87, 136
    paranoid, see Paranoid
    and partner's claims 100
    of pregenital enjoyment 136
    –p oneness in children 74, 161
    and wishes in the new begin-
        ning 192
Aphrodite, one conception of love
    73, 78, 80
    Eros and 73–89
Ars amandi [see also Genital, Love]
    78, 131, 138, 207

Asexual
    fore-pleasure always – 77
    forms of life 38–40
    propagation 19–20, 24, 33–4
Associations, free
    and learning 205
    and the analyst 260–2
Auto-erotic [see also Egoism, Nar-
    cissistic]
    gratification as substitute 123,
        194
    gratifications [see also Gratifica-
        tions] 59, 162
    gratifications impossible in the
        new beginning 245
    stage 62, 123, 192, 194
Auto-erotism [see also Egoism,
    Gratification, Masturbation,
    Narcissism] 50, 52–3, 63,
    65, 123, 194
    always analysed 56
    a biological concept 63, 65
    as biological foundation of
        secondary narcissism 123
    Freud on 58, 125–6, 195
    independent of external world
        122, 125
    and mother-child relation 123
    preliminary stage to object-re-
        lation 50
    primary 64, 122
    secondary nature of 53–9, 196
    simultaneous with primary love
        123
Automatic
    form of defence 202
    super-ego 208, 211
Automatism(s) [see also Rigid forms
    of reaction] 180–2, 185, 198
Autoplastic
    methods [see also Adaptation,
        Alloplastic] 40, 41, 210, 236
    method of gratification 125
    phase 194
Autotomy 85

Birth trauma 191
Bisexual 19, 39

Breast (good or bad) 144
Brother horde 137–8, 140

Cannibalistic, see *Oral-sadistic*
Case histories 75–6, 109–13, 141–2, 179–80, 182–3, 183–5, 189
Wolfman 54–5
Castration
anxiety 222
complex 129
conflict 60
threat of 54, 55, 98
Catatonic, never completely unresponsive 104
Catharsis 190
Cathexis (Investment of libido)
erotic 44, 48
narcissistic 45, 70
of objects 70
Character [Personality, see also *Ego, Individuality, Mind*] 47–8, 162, 166–71, 180, 224, 226
– analysis 37, 61, *159–73*, 225
and automatism 180–1, 185
as defence against over-excitation 170, 173
disturbances 61
and individuality 168, 180
– neurosis 227
strong and weak 167, 169, 171
to be interpreted first 210
– traits 42, 54, 170, 173, 181–5
and transference problems 185
Characterology 174, 180–2, 185
form-problem of 168–9
intensity problem of 168–9
Child(ren) [Infant, see also *Education, Infantile, Latency, Mother-child relation, Object-relation, Pregenital, Puberty*] 56–7, 59, 62, 194
adult eternally a child 133
– analysis, see *Child analysis*
anxiety prone 74, 161
defenceless against adults 170
'educated to analysis' 205
and environment, see *Child and Environment*

hostility in 95
insatiability of 91–2, 95, 102, 106, 144
language of – in literature 69
love for the mother *109–27*
mother as sexual partner 120–1 [see also *Mother*]
neurosis, see *Infantile*
observations of 57, 232, 257–8
orgasm-like states in 102
and parents 170, 197 [see also *Education, Parents*]
and passion 62
self-sufficiency of 115
Child analysis [see also *Child*] 56, 107, 197, 205, 217, 232, 244
final state after 57
and pregenital forms of love 57
Child and Environment [see also *Child, Education, Environment, Object, Object-relations*] 113, 144, 161–2, 169–70, 249
good understanding between 53, 55, 57–8
Civilisation [Culture, see also *Education, Environment, Society*] 43, 47, 69, 96, 101, 138, 140
responsible for form of love (object-relation) 63, 66–7, 131–2
Clinging [see also *Instinct to cling*] 61, 97–100, 115, 126–7
Coitus [Intercourse, see also *End-pleasure, Fertilisation, Mating, Orgasm*] 31, *72–89*, 160, 191, 207, 237
as an altruistic act 101
and death 34
identification in 101, 134–5, 137
interdependence of the partners 120, 125, 130, 135
more satisfactory than any perversion 76
physiological explanation of 31
primarily devoid of pleasure 88
Colonies (as against individuals) 26, 33

Compensation, demand for 199
Compromise formation,
 adult object-relation as 247
 character as 171
 pregenital love as 59
 symptom as 52, 53, 200
Conceptions [see also *Psycho-analytical terminology, theory*]
 dynamic, of mental processes 170
 negative 103, 150, 152
 genital love as negative conception 128
 using 'not yet' 103–4, 108, 151
Conflict(s) 47–8, 60, 82, 198, 200
Confusion of tongues 62, 197–8
Conscious
 control 85, 198, 220
 making the unconscious conscious 185, 189–90, 196, 203, 211
 recollection of early infantile experiences 95
Consciousness 198
 and internal organs 46
Consolation for loss of object 58–9
Constitution (innate) 48, 60, 62, 151, 197, 199
 environmental influences distorted by 60
 no constitutionally wicked or evil human being 62
Control analysis, see *Psycho-analysis, supervision*
Conversion [see also *Hysteria*] 44, 47, 209
Counter-transference [see also *Psycho-analyst, Psycho-analytic situation, Transference*] 163, 178–9, 181, *213–20*, 233, 250
 always libidinous 231
 and 'sterility' 179, 181, 187, 213, 218
 is transference 214–15, 218–20
Culture, see *Civilisation*

Death 32–4, 36, 40
 – instinct 44, 92, 143, 147, 150
 from internal causes 33

and mating (coitus) 34
and new beginning 40
and orgasm 78
threat of 170
wishes 110–11
Defence [Defensive mechanism, see also *Ego, Mind*, and under the specific headings] 110, 143, 145, 154–6, 170, 173, 200–2, 209, 222–4, 234
 interpreted first 217
 later forms of 87
 primal forms of 87
Defiance of ungratifying object (in children) 57, 59, 194
Defloration 88
Demands, see *Interests*
Dependence 148–9, 154–6, 250
 abnormal, as result of suppressed auto-erotism 123
 denial of 146, 148, 149, 154
 despondent 154
 on object of primary love 145
 perpetual 154
Depression(s) [Melancholia, Mourning] 146, 252–7, 263–4
 as basis of psycho-analytical theory 209–10, 226–7, 230
 common basis of all forms of 253–5
 difference from melancholia 253, 255
 in the new beginning 252–7
 normal 264
 therapeutic (benign) 255
Depressive
 fears 144, 153, 253, 257, 259–60, 264
 position 253, 258–60
 syndrome *244–65*
Destructiveness, see *Aggression, Hate, Hostility, Sadism*
Determination of sex 17
Development [see also under the respective headings]
 of instinctual aims and of instinctual object-relations 49, 51, 71, 102

Development of libido, see *Libido*
of object-relations, see *Object-relations*
Differentiation (sexual) 15, 17, 33–6, 30, 33, 35, 37–8, 41, 81
and death 33–4
fore-pleasure not differentiated 77
and individuality 34–5, 39
Dimorphism (sexual) 26, 35
Diploid generation 19, 36, 37, 81
Discharge
danger of 202, 203, 206
of excitation 74, 76, 82, 84, 85, 122, 159–62
restricted by education 86
through a neurotic symptom 172
Displacement 47, 209
in development of genitality 80
in perversions 76
Dreams, of analysed people 190
Drinking (Intake of fluids) 42
Dual-unity instead of primary object-relations 127

Eating (Intake of Solids) 42
Education [Upbringing, Training, see also *Environment, Civilisation, Society*] 42–3, 58, 86–7, 161, 236
and active love 66, 194
to analysis 205
and auto-erotism 123, 194
basic methods of 86
disastrous effects of 208, 212
and discipline 204
of the ego 200–12
errors in 171
and object-relation 123, 132, 136, 139, 194
amongst primitives 96, 101
and psycho-analysis 208–10, 212
and psycho-analytic treatment 205, 208
and repressed sexuality of parents 160, 170

responsible for anal-sadistic, phallic, genital, forms of love 63, 72
of the super-ego 209, 211–12
ununderstanding 195, 197–8
Educability *42–6*
of ego-instincts 42–3
Ego [see also *Defence, Mind, Split*] 46, 222
body ego 210
as condenser 202–4, 206–7
defence of the 201
education of the *200–12*
and endurance of tensions 201–2, 204–5, 207–8
early states of *90–108*, 212
form of love of the 126
functions of 210–11
and genital love 136
immature (see also *weak*) 149
interests of the 200
and introjected objects 252–4
– psychology 187, 196, 203, 209–10
and repression 173
strength of the 86–8, *200–12*
strength of the ego as capacity 202–3
structure of the (mental structure) 137, 202–3, 222–3, 231, 236–7, 246
strong 201, 207, 209
and sublimation 210
weak 93, 137, 143, 149, 153, 200
and working through 202 [see also *Working through*]
Ego-instincts *42–8*
Ego (Subject) and Object [see also *Mother and Child, Orgasm*] 95, 127
inequality of 149, 154
in a 'mystical union' 136
Egoism [see also *Love, primary, Reality testing*] 113–14, 124
in genital love 129, 139
naïve 114, 115, 120–2, 125
Embryogenesis and development of psychosexuality 13, 25

Emotional life [see also *Affect*]
development of 115–17, 120–5
Emotions, see *Affect*
End-pleasure [see also *Erotic, Erotism, Fore-pleasure, Gratification, Orgasm, Pleasure*] 73–89
absent in children 74, 161
alien to soma 81
capacity for 172, 210, 237
different from fore-pleasure 74, 77, 79, 82, 88
economic aspects of 82, 85
sexually differentiated 77
and suspension of pleasure principle 84
maybe traumatic 84, 87
Enjoyment, see *Pleasure*
Environment [see also *Child, Civilisation, Indifference, Reality, Society*] 23, 59, 60, 62, 67, 71, 97, 104, 122, 125, 151, 196, 229, 247–8, 259
demands of 200
and primitive needs 98
and new beginning 192–3
and reality testing 262
Eros [see also *Genital, Libido, Sexual*]
and Aphrodite 73–89
career of 11–28
conquering tendencies of 29–30, 35, 41
one conception of love 73, 78 [see also *Infantile sexuality*]
Erotic [see also *Genital, Libido, Sexual*, etc.]
cathexis 44, 48
component of ego instincts 42–8
sense of reality 50, 122, 125, 194
Erotisation [see also *Libido, Sexual*, etc.]
of ego instincts 42–8
in organic and functional diseases 47
Erotism [see also *Anal, Auto-, Genital, Oral*, etc.]
development of 51, 52

parental 119
pregenital 80 [see also *Pregenital*]
Erotogenic zones 51, 81, 101
instincts bound to 51, 58–9
Evacuation [see also *Anal, Gametocyte*] 26, 31
and the sexual functions of the male and female 27
Evolution, see under the respective headings
Excitation (Stimulation, see also *Tension*] 21, 24, 31, 74–7, 84–5, 122, 159–64, 172–3, 207
of component instincts 76
disproportion between discharge and – 74–5, 159–62
and fore-pleasure mechanisms 78, 82
optimal level of 85
overstimulation 160–5, 170–3
self-determined 163–4
External factors, see *Environment*

Father 116, 119, 121, 222
primal 138
Fear [see also *Anxiety*] 159–60, 167–71
of disproportionate pleasure 170
of being dropped 61
of retaliation (in the new beginning) 97
of the strength of an instinct 103
of withdrawal of love 170
Feeding and sexuality 15, 26, 38
Female 27, 33, 35
equal rights to male 140
and passive 77
potentially immortal 33
Fertilisation, external 14, 38
internal 21, 22, 23, 28, 29 [see also *Coitus, Mating*]
Fetishism 75
Fish symbol 12
Fixation 52–5, 151, 172
Foetalisation 133–4

Fore-pleasure [see also *Erotic, Erotism, End-pleasure, Gratification, Infantile, Pleasure, Pregenital, Tenderness*] *74–89*, 210
  and coquetry 83
  differences from end-pleasure 77, 79, 88
  and excitation 78, 82
  level of 98, 237, 245
  perennial 78–80
  and somatic functions 81
Frigidity 87, 88, 160
Frustration [see also *Indifference*] 60, 123
  and aim-inhibition 131
  leading to hate 146, 149, 194
  in the new beginning 62, 98, 246
  as source of sadism 92, 94, 144
  usually underestimated 196
  vehement reactions after 97–8, 102, 144, 247
Functional diseases (Neuroses) 47

Gamete(s) (Germ cells) 14–15, 32, 35–7, 81
  anisogamous 15–16
  and death 33
  as the individual 15, 32–4, 36–7, 39
  isogamous 15–16
  sexual differentiation of 15, 17, 18, 23
  sexual function of, see *Sexual*
  treated as excreta 20, 26, 30, 35
Gametocyte 16, 25–7, 35, 37
  and death 33
  sexual differentiation of 17, 23
  sexual functions of, see *Sexual*
Gametocyte-carrier [see also *Soma*] 16, 37
  and death 16, 20, 33–5
  sexual differentiation of 17, 23
  sexual functions of, see *Sexual*

Genital [see also *Genital love*]
  excitation 46, 172–3
  function, see *Genitality*
  gratification [see also *End-pleasure, Orgasm, Pleasure*] 67, 71, *73–89*, 129–30, 135–6, 236
    and civilisation 138
    exclusive in primal horde 138
    Shakespeare on – 138
  heat 133, 135
  identification 134–5, 236–7
  instinct 49, 229–30
    primacy of 222, 236
  masturbation 31, 75–6, 88
  point 172
  potency not identical with love 67
  transference 153–4
  union as regression 21, 26
  wish 82, 132–3
Genital love [Object-relation] 49, 52, 59, 60, 63, 66–7, 71, 80, 112–13, 124, *128–40*, 147, 229–30, 236, 264
  absent in primal horde 138
  and altruism 129
  asocial 139
  and fusion with tenderness 132
  and homosexuality 137
  as retardation 133–4
Genitality [Genital function, see also *Coitus, End-pleasure, Genital love, Mating, Orgasm, Sexuality, mature*] 24, 25, 29, 31, 46, *73–89*, 120, 137, 139, 172, 191
  as basis of genital love 132
  evolution of 28, 80, 134
  and foetalisation 133–4
  inexact use of 67
  mature 236, 239
  phylogenetically new 134
  in plants 27
  and reality testing 120–1
Germ cell, see *Gamete*
Gonad (Ovary, Spermary) 19, 20

Gratification [Satisfaction, see also *Aim-inhibition, Auto-erotic, End-pleasure, Fore-pleasure, Orgasm, Pleasure, Tranquil, quiet, wellbeing*] 59, 62, 67–8, *73–89*, 91, 123, 146–7, 162, 194, 197–8, 223, 245

automatic in primitive love 146

in genital love 129–30, 135–6 [see also *Genital love*]

genital mode of 67, 75, 85 [see also *End-pleasure, Genital, Orgasm*]

by objects 63, 124, 191, 245 [see also *Object*]

of parents in education 161–2, 170

pregenital, see *Fore-pleasure, Pregenital*

primitive in the new beginning 97, 191–2, 237, 246, 255

in the psycho-analytical situation 237, 255

quiet 98, 245, 247

Greed, see *Insatiability*

Group 138, 139, 140

fair share of the average member 140

– therapy 233

Guilt 97, 117

in a patient 109–10

Haploid generation 19, 35, 36, 37, 81

Hate [see also *Hostility, Object-relation, Sadism*] 5, 57, 93, 97, 111, *141–56*, 163, 169, 194, 247

barriers of 148–9, 154–6

behind anxiety 141–2

change into love 142–9

and character 168–9

as defence 110, 143, 154–6

early 94

equal status with love 147–50

frustration leading to 142–6, 194

and health 147–50

and inequality of subject and object 143

in the new beginning, see *New beginning*

and primary love 122

primitive and mature forms of 143, 147–8

secondary 111, 150

suspect of immature ego 149

true and pseudo – 111

theory of 140–9, 150

Health 147–50, 239

Heartbeat 42, 43

Heterosexual [see also *Genital, Sexual*, etc.]

relations in human evolution 138–40

Homosexual [see also *Perversion*] 75

love (relation) 137–8, 140

Homosexuality in a patient 111–12

Hostility 91, 92, 249 [see also *Aggression*]

in the phase of new beginning 97

unavoidable in infants 95

Human relation, see *Object-relation*

development of individual – 5

Hysteria [see also *Conversion*] 40, 208–10, 212, 223, 226

as basis of new technique 227

in children 56

Id 11, 127, 201, 208, 210, 222

demands of 200

– impulses 40, 45, 47

form of love of the id 126

Idealisation 155–6

in genital love 130–1

of object and instinct 130–1

Idealised object 261–3

Identification 100, 110–11

with the aggressor 155, 159

complete in coitus 101, 135

genital versus oral 134, 137

idealised (dependent) 155–6

with the faithless object 123

Identity, ego-object 101

Illness (physical) [see also *Organic*] *46–8*, 159
chronic and character 48
and new adaptation 47
Immortality
lost, of the soma 35
and new beginning 37–8
of unicellulars 33
Incorporation, see *Gametes, sexual functions of, Internalisation, Introjection*
Indifference [Carelessness, see also *Frustration, Hostility*] 93, 142–3, 246–7, 249, 251–2, 259
Individual(s) (in biological sense) 15, 26, 32–7, 39
dangers to individuality 32
and phylogenesis 33–4
sexual couples as 34
Individual(s) (in psychological sense) [see also *Character, Ego, Mind*] 118, 135–6, 139–40, 149
and his character 171
and his environment 59, 62
and society 171, 187
and limitations of psycho-analytical theory 223, 226–8, 230
and therapeutic aims 223
Individuality 39
and character 168, 180
and death 32–4, 36
and orgasm *28–36*
and sexual differentiation 34–5, 39
Infantile [see also *Child*]
amnesia, removal of 190, 222
experiences and the psycho-analytical situation 95–6, 98
form of love, see *Love, primary, Object-relation, early*
history, remembered after terminated analysis 190
material and final phase of analysis 189
neurosis 56, 93
Infantile mind (see also *Mind*]
divergent views of 92–6
Freud's description of 91–2

and insatiability 102–3
narcissistic 92, 107
not narcissistic 98–9, 107
Infantile sexuality [see also *Eros, Sexuality*] 74, 161
always object-related 194
narcissistic 103
no end-pleasure in 74
polymorph-perverse 90
and transference 186
Infantile situation [see also *Mother-child relation, Trauma*]
and adult transference 181
and character traits 182, 185
and fixations 53–55
repeated in the new beginning 98
to be interpreted first 216
and trauma 160, 163 [see also *Trauma, Traumatic*]
Inflammation 46, 47
and genital excitement 46
Inhibitions 152
Insatiability [Greed] 92, 95, 199
of children 91–2, 95, 102–3, 106, 144
of narcissistic people 105
in the new beginning 166, 193, 246 [see also *New beginning*]
and omnipotence 146
of patients 97–8, 144, 166, 193, 246
possible cause of 102, 144, 153–4
Instinct(s) [see also under specific headings]
aim, object and source of 228–30, 236
breakthrough of 223
to cling 61, 97–100, 126–7
component 44, 60, 76–7, 124
and erotogenic zones 51, 58–9
fear of strength of 103
and fixations 53
and new beginning 192, 197
prevalent 49, 228–9
repressed 222–3
theory of 174
ultimate goal of 101

Intercourse (sexual), see *Coitus, Mating*

Interdependence (instinctual), see *Coitus, Mother, Child, Mutuality*

Interests [Demands]
different for analyst and patient 114–15, 122
different for self and object 100, 142
of the ego and the id 200–1
identical in coitus 101
identical in mother-child-relation 116
of the object 124, 237–8, 252
of the partner 116, 134, 139
primary object has no interests 111

Internalisation 226–7 [see also *Introjection*]

Interpretation(s) [see also *Psychoanalysis, Psycho-analyst, Psychoanalytic technique*] 5, 157, 163, 198, 216–17, 246, 252
of character 210
of content 223–4, 233
'correct' 202, 216, 219, 224, 260–1
of defence 223–4, 234
'deep' 216
dynamic 223
of formal elements 224
'mutative' 225
and patient's reactions 201, 260
and strength of the ego 201
topic 223
of transference 225, 234

Intra-uterine existence 239

Introjection [see also *Internalisation*] 93, 134, 207, 231, 252–4
of archaic objects 253
and widening of the ego 203

Introversion 194

Investment of libido, see *Cathexis*

Isogamous gametes (sexually undifferentiated) 15, 16 [see also *Gametes*]

Jealousy 43

Language
adultomorph 144–5
baby language 69
of tender love 69

Latency 120, 131, 137

Learning 203–12

Libidinal (Libidinous)
economy 76, 86
experience, duality of 74
nature of character traits 42
sadistic tendencies 143, 153

Libido [see also *Cathexis, Libido, development of, Libido, organisation of, Love*] 31, 44, 46
genitopetal and – fugal flow of 31
greedy 91–2
narcissistic 45, 115, 124
object – 45, 124–5
oral 12
pregenital 12, 49–72, 88

Libido, development of [see also *Libido, organisation of, Object-relation*] 12, 25, 49–72, 165, 192, 194, 247
chronology of 50–1, 60, 64
phases in 49–51
anal-sadistic phase 194
auto-erotic and narcissistic phase 62, 192, 194
phallic phase 50, 56, 77, 194
polymorph-perverse phase 50, 90

Libido, organisations of 49–72, 228–9
anal-sadistic 54–5
oral 12
pregenital 12, 49–72, 88
theory of 59, 102

Life
asexual forms of 38–40
– instinct 32, 147, 150

Love (in general and in adult form) [Object-love, Mature or adult love, Active object-love, see also *Aphrodite, Ars*

Love (*continued*)
  amandi, *Eros*, *Genital love*,
  Genitality, *Love for the father*,
  Love for the mother, *Love*, *primary*,
  Object-relation] 41, 52, 66,
  69, 70, 72, 80, 99, 124, 126,
  128–40, *141–56*, 162, 165,
  194, 196, 198, 247–8, 259
  as aim-inhibition 124–5, 131
  altruistic 70, 110, 112
  ambivalent 128
  anal (anal-sadistic) 49, 53–5,
    59, 62–3, 66, 71–2, 124, 128,
    229–30
  in animals and plants 32
  no bounds 149–50
  capacity for 166–7, 169, 198–9
  changing primitive into mature
    151–2
  and character 168–9
  development of 51–62, 71–2,
    121, 124, 126
  different conceptions of 73
  equal status to hate 147–9
  falling in love 32, 137
  free of anxiety 159, 165
  genital, see *Genital love*
  and health 147–8
  inability for 111–12, 159
  and increase of tension 66
  infantile 91
  – making 131–2, 135, 138 [see
    also *Work of conquest*]
  narcissistic 59, 70, 124
  and new beginning 166, 197–
    9, 237–8, 245
  of old people 67
  oral (oral-sadistic, greedy) 49,
    53, 59, 63, 66, 106, 124, 128,
    134, 229–30
  passionate, see *Passion(ate)*
  phallic 50, 53, 56, 59, 77, 94,
    129
  – poetry 131
  postambivalent 128
  possibilities of 169
  pregenital 52, 55, 57, 59, 66,
    128, 132, 146 [see also *Object-
    relation*, *pregenital*]

  principles for classification 124
  and reality 44, 120–1, 124,
    135, 137
  refined forms of 138
  sadistic [see also *Love*, *anal-
    sadistic*, *oral-sadistic*] 128
  sensual [see also *Passion*] 67–8,
    124–5
  a source of suffering 170
  tender 68–9, 93
  transference –, see *Transference*
  withdrawal of 170
  work of conquest, see *Work of
    conquest*
Love, primary [Archaic, Passive,
  Primitive, object-love, see
  also *Love*, etc., *Mother-child
  relation*] 61, 63, 69–71, *90–
  108*, 113, 123–4, 127, 142,
  150–3, 155–6, 194–5, 198,
  247–8, 252, 257–60, 263–5
  in adult, characteristic triad of
    154
  and blissful expectations 142
  change to hate 142, 148
  controversy about 143–6
  egotistic 70, 100, 110, 112–13,
    115
  no fear inherent 260
  and greed 144–6
  and hate 122
  and naïve egoism 116, 120
  narcissism as defence 115
  and omnipotence 145
  oral erotism as expression of
    106, 113–14
  original aim of 61, 63
  and reality testing 113–17,
    119–20, 125–6
  regression to 148–9
  roundabout ways of 63, 66
  sexually not differentiated 116
  unscrupulous 111
Love for the father 116
Love for the mother, peculiar
  nature of 109, 114–6

Male(s) 27, 35, 138, 140
  and 'active' 77

Male(s), development of sexual functions in 27
  equal rights to females 140
  the first mortals 33
Malignant growth 45
Manic syndrome, in the phase of new-beginning 97
Masculinity complex, in a patient 110–11
Masochism 75, 150, 170, 246
  clinging as precursor of 100
  co-operation of partner in 83
Masturbation [see also *Auto-erotism*]
  anal 75
  genital 31, 75–6, 88
Maternity [see also *Mother, Mother-child relation*]
  civilised 120
  instinctive 117, 119–20, 122
Mating [Copulation, Pairing, see also *Coitus, Genital, Genitality, Orgasm, Union*] 14, 17–18, 20, 24–6, 28–9, 31, 35–6
  and death 34–5
  organs 22–3, 29–30
  as regression 27
Maturity [see also *Adult*] 136–7, 142–3, 148–9
  and neoteny 133–4, 137
Melancholia, see *Depression*
Mental development [see also *Mind, development of*]
  biological theory of 49, 90–1, 228–9
  early stages of 258, 262–5
  and object-relations 229–30
  primary object-relation an unavoidable phase of 59, 101, 263–4
Mental structure, see *Ego structure*
Metagenesis 20, 24
Mind (Psyche)
  archaic strata of 84
  development of [see also *Mental development*] 258, 263–5
  dynamic factors in 190
  early stages of 91, 92, 95, 96, 98, 260

and fore-pleasure 82
  infantile, see *Infantile mind*
  parts of 252–3 [see also *Split*]
  structural defects of 190, 196–9
  struggle within 252–5
Mistrustful (Suspicious), see *Paranoid*
Monogamy, demand for 139
Mother [see also *Maternity, Mother-child relation, Parent*]
  'bad' 117
  child, an object of gratification for the – 119–21
  'good' and 'bad' 144, 197
  'gruesome' 118–19
  – love *109–27*
  and naïve egoism 117–22
  turning away from the child 119–21
Mother-child relation [see also *Child, Infantile situation, Maternity, Object-relation*] 99–104, *109–27*, 146
  and abortion 118–19
  and auto-erotism 123
  instinctual interdependence in 102–3, 119–21, 125
  inequality of the partners 122
  sexually not dimorphous 146
Mouth, primitive 13, 25, 28 [see also *Oral*]
Muscle(s)
  activity of 42–3
  appearance of, in ontogenesis 13, 75
  muscular tension as defence 87, 88
Mutilation, operative, as substitute of new beginning 38
Mutuality [Interdependence]
  in coitus 120, 125, 130, 135
  in enjoyment 170
  Ferenczi on 120
  in genital love 135–6, 147
  in mother-child relation 119–20, 122
  in patient-analyst relation 246, 249

Narcissism [see also *Auto-erotism, Egoism*] 45, 55, 59, 63–5, 113, 252, 254–5
absolute, impossible 104
Freud on 64, 70, 125–6, 195
and infantile mind 98–9, 107
and infantile sexuality 103
and insatiability 105
limits of 70
as preliminary stage to object-relations 50, 64
primary 94, 103–8, 150, 258
and reality testing 63
(always) secondary 63–5, 98, 102–8, 193, 258–9, 263
Narcissistic
attitude 113
cathexis 45, 70
character of infantile mind 92
features 258, 264
libido 45, 115, 124
love 59, 70, 124
phase 62
states 104–8, 193–4
tendencies 143, 153
Need to be loved 113
of the children neglected 161
New beginning *36–41*, 61–2, 97–9, 102, 127, 165–6, 191–3, 196, 237, 240, *244–65*
character analysis and *159–73*
and death 40
hate in 67, 98, 246
theoretical problems of 192, 195–7
Nursing, proper 144

Object(s) [Love-object, Sexual-object, see also *Partner, Object of primary love, Object-relation*] 52, 56, 59, 70, 72, 82–4, 94–5, 97, 101–2, 104–6, 123, 228–30, 236, 255, 257
activity directed towards 97–9
always ambivalent (willing and reluctant) 135, 138–9, 147
analyst a recalcitrant – 153
archaic, see *Object(s) of primary love*

'bad and good' 93, 99, 116
and change of hate into love 149
co-operation of 82–4 [see also *Partner*]
depressing 263
exchangeable (physiological) 229
genital [see also *Partner*] 83–4, 135
idealised 130–1, 261–3
identification with 100, 123
inanimate (in perversions) 82
incestuous 82
infant and 94–5, 101–2, 104–6
interests of 100, 124, 142, 237–8, 252
libido, see *Libido, object*
loss of 88–9
'lovable' 198
persecutory 262–3
the real dangers 170
regard and consideration for 133–4, 138–9, 145, 152
reluctant 99
and transference 153–6, 174–5, 178–9, 185, 187, 213–14
transitional 263
ungratifying 57, 59, 194
wishes of 122, 135
withdrawal from 227, 230
Object(s) of primary love [see also *Mother*, etc.] 136, 145, 229, 253, 255, 261–2
absolutely unselfish 110–12
and analyst's behaviour 152
only an object (a thing) 145
are objects of ego-instincts 125
and respiration 145
taken for granted 145–7, 152
Object-relation(s) [Sexual object-relation, see also *Hate, Love, Mother-child relation, Object*, etc.] 53, 58–9, 63, 123, 132, 136, 139, 194, 199, 225–7, 229–34, 236, 247
adult (always sexual) 147, 247, 263–4 [see also *Genital love*]
ambivalent 111, 115, 143

Object-relation(s), anal (sadistic) 54–5, 59, 124, 264 [see also *Love, anal*]
and auto-erotism 50, 56, 58, 59, 122–4, 196
as basis of psycho-analytical technique 227, 230, 234
biological basis of 49, 51, 53, 64
and character 169–70
chronology of 94, 263–4
and civilisation 63, 66–7, 131–2 [see also *Civilisation, Society*]
and clinging, see *Clinging*
always demonstrable 56–61, 104, 194–5
depressive 252, 254–5
development of 49, 51, 71, 72, 102, 124–5, 229–30, 232–4, 262–3
development of, Freud's views on 125–6, 195
and dual unity 127
early [see also *primary*] 58–61, 93, 97–8, 102, 105, 107, 259
early, Freud's views on 58, 72
genital, see *Genital love*
and individual history 55, 72
and narcissism 50, 64, 103 [see also *Narcissism*]
in neurotics 52, 230
in the new beginning, see *New beginning*
oral (sadistic) 50, 58, 90, 92, 106 [see also *Love, oral, Love, primary*]
original aim of 247
paranoid 250, 252, 254
phallic 50, 53, 56, 59, 77, 94, 129
plane of 255
pregenital 53, 56, 66, 67, 71–2, 124 [see also *Love, pregenital*]
preliminary stages of 50
and the prevalent instinct 13, 49–51, 228–9
primary (archaic, passive, primitive) 59, 98, 101, 127, 150–6, 193–5, 250, 263–4 [see also *New beginning*]
primary, as condition for changing mental structures 155
and reality testing, see *Reality testing*
no repression without – 196
and termination of analysis, see *Psycho-analysis, termination of*
two-person-relation 145–6, 153
Obsessional neurosis 54, 209
as basis of theory 209–10, 226–7, 230
in children 56
ego in 209
Oedipus complex [situation, see also *Pre-oedipal*] 60, 90, 107, 186, 191, 222
negative 53, 56, 59, 72
and reality principle 117
Old age, and orgasm 78, 81
Omnipotence 92, 145, 153
as defence against a feeling of impotence 145
denial of dependence 146, 154
and 'oral greed' 146
Ontogenesis [see also *Phylogenesis, Recapitulation*] 39, 45, 229
Oral [see also *Mouth*]
greed 144, 146 [see also *Insatiability*]
instinct [erotism] 49, 58–9, 229–30
instinct and ambivalence 51
instinct becomes auto-erotic 58–9
incorporation [sexual function of the gametes] 25–6, 113
libido 12
love, see *Love, oral*
object-relation, see *Object-relation, oral*
– sadistic (cannibalistic) object-relation, see *Object-relation, oral-sadistic*
sucking 27, 99
zone (in mating) 14
Organic diseases [Organ neuroses, Psychosomatic illnesses, see also *Illness*] 46, 47, 159
psychogenic 44

Organic, mysterious leap into 210

Organisation, see *Libido, organisation of*

Organism 43–6

Orgasm [see also *Coitus, End-pleasure, Genital, Genitality, Mating*] 25, *28–36*, 41, 62, *73–89*, 101, 160
and anxiety 74, 87, 136
and death 78
and end of analysis 191, 237
and endurance of tension 207, 237
and extra-genital perversions 31, 77
and genital love 130, 136
and individuality *28–36*
intensity of 31–2, 35
'mystical union' 136–7
none on pregenital level 31, 62, 74
– like states in children 102

Orgastic
function 207
potency 191

Orthogenesis 44, 45

Paranoia [Persecution]
as basis of psycho-analytical theory 226
infantile 93

Paranoid [Persecutory, Suspicious]
anxieties (fears) 250, 257, 259–60
atmosphere 71, 162
position 250, 254, 258–60, 263–4
sensitivity 101, 105, 114
syndrome (picture) 97, 153, *244–65*

Parents [see also *Education, Father, Mother*] 119, 160–2, 170, 197

Partner(s) [Genital partner, Sexual partner, see also *Object*] 66, 68–70, 83, 99, 100, 122, 146, 163, 196, 236, 251

demands on 160
faulty reality testing with regard to 101, 120
identification between 101, 135
interests of 116, 134, 139
lasting harmony between 135, 139
–'s love frightening 112–13
'mystical union of' 136–7 [see also *Sexual union*]
perpetual emotional tie to 130
regard and consideration for 134, 139
relation to 129–30
work of conquest, see *Work of conquest*

Passion(ate) [Sensual] 57, 62, 67–8, 97–8, 124–5, 131, 133, 139, 193

Passive object-love, see *Love, primary*

Patient(s) [see also *Case histories*]
and his analyst 114–15, 122, 153–6, 237–8, 245–9, 260
in the analytic situation 151–3, 224–5, 231 [see also *Psychoanalytic situation, Transference*]
and barrier of hatred 154
deeply disturbed (hopeless) 199, 245
demands of 152, 159
and degree of tension 88, 160–5, 170–3
and dependence 154–5
inability to surrender themselves 71, 87, 159–66, 197–9 [see also *Paranoid syndrome*]
insatiability of 97–8, 144, 166, 193, 246 [see also *Insatiability*]
in the new beginning, see *New beginning*
and production of symptoms 44–5
reaction to the ending of a session 180
reaction to an interpretation 201, 260 [see also *Interpretation*]

Patient(s), response to psycho-analytical technique 5
silent 182–3, 216, 233–4
Penis 23, 29
Persecution, Persecutory, see *Paranoia, Paranoid*
Personality, see *Ego, Individuality, Mind*
Perversion [Perverse, see also *Pregenital* and under the respective headings]
only excitation, never real gratification 75–6
and fore-pleasure mechanisms 31, 77 [see also *Fore-pleasure*]
genitality never perversion 77
and inanimate objects 82
– like states in the new beginning 97 [see also *New beginning*]
and skill in sexual act (Ars amandi) 78, 131, 138, 207
Phallic, see *Love, Object-relations*, etc.
Phantasy [see also *Reality*] 94
Phylogenesis [see also *Ontogenesis, Recapitulation*] 40, 45, 81
and environmental changes 28
genital function in 134
and the human id 11
of (psycho)sexuality 13, 26, 27
Playfulness [see also *Aim-inhibition, Fore-pleasure, Pregenital, Tender*] 57, 62, 68
playful aggressive mode of gratification 62
Pleasure [Enjoyment, see also *End-pleasure, Fore-pleasure, Gratification, Orgasm*] 42, 73–89, 98, 166
and anxiety 160–2
capacity for 169, 198, 208
development of 52
external and internal resistances against 133
and new beginning, see *New beginning*
preconditions for 170

primal form and ultimate aim of 61, 63, 67, 70, 84–5, 98
– principle 84–5, 207
Polymorph-perverse 50, 62, 67, 90
Potency [genital, see also *Coitus, Genital(ity), Orgasm*] 67, 88, 191
Preconscious 40
Pregenital [see also *Fore-pleasure, Perverse*]
gratifications 73–89, 134, 136, 138–40
level 31, 62, 74
libido 12, 49–72, 88
love, see *Love, pregenital*
transference 153–4
Pre-oedipal states [Relations, see also *Love, primary, Mother-child relation, Object-relation*] 90, 108, 109
Primal scene 54
Primary aim of sexuality 61, 63, 67, 70, 84–5, 98
Primary love, see *Love, primary*
Processes
primary 206, 210
secondary 206
Progression, by regression 27, 41
Projection 93, 230
and shrinking of the ego 203
Psyche, see *Mind*
Psycho-analysis [Analysis, see also *Psycho-analytic clinic, Psycho-analytic therapy*, etc.] 152–6, 205, 208–10, 212
after analysis ('Nach-analyse') 188–9
character analysis 37, 61, 159–73, 225
of children, see *Child analysis*
control, see *supervised*
and education 205–10
genetic method in 90
interminable 154
of neurotics 52
of psychotics 107, 205, 217
and strengthening the ego, 208, 211

Psycho-analysis, supervised (control) 217–18, 224, 240
symptom – 225
terminated 44, 159
termination, see *Psycho-analysis, termination of*
training 167, 170, 179, 218, 240–1
transference 225
Psycho-analysis, termination of 56, 188–91, *236–43*
after the 57, 190, 240
clinic of 237–9
criteria for 159, 192, 236–7, 241–3, 247–9
theoretical descriptions of 189–91, 197–8
Psycho-analyst [Analyst, see also *Counter-transference, Psychoanalysis, Transference*] 238, 260–2
behaviour of the 5, 152, 178, 201, 213, 231
conscious control of 220, 231
and description of his experiences 260–1
faulty reality testing with regard to 101
gratifications of 231–2
language of 232, 260
and new beginning, see *New beginning*
as an 'object' 152–3, 155, 213
and patient 97, 114–15, 127, 153–4, 237–8, 245–9
as a 'real' person 153
and transference *213–20*
unconscious of 218–20
a well-polished mirror 213, 219
Psycho-analytic atmosphere
personal contributions of the analyst to 214–20
creating a – 234
Psycho-analytic clinic [Clinical experiences, see also *Psychoanalysis, Psycho-analytic therapy*] 260–2
in the end-phase of analyses 238, 242

more exact than theory 226–7
Psycho-analytic cure, see *Psychoanalysis, Psycho-analytic therapy, Psycho-analytic work*]
Psycho-analytic situation [relation, see also *Patient, Psychoanalyst, Psycho-analytic atmosphere, technique, Transference*] 5, 95–6, 98, 151–3, 162–4, 178, 211, 224–5, 227, 231, 237
always artificial 205
analyst's account of 260–1
character traits in 189
and education 205
and end of session 180–1, 205, 215
formation of 215
formal elements of 96, 224
gratification in 231–2, 237, 255 [see also *New beginning*]
independent of analyst 153
always an object-relation 231–2, 234
and the Oedipus complex 186
and primary object-relations 152–6
and the problem of the cushion 214–15
transference revived by 225
Psycho-analytic technique [see also *Psycho-analysis, Psychoanalyst, Psycho-analytic atmosphere, Psycho-analytic therapy* 5, 71, 151–2
absolutely correct 213, 216, 218–20
active (Ferenczi) 163–4
and the analyst's descriptions of his experiences 260–1
changes in *221–35*
classical 166
and the cushion 214–15
and the end of the session 180–1, 205
and hate 152–3
and the id 201
improvements in 107, 199, 225, 227, 232

Psycho-analytic technique, individual variants of 178, 214–19, 240, 260 [see also *Psycho-analyst*]
and new beginning 192, 199, 245–7 [see also *New beginning*]
and object-relations 227–8, 230, 234
obviously 'faulty' 261
and passivity 97, 164, 178–9, 214
and the patient 217, 260–1 [see also *Patient*]
with a silent patient 232–3
and sterility 213–18
and the strength of the ego 201, 211
and theory 5, 261 [see also *Psycho-analytic theory*]
and transference 218–19, 225 [see also *Transference*]
Psycho-analytic terminology 228, 230–1, 234, 260
confusion in 102
differences in 91, 94
inadequate 226–7
inexact 65, 251
numbers and 235
and physiological bias 228, 230
Psycho-analytic theory [see also *Psycho-analytic terminology*] 59, 102, 260–1
bias in 223, 226, 228–31, 234–5
biological basis of 49–51, 67
and chronology 50–1, 60, 64, 94, 258, 263–4
clinical basis of 209–10, 226–7, 230
divergent views in 59–60, 65, 90–5, 102–3, 106, 127, 150, 167, 260–5
dynamic (functional) and structural (topic) approaches in 222–3
ego in *90–108*, 187, 196, *200–12*, 222–3, 231, 236–7, 246
and extrapolation 104, 107–8, 125

of hate 192, 195–7
limitations of 223, 226–8, 230, 234
of narcissism 63–5, 98, 103–5, 193, 258–9, 263
negative concepts in 103–4, 108, 150–2
and numbers 235
and object-relations 225–31, 234–5 [see also *Object-relations*]
physiological basis of 223, 226, 228–30
and projective geometry 235
and psycho-sexual disorders 172–3, 227
and technique 5, 261
uncertainty of 53, 63–4, 67
undervaluation of quiet gratifications 102, 144
Psycho-analytic therapy [treatment, see also *Psycho-analysis, etc., Psycho-analytic clinic, Recovery, Working through*] 40–1, 44, 170, 179
and anxiety 154
aim (goal) of 45, *188–94*, 202–3, 208, 211, *221–35*
aim of, Freud on 190, 222–3
average duration of 219
and blissful expectations 154
constant elements in 211
and the ego 200–12
end (phase) of 56, 61, 97, 188–9, 191–2, 198 [see also *Psycho-analysis, termination of*]
and hate 149, 154
a 'natural' process 188, 238–40
and new beginning, see *New beginning*
of organic illnesses 46
recollection in 162–3, 165
repetition in 114, 162–3, 172, 191, 224, 257
results of 218–19, 240, 247–8, 251, 255
and super-ego 208–11
therapeutic process 151–4, 199, 201

Psycho-analytic work 97, 151–2, 219
Psycho-sexual [see also Sexual] development as recapitulation 11–13, 25–7
parallels *7–41*
Psychotics 205
analysis of 217
Puberty and end-pleasure 78, 87
Punishment 169–70

Rationalisation 180
Reaction formation 66, 203, 263
Reality [see also *Civilisation, Environment, Interests, Object, Society*]
adaptation to, see *Adaptation*
erotic sense of (Ferenczi) 50, 122, 125, 194
and phantasy 94
principle and love for the father 116–17
relation to 44, 65
no repression without 196
Reality testing [sense, see also *Reality*] 63, 65, 71, 236–8, 262–3
development of 124, 136
as ego function 211
and emotional life 120–3
faulty 101, 113–17, 119–20, 143, 146, 153, 259, 262–3
and genital love 135, 137
and hate 147–8
infantile form of 136
and love 124
uncertain chronology of 94
unnecessary in mother-child relation 102
Recapitulation (of phylogenesis in ontogenesis) 11–13, 25
Recollection (in analytic treatment) 162–3, 165
Recovery, processes of 188–90, 192 [see also *Psycho-analytic treatment*]
Reduction
of the nucleus 16, *36–41*
of the system 38

Reflex 43–4
Regeneration 33, 38
Regression 37–8, 41, 44, 52, 55, 60, 82, 151, 172, 246, 248
to archaic forms of love 148–9
to asexual forms of life 39
to auto-erotic phase 123
defence against 154–6
emerging from 151
Freud on 55
intra-uterine 71, 194
mating as 27
in ontogenesis 39
and progression 27, 41
thalassal 28, 194
Relaxation
after orgasm [see also *Tranquil, quiet, well-being*) 30
Repetition, see *Psycho-analytic therapy, repetition in*
Repression (Repressed) 163, 165, 174, 186, 196, 222–3
in perversions 76
'successful' 173
Resistance(s) 65, 174, 222
in analysed people 190
'internal' 207
overcoming of 190
Retardation 133
principle of 13
Respiration 42, 43
Return [see also *Regression*] to the mother's womb (to the sea) 39, 71, 194
Rhythmic movements 83–4
Rigid forms of reaction [see also *Automatism*] 167, 169, 180–1, 247–8
causes of 170
liberation from 40, 171, 211

Sadism 62–3, 75, 143–4, 197
always analysable 62
clinging as precursor of 100
and co-operation of partner 83
as derivative of anal erotism 51
of the parents 170
primary 92, 94, 150

Sadistic [see also *Anal-sadistic*, *Oral-sadistic*]
love, see *Love, sadistic*
tendencies 143, 153, 230
Satisfaction, see *Gratification*
Schizophrenia
as basis of psycho-analytic theory 226
in children 56
Scopophilia 75
Self, see *Ego*
– love, see *Narcissism*
Sensual, see *Passion*
Sexual [see also *Psycho-sexual*, *Sexual aims*, *Sexual functions*, *Sexuality*]
differentiation, see *Differentiation*
dimorphism, see *Dimorphism*
disorders and psycho-analytic technique 227
excitation (stimulation) 21, 24, 207 [see also *Excitation*]
excitation of children 160
organs, development of 20–6
union [see also *Coitus, Mating*] 14–15, 26–7, 30, 32, 36–7, 39, 41, 136–7
Sexual aims [see also *Aim-inhibition, Fore-pleasure, End-pleasure, Gratification, Orgasm, Pleasure, Tranquil, quiet, well-being*]
development of 49, 51
earliest 61 [see also *Love, primary*]
passionate (sensual) 57, 62, 67–8 [see also *Passion*]
playful 57, 62 [see also *Playful*]
ultimate 61, 63, 67, 70, 84–5, 98, 194–5
Sexual function(s) [see also *Genital*, etc., *Sexual union*] 73–89
complexity of – in fungi and worms 18–19, 28–9
development of 5, 17–28
of gametes and gametocytes 15–19, 26–7, 31
of gametocycte-carriers, see *Soma*
in males and females 27–8
original forms of 26

in plants and animals 18–21, 26–9
and somatic functions 15, 19, 30 [see also *Soma*]
Sexuality [see also *Erotism, Libido, Gratification, Pleasure,* etc.]
aims of, see *Sexual aims*
and death 32
development of 11–13, 25–7
difference between male and female 27
and feeding 14–15, 26–7, 38
identity of biological and psycho-analytic conceptions of 23
infantile, see *Infantile sexuality*
intake of solids and fluids 14, 26
mature (adult), see *Genital(ity)*
always object-orientated 124
phylogenesis, see *Sexuality, development of*
pregenital versus genital 25 [see also *Genital(ity), Pregenital*]
and work of assimilation 26–7
Society [see also *Civilisation, Education, Environment*] 171, 209
and character 171
and genital love 134
and the idea of 'average share' 140
and the individual 171, 187 [see also *Individual*]
and maternal rights 119
and transference 175
Soma [see also *Gametocyte-carrier*]
always diploid 35
and death 16, 20, 33–5
erotisation of 17, 19, 20, 24–5, 30, 33, 35
and fore-pleasure 81
and gametes 20, 26, 30, 35
and orgasm 81, 82
regenerative powers of 33
sexual differentiation of 17, 23–4, 30, 33, 81
sexual functions of [see also *Coitus, Mating, Sexual union*] 15, 19–22, 24, 26, 30–2

Spasm, tonic and clonic 87, 88
Spastic toleration, of excitement 164
Split 93, 197, 249–50, 252, 254–5, 262
Splitting processes 143, 153, 231
Starving, as reduction of the system 38
Stimulation, see *Excitation, Tension*
Strain, see *Excitation, Tension*
Sublimation 210
Super-ego 169, 198, 200, 204, 206–8, 210–11, 222, 252, 254
  and endurance of tensions 207–8
  pedagogy of 209, 211–12
Supervision, see *Psycho-analysis, supervised*
Surrender 163, 166, 248–9
  to enjoyment 160
  fear of 159–60, 171
  to love (and hate) 162
Suspicious, see *Paranoid*
Symbol(s) 12, 175–6
  of termination of analyses 238–9
Symptoms, neurotic 44–5, 52–4, 200, 222
  as defence against genital excitation 172–3
  is also a distorted object-relation 230
Synthesis, by regression 27

Tenderness [see also *Aim-inhibition, Fore-pleasure, Playfulness*] 57, 61, 68–70, 100, 121, 132, 137, 139
  demands for 112
  etymology of 132
  Freud on 68, 131
  pregenital, see *Pregenital*
  tender love 124, 131, 132 [see also *Love*]
Tension [strain, see also *Excitation*] 58, 160–5, 170–3, 201–2, 204–5, 207–8, 236–7
  in coitus 83–7, 191, 207, 237
  and learning 204–5, 211–12

libidinous in education 86–7
  in love 66
  as measure of ego strength 86, 200–2
  optimal level of 231
  in the psycho-analytic situation 231
  relief of 85, 88
  and repression 186
  and transference 177–8, 231
Training (analysis), see *Psycho-analysis, training*
Tranquil, quiet sense of well-being [see also *Fore-pleasure, Gratification*, etc.] 30, 84, 98, 102, 144, 245, 247
  undervaluation of – by theory 102, 144
Transference [see also *Patient, Psycho-analytical situation, technique*] 43, 96, 107, 153, 162, 174–5, 181, 186, 208, *213–20*, 224–6, 231, 233–4, 247, 249–50, 255
  aims and causes of 177
  often automatic 181–2
  always childish 186
  and economy 179–80, 185
  of emotions *174–87*
  hate no solution of 122
  on inanimate objects 174–7, 213–14
  individual and social 187
  and insatiable demands 199 [see also *New beginning*]
  and love 176, 257 [see also *Love, primary*]
  may be one-sided 214
  always an object-relation 225–6
  patterns of 178–80, 185
  pregenital and genital 153–4
  primary 154–6
  to 'real' objects 153–4
  and repetition 114, 122, 257
  not resolved 154
  social value of 186
Trauma [see also *Infantile*] 60, 160, 163, 238, 246–7

Trauma, of birth 71, 191
  and coitus 84
  and fixation 52, 53
Traumatic
  pre-traumatic state 246–8
  situation 92
Two-person relation [see also
  Object-relation, Transference]
  145–6, 153

Unconscious 174, 179, 196, 222–3
  in analysed people 190
  making the – conscious 185,
  189–90, 196, 203, 211
  and recovery 189–90
Union, sexual, see Coitus, Mating,
  Sexual union
Unpleasure, acceptance of 236,
  254, 257, 263–4 [see also
  Adaptation, Reality]
Utraquism (Ferenczi) 40

Wish(es)
  death – 110–11
  earliest 62, 84–5, 97–8, 247,
  263
  if frustrated, vehement demands 62, 98 [see also Hate,
  Love, primary, New beginning]
  primitive in the new beginning
  61, 97, 191, 245–6, 249, 251,
  253, 255
  renouncing of 254
  to touch or being touched 97,
  99, 100, 165, 245
'Work of conquest' (in genital
  love) 135, 136, 146–7
  and fore-pleasure 83, 135
  and genital transference 153
Working through 160, 162, 166,
  189, 202, 212
  and strengthening the ego 202

Yoga 45

INDEX OF AUTHORS

ABRAHAM, K.
  12, 13, 50, 51, 106, 229, 253
ALEXANDER, F.
  232
ANGELUS SILESIUS
  171
BALINT, A.
  5, 6, 58, 61, 63–5, 83, 95–6,
  100–1, 108–27, 194, 211,
  213–20, 262
BOLK, L.
  133
BORNSTEIN, B.
  56
BORNSTEIN, St.
  56

BREUER
  210, 221, 227, 232
CICERO
  81
FEDERN
  203
FENICHEL, O.
  128, 200, 254
FERENCZI, S.
  5, 12, 21, 28, 31, 35, 40, 46, 50,
  61, 74, 80, 82–3, 85, 87, 96,
  119, 124–5, 136, 162–4, 191,
  194, 200, 205, 217, 224, 232,
  246–7, 250, 254
FRENCH, Th. M.
  206, 232

FREUD, A.
87, 205, 208–9, 217
FREUD, S.
5, 11, 12, 13, 30, 32, 45, 49–50,
54–6, 58–9, 62, 64–5, 68,
70–1, 84, 88, 91–2, 96, 104,
125–6, 130–1, 135–6, 162,
164, 166, 190, 194, 200–3,
205–6, 210, 220, 221–8, 232,
253–4
FROMM-REICHMANN,
Fr.
56
GLOVER, E.
94, 216
GOETSCH
38
HARTMANN, M.
32, 37, 38
HERMANN, I.
61, 77, 96–7, 99–100, 126–7
HOFFMANN, E. P.
126–7
KAISER, H.
223
KEITH, Sir A.
133
KLEIN, M.
51, 196–7, 200, 225–6, 230–1,
244–5, 249–50, 252–3, 258–
61, 264–5
KOVACS, V.
87, 191
KRIS, E.
228
LAGACHE, D.
257
MACK-BRUNSWICK, R.
54
MEAD, M.
66
MEISENHEIMER, J.
19
NUNBERG, H.
128, 200

PASCHER
38
PETO, E.
124
PFEIFER, S.
85
RANK, O.
64, 80, 191, 207, 217, 232
REICH, W.
80, 191, 232
RICKMAN, J.
234–5
RIVIERE, J.
92–4
ROHEIM, G.
66, 117
ROSEN, J.
231
ROTTER-KERTESZ, L.
126–7
SACHS, H.
6
SADGER
63, 75, 79
SHAKESPEARE
130
SCHAUDINN
37, 39
SCHOPENHAUER
81
SHAW, G. B.
41
STERBA, E.
56
STRACHEY, A.
132
STRACHEY, J.
217, 225
WÄLDER, R.
94–5, 105
WELLS, H. G.
81
WINNICOTT, D. W.
263
WOODRUFF
32